The Megalithic Monuments of Western Europe

The Megalithic Monuments of Western Europe

THE LATEST EVIDENCE PRESENTED

BY NINE LEADING AUTHORITIES

EDITED BY COLIN RENFREW

with 74 illustrations

THAMES AND HUDSON

Maps by H. A. Shelley

First published in Great Britain in 1981
by Thames and Hudson Ltd, London
as Part II of *Antiquity and Man:
Essays in Honour of Glyn Daniel*,
edited by John D. Evans, Barry Cunliffe
and Colin Renfrew.
Paperback edition 1983

Printed and bound in Great Britain

Contents

Preface   6
COLIN RENFREW
Disney Professor of Archaeology, University of Cambridge

1   Introduction: The Megalith Builders of Western Europe   8
COLIN RENFREW

2   The Megaliths of France   18
P.-R. GIOT
Director of Research, Laboratoire de l'Anthropologie, Préhistoire,
Protohistoire et Quaternaire Armoricains, University of Rennes, France

3   The Megalithic Tombs of Iberia   29
ROBERT W. CHAPMAN
Lecturer in Archaeology, University of Reading

4   Megaliths of the Central Mediterranean   42
RUTH WHITEHOUSE
Lecturer in Archaeology, University of Lancaster

5   Megalithic Architecture in Malta   64
DAVID TRUMP
Staff Tutor in Archaeology, Board of Extra-Mural Studies, University of Cambridge

6   Megaliths of the Funnel Beaker Culture in Germany and Scandinavia   77
LILI KAELAS
Director, Arkeologiska Museum, Gothenburg, Sweden

7   Megalithic Graves in Belgium – A *Status Quaestionis*   91
SIGFRIED J. DE LAET
Director, Seminarie voor Archeologie, University of Ghent, Belgium

8   Chambered Tombs and Non-Megalithic Barrows in Britain   97
LIONEL MASTERS
Lecturer in Archaeology, Department of Adult and Continuing Education, University of Glasgow

9   The Megalithic Tombs of Ireland   113
MICHAEL J. O'KELLY
Late Professor of Archaeology, University College, Cork, Ireland

Index   127

Preface

THE MEGALITHIC MONUMENTS of western Europe have long attracted the attention of those interested in the early past of mankind: among their number are some of the most spectacular and romantic constructions of the prehistoric period. Indeed for a long time they constituted, for the areas in question, almost the only known vestiges of the period of the early farmers, the 'Neolithic'.

The term 'megalithic' (literally 'large stone') is generally extended to include also the contemporary chambered tombs made of smaller stones. Some of the more ambitious examples were seen by earlier archaeologists as too sophisticated to be the unaided work of the barbarian inhabitants of early Europe. Instead they were regarded as the product of more 'advanced' builders, who must (it was assumed) have come from, or at least have been influenced by, the civilized lands of the east Mediterranean.

This explanation, based upon assumptions of the diffusion of culture from the civilized world of the Orient, was occasionally questioned by sceptical scholars, but it has only recently been abandoned by the majority of workers in the light of radiocarbon dating. The very early radiocarbon dates for some of the megalithic tombs, notably those of Brittany, at once called the traditional picture into question. The recent correction of the radiocarbon time scale through the bristlecone pine calibration showed that the true dates, in calendar years, were even earlier. It then became clear that the megalithic monuments of Europe were the earliest such constructions in the world. Indeed they are the earliest buildings still standing today.

This very early dating throws into relief a whole series of new and interesting problems, some of them of worldwide rather than simply European significance. The whole question of origins reasserts itself: if they are not the result of Near Eastern influences, how did they in fact originate? What factors determined the distribution of these constructions along or near the coasts of Atlantic Europe, and their virtual absence from eastern or south-eastern Europe? How, in fact, should we set about explaining the emergence of building activities of this kind, resulting in the construction of great monuments, by early farming communities – whether in Europe, or India or Polynesia or in north America? As concerns Europe, should we imagine a single origin for the megaliths, or did the process which led to their first inception in one area result in an analogous way in the development of similar burial practices involving large monuments in other areas not at all in contact with the first? Current specialist opinion inclines to this latter notion of several independent origins, but does this adequately account for the resemblances seen between the various areas? These are some of the questions which now have to be answered, and in a general way they are just as relevant to the mound builders of north America or to the monument builders of Polynesia as to the European megalith builders.

Underlying these problems about the form and appearance of the monuments are other issues which may ultimately be more significant. What were the functions of these monuments in the societies which created them? If they served as a focus for ritual, what can we infer about the contemporary beliefs and ideologies? They were built by people with a well-defined social structure: what can we infer about this, for instance from an estimation of the manpower which had to be mobilized for their construction? These and other questions about the customs and motives of their makers present themselves with renewed force now that the old diffusionist explanations in terms of a Near Eastern origin are no longer tenable.

In the light of these various issues, some of them more difficult today than they seemed twenty years ago, a survey of the megalithic monuments of Europe, for each of the areas of their principal occurrence, seemed a timely undertaking. The essays here, each contributed by the principal authority for the region in question, were written in honour of Glyn Daniel, the leading authority on the megaliths of Europe, and over many years the enthusiastic champion of their study. They first appeared together in the central section of the Festschrift, *Antiquity and Man*, edited by John D. Evans, Barry Cunliffe and myself (published by Thames and Hudson in 1981), which was presented to Glyn Daniel on the occasion of his retirement from the Disney Chair of Archaeology in Cambridge. As a coherent review of this still controversial subject, they are reprinted here in tribute to the encouragement which Glyn Daniel has given to all those seeking to learn more of these intriguing monuments.

The author of the final essay, Professor Michael O'Kelly ('Brian' to his many friends), is sadly no longer with us: his death in October 1982, just prior to the publication of his *Newgrange*, the definitive account of his excavations at that great monument, was a great loss to Irish and indeed to European archaeology. It is appropriate that this present, up-to-date survey of the European megalithic phenomenon should conclude with his own account of what was, he persuasively argued, its outstanding product.

Colin Renfrew

1 Introduction: The Megalith Builders of Western Europe

Colin Renfrew

And I remember after dinner walking down to the great Carnac alignments and in the moonlight wandering along those miles of serried, large stones, their dark shadows a reminder of their darker past and our ignorance of their makers and builders. For me that was a great and personal moment, and I knew then what I know even better now: that these megalithic monuments of western Europe would exercise an irresistible fascination for me for ever. . . . The past was alive. It was no archaeological manifestation which specialist scholars could study and argue about. It was something real which everyone could understand or try to understand, something which was the beginning of their own cultural past in western Europe.

Glyn Daniel (1963, 25–6)

IN THESE words, taken from that most admirable archaeological *vade mecum*, *The Hungry Archaeologist in France*, and in the introduction to his less personal yet more systematic volume *The Prehistoric Chamber Tombs of France*, the author of *The Megalith Builders of Western Europe* described the undergraduate holiday in 1934 which made him for life 'an *aficionado* of megaliths'. They convey some of the enthusiasm and of the keen sense of problem, as well as the Celtic eloquence with which generations of undergraduates at Cambridge have been introduced to this subject. No-one who has read archaeology at Cambridge over the past forty years or who has seen the television programmes which he has done so much to encourage can altogether have escaped its fascination, as a number of the succeeding chapters reflect. I count myself fortunate to have first visited those Carnac alignments and the other great monuments of the Morbihan in the company of Glyn and Ruth, together with a number of his students and of my own.

Interpretations may change, and chronologies, but the attraction of these structures, which we may recognize not only as 'the first surviving architectural monuments in north-western Europe' (Daniel 1958, 13) but of the world, does not diminish. It is appropriate, then, that as a tribute to the scholar who has contributed so much to their understanding, and to the teacher who has consistently promoted an aware-

ness of their problems, we should review the *status quaestionis* as it rests today, some four decades after his first substantial contribution to the subject. Succeeding chapters will take a regional approach – as is entirely necessary, since we all now realize that the megaliths were not a unitary phenomenon, and that the very use of the term 'megalith' to class together such a disparate variety of monuments, of several independent origins, is to impose a classification which owes more to our own assumptions than to any inherent unity in the material. Yet to adopt a cross-cultural approach is very much in harmony with current archaeological thought – to compare phenomena which appear to us as similar, irrespective of limitations of space and time, and to look for broader regularities of culture process. Surely there can be little doubt that these megalithic constructions, however independent their origins may be, *do* strike the eyes of the modern observer as in some ways similar? This, I shall argue, is because they fulfilled a similar function, or many of them did, as territorial markers of segmentary societies. So indeed did some of the comparable monuments in other parts of the world – in Polynesia, for instance, as well perhaps as some of those of India or Japan – which earlier generations of scholars sometimes linked together with those in the West as part of a unitary phenomenon, sharing a common origin, just as they did the monuments of western Europe until the past decade.

This shift in opinion, which owes much to the development of radiocarbon dating and its tree-ring calibration, need not be surveyed in detail here. It is admirably reviewed in successive editorials in *Antiquity*, the one international journal (other than *Radiocarbon* itself) which from the outset showed an acute awareness of the problems and results of radiocarbon dating, and their bearing upon the prehistory of Europe, including the stone monuments. I well remember, in the early 1960s, the Editor in his gown, entering the lecture room in Downing Street, on many an occasion clutching a letter from some eminent European scholar, and proclaiming the latest radiocarbon date with all the triumph (or sometimes the consternation) with which others might announce the racing results from Newmarket. Their significance was debated at many a supervision, sometimes over a restoring glass of Muscadet.

The now traditional view, which owed much to the 'modified diffusionism' (Daniel 1962, 95) of Gordon Childe, was set out afresh, with several useful insights in 'The Dual Nature of the Megalithic Colonisation of Europe' (Daniel 1941), and reviewed more comprehensively in *The Megalith Builders of Western Europe* (Daniel 1958). In one of the earliest considerations of the impact of radiocarbon dating upon the whole scene, 'Northmen and Southmen' (Daniel 1967), the alternative case was argued for the independent development of the monuments in several areas 'due to the separate traditions of the Northmen and the Southmen in the fourth and third millennia BC'. The new, independent view has recently been stated still more trenchantly (Daniel 1978):

> It should now be clear to all serious and unbiased students of megaliths that these structures of great stones came into existence in many separate societies: Malta, the toe of Italy, Bulgaria, Almeria, the Algarve of Portugal, Brittany, the northern European plain of NW Germany and Denmark, southern Britain and Scotland. Whether to these nine areas we should add Ireland is a matter for discussion.

These regions, with the exception of Bulgaria, are indicated in ill. 1, drawn by Ruth Daniel (Daniel 1958, 26), a map which today serves to illustrate the variety and the inhomogeneity of the megalithic phenomenon in Europe as elegantly as it once suggested their unity and affinity.

There is little more that need be said at a general level about their origin. I have recently set out one outline explanation (Renfrew 1976), and the authors of the chapters which follow have their own views and arguments for each region in turn. Instead I wish to turn to the inferences about society which we may hope to make on the basis of a study of the megaliths. It is my belief that some more coherent theoretical base is required for this purpose than has yet been propounded. In approaching these remaining indicators of Neolithic activity in north-western Europe there are assumptions which have to be made, and which I think are justifiable.

The first is that the construction of these monuments represents *a serious, coherent, indeed patterned activity*. We may not know the precise motivation of their builders, or have direct insight into the content of their beliefs. But that does not condemn us to regard them as irrational, eccentric, unpredictable manifestations by some manic sect: in the words of the Revd George Barry (1805, 102) writing of the chamber tombs of Orkney, 'inflamed almost to madness by the peculiar genius of their religion'.

1 *Distribution of the megalithic tombs of Europe, drawn by Ruth Daniel.*

The evidence is clear that many of them relate to the disposal of the dead, but we need not assume that this was their primary purpose. One can, if one wishes, dispose very readily of the dead without building great tombs for them. We need not assume that they all had the same purpose, or functioned in the same way. If the megaliths do not represent a unitary phenomenon, they can hardly be approached with a single, specific explanation.

Monuments in Space

A convenient initial approach is a spatial one. It need not involve any very elaborate locational analysis, but does require the consideration of the way in which various kinds of activity take place in space.

It is a commonplace in archaeology today to adopt a systems approach, and for heuristic reasons to speak of different subsystems of the culture system. One may consider the spatial patterning of different kinds of activity in a rather similar way. In that sense it can be meaningful to speak of *ritual space* – referring to the way people divide up the countryside as far as ritual and symbolic categories are concerned, and the manner in which they use space for ritual activities. *Locality space* simply refers to the everyday spatial behaviour of the inhabitants of a particular locality, conceived as the minimum settlement unit, be it homestead or village. *Kinship space* implies a two-dimensional map of the kin-relationships of the individual, which is clearly crucially determined by residence rules. *Political space* maps territorial aspects of the exercise of power. *Burial space*, with which we shall be particularly concerned, reflects spatial aspects of the burial process, relating place of life to place of death and place of burial in a structured way.

To consider such things in spatial terms is not at all to imply that they are spatially *defined*. The formal group, which is generally both the effective reproductive unit and the effective local political unit, may well be defined in kinship terms. But it will still have a territorial behaviour. In some cases, particularly when sedentary agriculture is practised, the local group – that is to say the people who occupy a given tract of land or locality – is effectively much the same as the formal group.

Langness, quoted by Brookfield and Hart (1971, 230–2), has examined the intersection of 'local' and 'formal' groups in the East New Guinea highlands, and found a high degree of overlap. Moreover he has suggested that the ideology of patrilineal descent there, patrilocal residence and group exogamy, is a cognitive model, conceived by the community, an *a posteriori* explanation of a reality in which the sheer *fact* of residence in a locality can determine so-called 'kinship'.

As an example of a particular and perhaps special kind of patterning in burial space, one may take the famous case of the Merina of Madagascar, as described by Maurice Bloch (1971). The Merina, however far they live from the old, traditional heartland of their country, the Imerina, trace back their descent to ancestors originally resident there in localities which they call *tanindrazana* – which one might translate roughly as 'old ancestral home'. They join in the maintenance of communal tombs in this place. On death they are first usually buried locally, where they lived, for a short space of time. Then at a ceremony at least two years afterwards, the *famadihana*, the remains are, with great expense and with the participation of a wide group of kinsfolk, and many guests, solemnly translated to the family tomb. This is an interesting example, not because it offers a supposed 'parallel' for any specific archaeological case, but because it exemplifies the potential difference between life space and burial space in some communities.

In working back from the archaeological remains, there are of course many difficulties, often hard to foresee. For instance, among the LoWiili of the Voltaic-speaking peoples of the Niger area, the actual burial of the dead is not carried out by the close kinsmen of the deceased, but by immediate neighbours who must not be members of the same lineage as the dead (Goody 1967, 100). These complementary funeral groups are usually patrilineages. Burial is generally in the courtyard of the deceased's home (*idem*, 92). The archaeologist must accept the likelihood of various counter-intuitive patternings of this kind. But the behaviour *is* nonetheless patterned – and in this case the spatial outcome is not altered.

Settlement and Burial

One further point which we need to consider in the case of many of the European monuments, is the lack of settlement remains. Only occasionally, for instance in the admirably thorough researches by Strömberg (1971) at Hagestad in Skåne, have settlements associated with megalithic tombs been adequately documented. In many cases they have not been found because they were scanty, and in particular because settlement was dispersed, in scattered household units, rather than aggregated in villages, as reflected in the tell communities of south-east Europe or the villages of the LBK people. Marshall Sahlins has remarked that 'Maximum dispersion is the settlement pattern of the state of nature' (Sahlins 1972, 97).

The choice between aggregation and dispersion is not a casual one. As Brookfield and Hart (1971, 226) noted:

> Why should people tolerate distance when they can virtually eliminate it by living in scattered and if need be mobile homesteads. People aggregate because there are advantages in so doing, whether for common work, co-ordination of efforts in the raising of prestations, in defence, or for the company and social security enjoyed in a group. Such benefits will increase up to a certain group size, but in the absence of division and specialisation of labour will not continue to increase in direct proportion to growing group size. If we can conceive of a 'curve of benefits' arising from aggregation, the point at which this curve peaks represents optimal group size. If while still rising it intersects a curve expressing toleration of distance, the intersection will represent a sub-optimal maximum size.

Thus the documentation of a dispersed settlement pattern, if we can document it, will tell us not only something of the organization of society, but by implication the constraints operating on it, which are in part ecological and in part related to the way the land is exploited. We are at once introduced into a consideration of environmental questions, and of agricultural intensification. Let us now look at some hypothetical arrangements indicative of life space (locality space) and death space (burial space), which cover a number of relevant possibilities. These are set out in ill. 2.

The first (ill. 2, 1a) is the case of an aggregated village settlement with a dispersed burial pattern. (If we were concerned with ritual space, the crosses could indicate shrines or other ritual foci.) One possible example is given by late medieval churches in Greece, for instance in the Greek islands. In some instances settlement is nucleated, in villages, yet the lands of individual families are often accompanied by a small church, effectively a rural family chapel, in which the dead were traditionally buried. This may be a case, like the Merina one, where a former locality space (in this case a former pattern of dispersed settlement) is formalized and retained in ritual or burial space, while a new locality space (centred on the village settlement) is established. It may be that such ritual lag is a very common phenomenon, which we must expect to see often in burial arrangements.

This case of the village with its own accompanying cemetery (ill. 2, 1b) is very much more frequent, pertaining probably to the majority of farming villages both today and in the past. The cemetery can occasionally contain monumental tombs, sometimes for family use. This is perhaps the explanation of the chambered tombs comprising the cemetery in the small fortified township of Los Millares in Spain.

In some cases (ill. 2, 1c) the village has a single, communal tomb. An archaeological example may be offered by the tombs of Mesara in Crete (although sometimes these come in pairs). It has, however, also been suggested that in some cases they served an essentially dispersed settlement pattern.

Intramural burial within village settlement (ill. 2, 1d) is rarely monumental, and is sometimes restricted to children. The Early Neolithic village of Nea Nikomedeia in northern Greece offers a well-known example.

A similar, if perhaps somewhat arbitrary division may be made out for the various spatial modes of burial associated with dispersed settlement. The first is dispersed burial (ill. 2, 2a), where the burial facility is adjacent to the homestead, or at least to the land cultivated. This is exemplified by the custom in some Polynesian islands, for instance the Tuamotus, and some of the smaller marae of Tahiti.

Cemeteries are not, of course, restricted to nucleated populations, and can accompany a dispersed

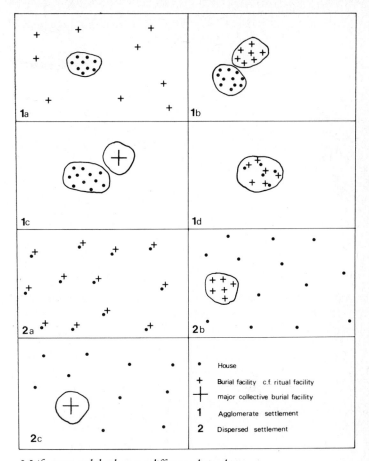

2 Life space and death space: different relationships between settlement pattern and the location of burial facilities.

pattern of settlement (ill. 2, 2b). The cemeteries of many mobile communities are comparable here, for instance the barrow cemeteries of some Iron Age groups in eastern Europe, as well, perhaps, as some of the Bronze Age barrow cemeteries of Europe.

Communal burial within a single burial facility is also logically possible for the dispersed population of a region (ill. 2, 2c). This seems to have been the practice at the larger image ahus of Easter Island. It is tempting also to suggest that the great hypogeum of Hal Saflieni in Malta represents a pattern of this kind.

This treatment of the possible conjunctions of settlement pattern and burial practice leads naturally to the consideration of the circumstances in which a given burial configuration may imply a specific settlement pattern. In particular in what circumstances does a dispersed pattern of monumental tombs reasonably imply dispersed settlement, a configuration approximating

11

to that of pattern 2a, and the existence of what may be termed a segmentary society?

Segmentary societies (Renfrew 1976, 205) 'are small-scale societies, and frequently non-literate. In particular, they display segmentary organization, which implies the repetition of equivalent groups. They are cellular and modular: cellular in that the groups are clearly defined and operate in many ways independently, and modular in that they are of approximately the same size. The segments are autonomous, economically and politically, and usually number between 50 and 500 persons. In segmentary societies the primary functioning unit – normally a residential unit, whether a village or an association of dispersed houses – is the primary segment, a self-sustaining perpetual body, exercising social control over its productive resources.'

This definition as it stands is a very general one but, if it can be shown to be appropriate in a particular archaeological case, it can certainly be informative. It can lead to inferences about the social organization in question, some of which may be opened to testing by other categories of evidence.

When confronted by a dispersed pattern of burial, as so often is the case for megalithic monuments, it is clearly relevant to ask at once whether the settlement pattern may be an agglomerate one (pattern 1a). One is therefore led to look for village settlement. Its absence may carry some of the dangers of negative evidence, yet an intensive field survey of the local region should, in the absence of pronounced geomorphological change, be capable of documenting the presence or, it is hoped, absence of nucleated villages.

Secondly, the term segmentary society is only appropriate when the groups in question are not subordinate parts of an effective and larger unity. It is

therefore relevant to search for a hierarchy, which in this case will presumably be revealed, if at all, in the burial monuments themselves. Inevitably some will be larger than others. One appropriate procedure, in the absence of rich grave goods, is to calculate the approximate man-hour input required to construct the monument. If a real hierarchy of monuments exists, the levels in the hierarchy may be expected to differ by a factor of about 10 in their labour requirement in man-hours. An order of magnitude difference of this kind may well reflect a real, social hierarchy, while a difference by a factor of only 2 is less impressive or persuasive.

Such a hierarchy may be argued for the Neolithic field monuments of southern Britain (ill. 3; see Renfrew 1973), where the long barrows represent a labour investment of some 10^4 man-hours, the causewayed camps 10^5 man-hours, the great henges 10^6 man-hours, and the two prime monuments – Stonehenge and Silbury Hill – an investment well in excess of 10^7 man-hours.

The analysis so far is not a rigorous one. Nor have we yet formulated precise spatial criteria for recognizing *dispersed* monuments. Of course, they do not have to be regularly dispersed, in a lattice. There may be cases where two or three are together. But evidently they should not show close bunching.

There is, however, an independent test of these ideas, in terms of the availability (to the territories defined by the dispersal of the monuments) of resources adequate for survival, especially arable land. A dispersed pattern of monuments in mountain highlands might have very different connotations. The distribution of megalithic cairns in the Scottish island of Arran, in relation to arable land, is a case in point. Considered in their own right in the light of the foregoing discussion, they might well be taken as suggesting a segmentary society in Neolithic times. The presence of a convenient area of arable land within the territory of nearly every cairn, as simply if rather crudely defined by the construction of Thiessen poly-

3 Socio-spatial hierarchy in Neolithic Wessex. Henges replaced causewayed camps in the Late Neolithic period, c.2500 BC.

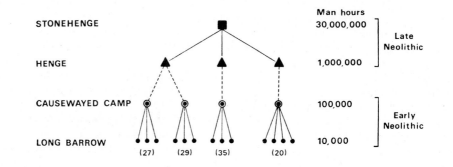

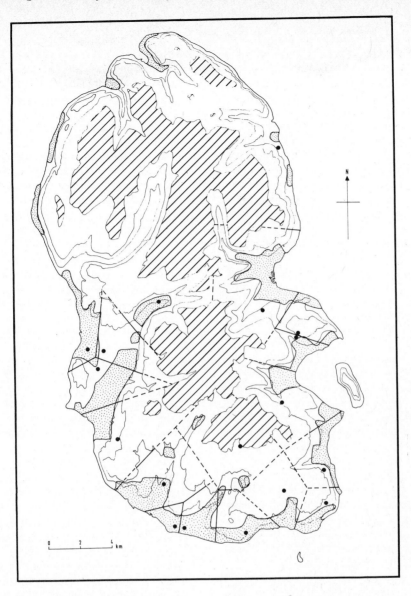

gons (ill. 4) constitutes a positive response to the test.

A thorough consideration of the relation between burial and settlement along the lines indicated could doubtless lead to a series of inferences and alternatives, which particular burial arrangements might offer concerning the social structure of the parent populations. One such is certainly, as argued above, the *hypothesis* that a dispersed pattern of monumental tombs, in the absence of agglomerate settlement, would lead to the inference of a segmentary society, as defined earlier. An independent test of the hypothesis is suggested in terms of the land use potential of the different territories, defined on the basis of the distribution of monuments.

4 Distribution of the chambered cairns of Arran, with notional territorial divisions indicated by means of Thiessen polygons, and with modern arable land shown by stippling. (Contours at 100 m intervals.)

Orkney and the Boyne

The megalithic tombs of two areas of Europe have recently been investigated in a manner relevant to our discussion. The first is Orkney, at the extreme north of the British Isles, where the great concentration of chambered cairns has for long excited the attention of scholars. I had the privilege of directing there a programme of researches, of which the main activity was the excavation of the chambered cairn at Quanterness. The distribution of such monuments in the Orkney islands in general leads to the hypothesis set out above. Only the celebrated monument of Maes Howe, together with the two henge monuments with their stone circles, the Ring of Brogar and the Stones of Stenness, represent a substantially greater input of man-hours, suggesting the possible inference that a hierarchy in scale of monument may here reflect some hierarchy within the society.

One important result of the project was to demonstrate through radiocarbon dating that Maes Howe was probably constructed some centuries after Quanterness. Moreover the radiocarbon dates obtained by Dr Graham Ritchie for the Stones of Stenness during his excavations there suggest that both that monument and the Ring of Brogar are the contemporaries of Maes Howe, and thus later than Quanterness and its sister cairns. During the period of the construction of Quanterness and its earlier use, there is no evidence to suggest a hierarchy of monuments, such as becomes apparent later.

The other important result at Quanterness, within the context of the present discussion, was the recovery of much human skeletal material, which permitted an estimate of the size of the group served by the tomb. This lent valuable confirmation to the original hypothesis. Further details of the project are available in the final report. Here it may be sufficient simply to set out the summary of conclusions as reached there (Renfrew 1979, 218–19):

1. At the time of its early use the cairn at Quanterness was not stratified in a hierarchy above or below monuments of different scale.

2. Quanterness was an equal access tomb, with balanced representation of both sexes and all ages (despite a low average age).

3. No prominent ranking is indicated among the tomb occupants, either by disparity in grave goods or difference in funerary practice (although three grave inhumations were noted).

4. Elaborate burial practices were documented; inhumation within the chambered cairn was among the last stages in the treatment of the deceased.

5. The chamber was in use for at least five centuries.

6. The size of the group using the cairn may have been of the order of twenty.

7. The labour required for the construction of the monument, about 10,000 man-hours, could without difficulty have been invested in the space of just a few years by such a group, perhaps with the assistance of neighbouring groups.

8. Quanterness is just one of a number of similar Orcadian cairns of comparable scale.

9. The distribution of these cairns is fairly dispersed, suggesting that the corporate group using each was largely a locality group, although it could at the same time have been formally organized as a descent group.

10. A subsistence base of mixed farming is inferred (although reference to the settlement site at Skara Brae is necessary to document the cereal component), with the exploitation of game (deer – not necessarily wild), birds and fish.

11. Vegetation was open and treeless, and the environment much like that of today (with little geomorphic change).

12. Late in the period in question just a few monuments of larger scale were constructed in a single central area, implying the emergence of some form of centralized organization.

The conclusion therefore is that the data from Quanterness do firmly support the notion of a segmentary society in Orkney at this time. The development late in the Neolithic of monuments of greater scale, suggesting a measure of centrality, is interesting in view of the comparable pattern of development in southern Britain.

It is interesting to compare the development towards a more centralized society in Orkney and in Wessex with the somewhat different pattern in Ireland demonstrated by Darvill (1979). He has shown graphically (ill. 5) how the court cairns represent a dispersed pattern, while the passage graves show a marked tendency to congregate in groups. He argues that in general the court cairns represent an earlier stage in Ireland than the passage graves, although with some evidence for a chronological overlap. In terms of the model developed above, the court cairns would represent pattern 2a of ill. 2, while the passage graves would represent pattern 2b. The court cairns may perhaps be interpreted as the territorial markers of segmentary societies, within the perspective adopted here. But just as in the case of the unchambered long barrows of Wessex, this need not imply that all the dead were ultimately deposited there: the scarcity or lack of human bones reported from them suggest the contrary. At Quanterness, on the other hand, there is the clear suggestion that the entire group was destined for deposition in the tomb, although the process of excarnation after death has resulted in the loss of much skeletal material.

On the other hand, the passage graves of Ireland show an altogether different pattern, well exemplified by the most famous of the cemeteries, on the Boyne River. For here the development did not lead to just

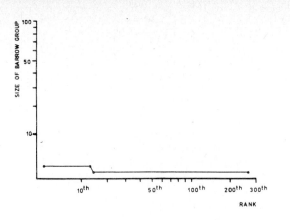
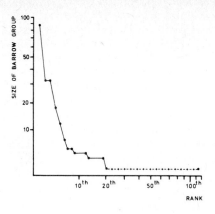

5 Dispersed versus agglomerate distribution: rank-size plots for clusters of court cairns (left) and passage graves (right) in Ireland. Monuments are said to cluster if they lie within 800 m of each other. (From Darvill 1979.)

one or two major monuments, analogous with Brogar/Stenness or Stonehenge/Silbury, but to a concentration of no fewer than 32 tombs, a figure itself surpassed by the 89 passage graves at the Carrowmore cemetery.

The Boyne case therefore exemplifies something very different from the Orkney one. In a certain, objective sense it may be seen as the formation of a 'hierarchy', but let it be stressed that the implications of a 'hierarchy' in terms of funerary monuments in this way is something whose social correlates remain to be explored.

Clearly a single 'collective' tomb – and by collective in this case we mean for multiple burials, occurring successively over a long time period – does of itself *define* a social group, in the strict objective sense of those persons who are buried within it. Behind it must lie a *real* social group, in the sense of a community or lineage or whatever, of persons – some corporate body, whose membership is a necessary criterion for burial in the tomb, although not necessarily a sufficient one.

A cemetery of such tombs, whether at Los Millares or the Boyne, is therefore a group of groups – that is where the objective hierarchy comes in. At Los Millares that might mean simply an agglomerate settlement whose population may be divided into a number of burial groups, which may in fact represent lineages. An Irish passage grave cemetery, where there is no corresponding agglomerate settlement, must again, in the larger sense, represent a burial group – those persons who were buried there. Behind that lies a corporate body, whose membership is presumably a necessary criterion for burial in the cemetery.

Such burial is therefore tribal behaviour, if we may use the term 'tribe' in this loose way. But already the emergence of a centre – for surely the cemetery is at least in ritual and burial terms a centre – hints at something beyond the symmetrical and mechanical solidarity of the tribe. It is the essence of a chiefdom society

that it is centred, asymmetrical, and has some elements of organic solidarity. The emergence of a centre is one criterion here, although another is that of personal ranking, which has not been established in this analysis, although it could be for the Boyne cemetery. Other criteria include the mobilization of manpower, as reflected in southern England by Stonehenge, Silbury Hill etc., and to a lesser extent by the Ring of Brogar. The Irish passage grave cemeteries thus hint at some measure of group, of centralization, in the society of the time.

The simple demonstration of a 'group of groups' (although a hierarchy in the strict spatial sense) does not, however, of itself document or even suggest a hierarchy of persons. Nor has any systematic study yet been undertaken of the scale of monuments (in man-hour terms) *within* an Irish passage grave cemetery. So to speak of a chiefdom in the Irish case would appear premature – even if the term be accepted for the Wessex of Stonehenge or for the Orkney of the Ring of Brogar and Maes Howe. The Irish passage grave cemeteries appear to document a different and distinctive configuration, pattern 2b of ill. 2. That is a feature of particular interest.

I would like finally to return to the dispersed settlement pattern which is sometimes implied by the dispersed burial pattern with which we began. Why does this burial pattern occur? Art Saxe (1970, 119) was the first archaeologist to offer a coherent answer:

To the degree that corporate group rights to use and/or control critical but restricted resources are

15

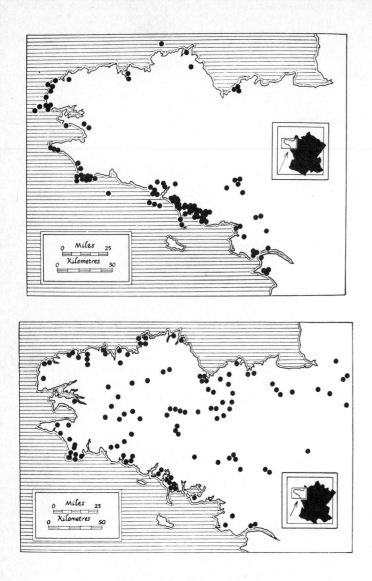

6 Contrasting distributions of the passage graves (above) and allées couvertes (below) of Brittany, drawn by Ruth Daniel. (From Daniel 1960.)

the most obvious is arable land. Grahame Clark in a recent paper (1977) has drawn attention to a different resource, notably in Bohuslan in western Sweden, where the rationale of the pattern may be access to maritime resources. This may well be a non-arable instance of the phenomenon Saxe describes.

Chapman (1981) has recently examined this notion for prehistoric burial in Europe as a whole – naturally including non-megalithic cemeteries within his scope – and finds that it works well. In general, for instance, one does not expect swidden agriculturalists, for whom land itself is not the critical resource, to use formal disposal areas in this way.

The question as to why the formal disposal should be megalithic takes us further. I have already suggested (Renfrew 1976) that these monuments are intended as territorial markers, conspicuous signalling devices in relation to land, to territory, to the most frequent critical resource. This suggestion is in harmony with, although it goes beyond, Saxe's hypothesis. There may be sound demographic reasons why the resource in question – land – became critical first along the Atlantic façade.

There is room, of course, for much more work to follow up these ideas. But if their general drift is accepted, we have a new insight into an important period of European prehistory. The Neolithic of western Europe, far from being extremely poor in settlement data, is seen instead as exceptionally rich in information bearing upon land use, settlement pattern and population. For while it remains true that preserved domestic, residential structures are in general rare, and likely to remain so, the chambered tombs – under the conditions which we have discussed – offer us as comprehensive a pattern of settlement data as we can expect to obtain from prehistoric times. The signalling devices were built to last, and in many cases they continue to signal.

A whole series of survey techniques has recently been developed or adapted to archaeology, some of them springing from the initial insights of the 'site catchment analysis' of Eric Higgs and Claudio Vita-Finzi. Now of course burial facilities are not residential sites, and the same locational constraints do not hold between tomb and field as between homestead and field. But while the relationship may not be direct or invariable, there is reason to suggest, as stressed in the assumption made at the outset, that it is patterned.

Much work remains to be done, indeed it is only beginning, with the detailed surveys like those in Arran by Roger Mercer, and in Rousay by my colleague the geomorphologist Donald Davidson. Environmental variables have to be taken into account. I forecast, however, that the megaliths will be found to be capable

attained and/or legitimised by means of lineal descent from the dead (i.e. lineal ties to ancestors), such groups will maintain formal disposal areas for the exclusive disposal of their dead and conversely.

Here 'formal disposal areas' for the dead are implicitly linked with lineal descent groups. We have seen earlier that this is not a necessary linkage, but it is a frequent and a plausible one. Saxe goes on to equate the use of such formal disposal areas with the control, by such lineages, of crucial but restricted resources, of which of revealing to us some of the best archaeologically documented segmentary societies of any period anywhere in the world.

Chronological problems will persist, whenever spatial distributions are studied, until the far-off day when every monument under consideration can securely be dated by means of radiocarbon. Yet already the broad sequences now available open up new perspectives in terms both of land use and social organization. Ruth Daniel's elegant maps (ill. 6) contrasting the distributions of the Breton passage graves and the *allées couvertes* (Daniel 1960) can be seen in this way, in the light of the useful ascription by Giot and L'Helgouach (1979, 172 and 293) of the former to the earlier fourth millennium BC, and the latter to the third millennium BC. The Breton passage graves no longer document, by their coastal distribution, the path of some colonists from Iberia: their pattern of location has, on the contrary, much to teach us of the economy

of their builders, as well as of their society. The inland distribution of the *allées couvertes* testifies, among other things, to the wider distribution of agricultural practice in the Armorica Peninsula at the later time.

The archaeological potential of these remarkable structures is far from exhausted, and each generation of archaeologists will no doubt find new ways of looking at them, and obtain fresh insights from them. The young traveller of today would do well to heed the sage advice of that young Celtic traveller of forty-seven years ago, who has since done so much to encourage and stimulate their study (Daniel 1963, 187):

But wherever your last meal in France, take back with you the memory of the great painted caves and the great megaliths – archaeological vestiges of a time when France was young, when Western Europe was young, and when neither Frank nor Anglo-Saxon had been heard of.

Bibliography

BARRY, G. 1805 *History of the Orkney Islands*, Edinburgh.

BLOCH, M. 1971 *Placing the Dead,* London.

BROOKFIELD, H. C. and Hart, D 1971 *Melanesia, a Geographical Interpretation of an Island World*, London.

CHAPMAN, R. W. 1981 'Emergence of formal disposal areas and the "problem" of megalithic tombs in prehistoric Europe', in Chapman, R. W, *et al.* (eds.), *The Archaeology of Death*, Cambridge, 71–82.

CLARK, J. G. D. 1977 'The economic context of dolmens and passage-graves in Sweden', in Markotić, V. (ed.), *Ancient Europe and the Mediterranean, Studies Presented in Honour of Hugh Hencken*, Warminster, 35–49.

DANIEL, G. E. 1941 'The dual nature of the megalithic colonisation of Europe', *Proc. Preh. Soc.* VII, 1–49.

1958 *The Megalith Builders of Western Europe*, London.

1960 *The Prehistoric Chamber Tombs of France*, London.

1962 *The Idea of Prehistory*, London.

1963 *The Hungry Archaeologist in France*, London.

1967 'Northmen and Southmen', *Antiquity* XLI, 313–17.

1978 Review of S. J. De Laet (ed.), *Acculturation and Continuity in Atlantic Europe: Papers Presented at the IVth Atlantic Colloquium*, in *Helinium* XVIII, 268–9.

DARVILL, T. C. 1979 'Court cairns, passage graves and social change in Ireland', *Man* XIV, 311–27.

FERGUSSON, J. 1872 *Rude Stone Monuments in all Countries: their Ages and Uses*, London.

GIOT, P-R., L'HELGOUACH, J. AND MONNIER, J-L. 1979 *Préhistoire de la Bretagne*, Rennes, Ouest-France.

GOODY, J. 1967 *The Social Organisation of the LoWiili*, Oxford.

RENFREW, C. 1973 'Monuments, mobilisation and social organisation in neolithic Wessex', in Renfrew, C. (ed.), *The Explanation of Culture Change: Models in Prehistory*, London, 539–58.

1976 'Megaliths, territories and populations', in De Laet, S. J. (ed.), *Acculturation and Continuity in Atlantic Europe, Papers Presented at the IVth Atlantic Colloquium*, Brugge, De Tempel, 198–220.

1979 *Investigations in Orkney*, Reports of the Research Committee of the Society of Antiquaries of London, 38, London.

SAHLINS, M. 1972 *Stone Age Economics*, Chicago.

SAXE, A. 1970 *Social Dimensions of Mortuary Practice* (Ph.D. Dissertation, University of Michigan) Ann Arbor, University Microfilms.

STRÖMBERG, M 1971 *Die Megalithgräber von Hagestad,* Acta Archaeologica Lundensia, ser.8, no.9, Lund, Gleerup.

2 The Megaliths of France

P.-R. Giot

ARCHAEOLOGISTS are usually aware of how artificial and risky it is to separate megaliths from their total cultural and chronological contexts. 'Rude Stone Monuments' do certainly present a few specific problems of their own, which can be studied in isolation, but there are great dangers in this. It provides scope for the 'lunatic fringe', who seem to be purveying their nonsenses ever more successfully around the world – even if some of them do from time to time have a brilliant idea or observe an interesting detail which had escaped the notice of the professionals. As they are a permanent nuisance to archaeologists, it is often difficult to give them due credit for the few ideas one owes them. Enough said; Professor Glyn Daniel, as a most distinguished editor of *Antiquity*, has had to fight many a fine battle against the lunatics and false druids.

Because most of us are drawn to those clearly visible piles of stone called megalithic monuments, we may be giving them – or those forms that have resisted destruction – undue importance. Conditions of conservation or preservation induce a differential destruction and can obliterate whole blocks of evidence. Perhaps archaeologists working in countries with no visible megaliths – or only a few, or unimportant ones – are spending their time more profitably in not getting involved in absorbing and exacting megalithic enquiries.

One great truth arises from recent excavations in France. Besides the most prominent types of megaliths and para-megalithic structures one has known about for a long time, there exist quite a range of other monuments, which appear nowadays to be unique or exceptional probably only because all the other examples have vanished. We are not even sure that the monuments we consider characteristic constitute an adequate sample of those built during their time, or even that they don't simply represent a collection of more durable chance survivals. At least we now know that beside them once stood an array of wooden or part-wooden-and-part-earthern structures which were perhaps just as important as – or more important than – the stone ones. Megaliths, like icebergs, may always have features or characteristics hidden from view.

Twenty years ago or so Professor Glyn Daniel wrote a book about the prehistoric chamber tombs of France. It gave a useful although sometimes partial summary of the evidence available up to the 1950s. It was, however, conceived and constructed in pre-radiocarbon days and for this reason did not have the impact which it might otherwise have deserved, nor of course could it anticipate the results (and the radiocarbon datings) which were to emerge from subsequent excavations in Brittany and elswhere (Daniel 1960). This was the time when the maximal contraction of the chronological concertina was in fashion and inevitably with its subsequent expansion, many concepts have had to be changed. This being said we should acknowledge how stimulating to further work was this summary statement of the position – even if the stimulation has sometimes been in reaction rather than in agreement.

Statistics and Surveys

Last century, people were very enthusiastic in France about the idea of counting for each *département* or province the total number of recorded monuments of different types, as if it were a competition, and on this basis they would produce elaborate density distribution maps. Counting the stones of alignments as menhirs and then adding the result to the dolmens could distort the statistics. Because of the amount of destruction, even with present information one should be very careful about utilizing these figures for districts which have been densely populated for a long time – subject to agricultural disturbance, urbanization, quarrying for building and road-making materials, or massive alterations in the Dark Ages.

Some recent detailed toponymic studies, such as those of B. Tanguy in Brittany (Tanguy 1976, 1979), have shown how numbers of presumed monuments may have left their names to fields, names recorded at the beginning of the last century in the original rolls. Districts without monuments today may have had nearly as many as other places less ravaged. Of course, in poorly populated areas such as the Causses plateaux of southern France one would not expect such devastation.

1 *French sites and place-names mentioned in the text.*

Megaliths, or any visible antiquities, are not popular with farmers practising modern methods of agronomy. One could multiply unhappy stories such as the following: recently an archaeologist was to re-excavate the well-known monument of Le Pouy de la Halliade, at Bartres (Hautes-Pyrénées). He had obtained a written agreement from the owner and the official licence from the authorities; possibly it was the monument scheduled as a 'dolmen' in that commune since 1887. A few days before this archaeologist was to begin his dig, a bulldozer was ordered and destroyed the site (Clottes 1975). Peasants are politically very powerful through their trade associations. Destroying a megalith, especially if the monument interests tourists or ramblers, even if the action is of no agricultural benefit, is a prerogative of independence and a clear manifestation of property rights. To go and show interest in a megalith can sometimes be fatal for the monument.

There have been many unhappy examples – especially after the operations of the *Remembrement*, the compulsory redistribution of the land, when amalgamations were taking place and all 'obstacles to the rational exploitation of the land' were being eliminated. The Ministry of Agriculture always seems to take note, sincerely or not, when it is told that an antiquity has been destroyed. But giving them in advance lists of monuments or sites to be respected and preserved has proved sometimes to be provoking martyrdom. The peasants are induced to bribe the bulldozer drivers and contractors and to pay for the additional work which will permit them to get a clean open space.

The administrative protection of megaliths by scheduling them as Historical Monuments has not always prevented destruction either. And even monuments bought by the state have escaped from public ownership through usucaption – the acquisition of right to property by uninterrupted possession – and are now again in private hands.

During the last century, the need for regional archaeological surveys eventually became apparent. These were initiated locally in some places at first, and then received official encouragement, although it never brought about a complete and uniform coverage of the country. Megalithic monuments were often incorporated in general archaeological inventories, or occasionally in special lists, some more detailed and descriptive than others. The fewer monuments there were in a district, the more precisely were they located, described and illustrated.

Some thirty years ago, an ambitious programme of inventories of French megaliths was proposed by Professor R. Vaufrey (Vaufrey 1943). It took a long time to become a reality and to find volunteers. At present the special volumes for some *départements* have been published in the collection of supplements to *Gallia-Préhistoire*: *Indre-et-Loire* (Cordier 1963), *Maine-et-Loire* (Gruet 1967), *Loir-et-Cher* (Despriée and Leymarios 1974), the *départements* of the Paris region (Peek 1975), *Lot* (Clottes 1977). The *Deux-Sèvres* (Germond 1980) has just been published. The work of Dr J. Clottes, being a doctoral thesis, has a more synthetic aspect; it concerns a southern *département* with very few menhirs and many 'dolmens' (498, although in fact the number now recognized is 500). Most of the other *départements* covered by the survey are moderately rich in megaliths, and some devoted research worker or other has managed to find the time and the resources to study each one. For all those involved it has been a heavy voluntary burden. Having to deal with so many menhirs can become monotonous after a while. But it is a matter for regret that some people who began work on the scheme, in Brittany for instance, have had to give up because of other pressing commitments.

In fact general synthetic works on the Neolithic cultures of whole provinces or groups of provinces, such as the Paris Basin (Bailloud 1964, 1974), Provence (Courtin 1974), the Centre-Ouest (Burnez 1976), give quite a lot of information about the megaliths,

and still more is to be found in the regional synthetic works on megalithic tombs, such as in the standard and classic one for Brittany (L'Helgouach 1965), which can now be supplemented by different revisions and general works (Giot, L'Helgouach and Monnier 1979; Giot, Briard and Pape 1979). There has been a huge amount of regional research in the same sense: in the North and Pas-de-Calais (Piningre 1980), in Normandy (Verron 1976), in Vendée (Chaigneau 1965, and Joussaume, in preparation), in Poitou (Germond and Joussaume), in the Charentes (the same and Gauron, and Mohen), in Aquitaine (Roussot-Larroque), in the Côte d'Or (Joly 1965), the Franche-Comté (Pétrequin and Piningre 1976), the Massif Central (G.E.M.A. 1973), the Grands Causses (Lorblanchet 1965, Maury 1967), the Lodévois (Arnal 1979), the Aveyron (Galtier 1971), the Gard (Audibert 1958 and 1962, Roudil since), the Hérault (Arnal 1963), Provence (Sauzade, in preparation), the Roussillon (Abelanet 1970), the Aude (Guilaine), etc. And we have probably not heard about all the unpublished doctoral dissertations and master dissertations involved either.

Recent Excavations

To obtain an idea of the number of modern excavations that have taken place over the past twenty years or so we have drawn on the information reports collected in *Gallia-Préhistoire*, amended by some other documents.

There have been approximately 250 small rescue excavations (before or after destruction), or cleaning up operations of already emptied tombs which can involve the sifting of spoil tips from older or clandestine excavations, a procedure very rewarding in the south of France. And in addition there have been 60–80 excavations of considerable importance, some very large-scale digs concerning complex multiple-chambered monuments or even groups of them. If we take into account the individual chambers we might arrive at about 120–140 monuments excavated or re-excavated minutely and on a large scale. If one also considers the amount of money involved (including the funds needed to conserve some of the major sites) the conclusion must be that never before has such an effort been expended on megaliths, even in the era of private amateur digging, which was always a quick affair. A possible total of about 400 monuments have thus been explored.

This research can be divided into two distinct but not mutually exclusive categories. On the one hand we have the large and complex megalithic structures of the Atlantic façade, from the Charentes to Normandy,

20

where problems of architecture and of the antiquity of the structures have been highlighted. On the other hand we have the tombs in the limestone, chalky or calcareous areas, where the good or better preservation of bone makes the delicate dissection of the contents of the tombs very profitable. (In those monuments where the bones have been leached out, some settling of the in-fill will have occurred at the least, and less precise information on burial rites will be available.)

Chronology

We are much better informed about megaliths than we have ever been, now we know that they were built over a span of at least 2,500 years (more probably 3,000 years), and that quite a lot of them are nicely linked by a series of complementary cross-datings through time.

The first megalithic chamber tomb to be radiocarbon dated (in 1959) was the central one of the Ile Carn cairn, at Ploudalmezeau (Finistère), and in fact from some material from my own first excavation there. The result caused a small sensation at the time, truly without any justification, as already quite a few dates were available from different Neolithic cultures in Europe which demonstrated the need to open up the chronological concertina. Of course some conservative scholars went on arguing for the old dates because they were obsessed by problems of origins and of beginnings. Cultures have no beginning and no end. They emerge gradually and spontaneously out of the mists of time. We are still living in a culture which is to an extent 'megalithic' in its inheritance.

In Central Europe particularly we still encounter scholars who seem uneasy about the early dating of the big monuments of the Atlantic façade of Europe. They consider them to be – from a comparative archaeological point of view – typically 'Chalcolithic' or 'Eneolithic' achievements. They are very annoyed by the many 'early' radiocarbon dates from Western European monuments, especially if these are calibrated. One should not forget that these radiocarbon dates, more and more numerous every year, are supported by corresponding TL dates, palynological evidence, geological evidence (sea-level variations for instance), and so on. Details may be made more precise by the new methods of the future, at least if they provide more precise dating, but now we can consider the principal lines of our chronological system to be good enough, at least if we assume that an approximation within five-to-ten per cent of the correct ages is sufficient.

At present we have about twenty-five radiocarbon dates or so of 5000 years BP or older for monuments of the Western façade, and probably a good hundred of later Neolithic or Chalcolithic date from megalithic and para-megalithic sites in all parts of the country.

Chronological Distribution of Collective Tombs

If we briefly synthesize this chronological information in a geographic model, we find a decrement when we progress from the Armorican Atlantic seaboard towards eastern or southern France.

Middle Neolithic collective graves (4000–2700 BC approximately) are found in Brittany, western Normandy, Poitou, Charentes, possibly Anjou and Touraine. A unique case is possibly a site on the coast of Aquitaine (Le Gurp). In the old typological language, these monuments would belong to the passage graves and their derivatives.

Late Neolithic collective graves (from 2700 BC onwards) are to be found in the Paris Basin, eastern Normandy, Champagne, Burgundy, Jura, the Massif Central, Aquitaine and the Pyrenees. In the traditional typological terminology, these monuments would fit into the categories of the gallery graves, the trenches and the rock-cut tombs.

Chalcolithic collective graves (from about 2200 BC onwards) can be found in Provence, the Alps, Languedoc and the Causses. They correspond to the meridional dolmens, to the rock-cut hypogea and the natural caves used as ossuaries. There is a small overlap since in these southern and south-eastern districts the Chalcolithic begins earlier than farther north, where the Late Neolithic tombs have been more often re-used in the Chalcolithic than really built anew, though this has certainly happened.

These chronological simplifications and their presentation may not be taken too seriously. The distribution pattern thus revealed is nevertheless remarkable. Ignoring contacts with Iberian megaliths through the Pyrenees, the apparent picture is that of a diffusion from the older monuments of the Atlantic façade towards the interior. Even if we don't want to use a diffusionist model, we can't get away from this fact.

We should not forget either that the Danubian Neolithic cultures buried their dead in single graves, as did also the principal Middle Neolithic culture of continental France, the so-called Chasséen (and its regional variants). The Chasséen tombs of southern France are quite often in small cists.

Typology

The greatest preoccupation of many megalithic scholars over the last thirty to fifty years has been with typological subtleties.

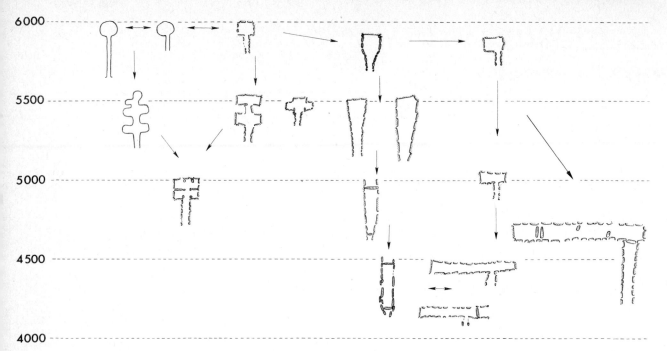

2 Chronological (years before the present) and typological relationship of the main types of megalithic tomb plan in Brittany, in a tentative chart of complete regional development.

In spite of its diffusionist flavour, Glyn Daniel's 1941 paper on the 'Dual Nature of the Megalithic Colonisation' has provided illumination for many megalithic-lovers over a number of years. Its principal merit was to reduce the different regional or local variants to two main successive types. Of course this paper did also dwell on the problem of 'origins'. As I have said above, these sorts of phenomenon may have no definite origins. They may appear spontaneously at about the same moment in quite separate population groups under approximately the same conditions, the societies being at about the same stage of development. Even if such an hypothesis is false, it has at least a provisional value, in exorcizing those questions which ask about the earliest megaliths.

The tendency today is to study typological problems in regional or local groups of monuments which are definitely linked. If ancient people in the past could reach most megaliths in a group on foot within a few days, one can assume that knowledge of some kind about the megaliths would spread. Elements from nearby populations might meet together on certain grand occasions, the most obvious even being for the transport of the biggest stones, so that plenty of men could have had the opportunity to see monuments in the course of construction. These contacts will have been the most likely means by which regional types became standardized, with of course the possibility that 'masons', 'architects' or 'engineers' moved about to give technical help or advice. One can't very well imagine 'academies' of megalithic architecture!

Even if information only circulated between distant communities through chance contacts or at best through the movement of middlemen, these people are likely to have been allowed to see the interiors of tombs in each community, or at least to have heard precise descriptions. But since most monuments were probably covered up under mounds, barrows or cairns there will have been great difficulty in obtaining an accurate idea of their dispositions from only an outside view – unless it proved possible to get inside that is. We are so accustomed to see exposed the inner skeletons of the megalithic monuments that we rather tend to forget when discussing typological or structural niceties that the interiors were no doubt hidden to the profane.

At least as a game or an exercise, one can tentatively build up phyletic trees with types of megalith from a region. As an example we present one for Brittany (ill. 2), which ties in with all the chronological evidence currently available, although some aspects are speculative. It shows that all the main types of tomb-plan known in that region can be fitted into such a chart. Of course the lay-out of tombs is only part of the

22

definition of each type – if types exist other than as ideas in the minds of modern scholars.

Mortuary Practices

Reading old publications leads one to doubt the accuracy of many observations of burial ritual, such as the practice of cremation in some instances, or more often the idea that megalithic chambers only contained secondary interments, as if they were used only as bone-houses after a *décharnement pré-sépulcral* in another place. But some nineteenth-century antiquaries did correctly observe cremated bones. And at least in northern Europe, modern excavations have proved that some megalithic tombs were utilized as repositories or charnel-houses.

Some descriptions of cremation actually concern inhumed bones which have been secondarily scorched by accident, either by torches, or when during a much later intrusion in a tomb a fire may have been lit.

The collective tomb of Neuvy-en-Dunois, Eure-et-Loir (Masset 1968), has produced an early but definite case of incineration. It was not a true megalithic structure, but simply a sub-rectangular pit, measuring 2.60 m by less than 2 m, with a depth of 1.20 m. It contained the remains of 22 to 24 individuals of both sexes and of all ages. All had been cremated, on a small hearth not very far away, positioned on their backs, with half-open arms. Earth and stones were laid over the bones, and there were a very few grave-goods. A radiocarbon date of 3300 ± 140 BC has been compared with that of the cases of cremation known from some of the very large barrows of the Morbihan.

At a later period, a very curious cremation trench was cut into the side of the cairn of La Hoguette, at Fontenay-le-Marmion, Calvados (Caillaud and Lagnel 1972). Of a total length of 12 m, 3 m cut into the already dilapidated cairn, leaving the greater part outside. The trench's mean breadth was 1.30 m, its depth more than 0.50 m. At least 16 corpses were represented, with some Seine-Oise-Marne (SOM) style pottery and other grave-goods. A radiocarbon date from the associated charcoal of 2350 ± 120 BC gives the best fit out of four dates. Apart from a few cases of incineration associated with inhumations in

3 The gallery grave of La Chaussée-Tirancourt (Somme) in the process of being excavated by C. Masset, in 1974. The photograph shows the oldest burial layer in a central compartment. The interruption to the left is due to an earlier excavation. In the right half of the picture are two incomplete primary burials, somewhat disturbed. In the left half, the bones are still more disconnected. (Photo C. Masset.)

4 *The hypogeum of Roaix (Vaucluse) during the excavation by J. Courtin, in 1966: the most recent burial layer, eastern part. A massive inhumation of piled up bodies. (Photo J. Courtin.)*

the Paris Basin, the tomb of Stein in the Netherlands is a good counterpart.

The same cairn of La Hoguette has given excellent information on the practices of the passage-grave builders. It contained 7 or 8 chambered tombs, the last being destroyed. Two chambers presented rather mixed up bones from 8 and 9 people respectively, in the first chamber with some protection of the skulls, in the second some partly connected bones; another disturbed chamber yielded the remains of 14 individuals, some bones still being joined together. Three other chambers produced bones of 14, 6 and 5 persons re-

spectively, most of them being crouched on their sides, with flexed limbs. This excellent excavation has shown clearly the importance of the flexed position. To keep an eight-month-pregnant woman as crouched as possible, her calcanea had been bored after her death.

In the second cairn of Vierville, Manche, also in the calcareous area of western Normandy, but less well preserved, at least one contracted skeleton lying on its right side has been discovered (Verron 1977). In an intact chamber of La Hogue, Fontenay-le-Marmion, Calvados, six skeletons were found dispersed; the early digs had encountered a protected skull.

The cairn of Le Montiou, Sainte-Soline, Deux-Sèvres (Germond and Joussaume 1978) has chiefly produced disordered bones, although there were indications among the older burials that the bodies were lying prone, bent knees towards the abdomen. In the celebrated group of cairns at Bougon, Deux-Sèvres (Mohen 1977), where tomb A had yielded about 200 skeletons in 1840, the first chamber of cairn E contained 5 or 6 people, the skulls against the walls, with a radiocarbon date of 3850 ± 230 BC. The bottom of chamber O contained 10 skeletons, bones still partly linked in a huddled position; half were children and radiocarbon dates of 3850 and 3650 BC are available.

Thus a very coherent picture of the mode of deposition of the dead comes out of this survey. In all the older types of megalithic tombs we have primary burials in a lateral and crouched position. New burials often dispersed the bones of the first occupants, and sometimes the skulls received greater attention. No case of specific removal of certain bones has yet been noticed.

If we pass on to the later monuments, similar conclusions also emerge from modern excavations. The *allée couverte* of La Chaussée-Tirancourt, Somme, the most northerly of its type (Masset 1972), contained well over 350 burials (ill. 3). The later burials greatly disturbed the earlier ones, but happily a few of the latter did at least partly survive intact. The first inhumations were distributed in compartments, the later ones in smaller cells or boxes. The compartments were divided off by lines of stones and possibly by wooden planks. This very meticulous dig, extending over eight years, has given a lot of information about the way the bones were treated and disposed of some time after their deposition. For instance, they could be packed so as to take up less space, sometimes when the flesh had decayed but the ligaments were still extant. At the beginning of the use of the monument, the corpses lay on their left side, with flexed legs; later, they may have been placed flat on their backs. At one period heads were turned towards the entrance of the tomb, at another towards the back.

The famous excavation of the rock-cut hypogeum of Les Mournouards, Mesnil-sur-Oger, Marne (Leroi-Gourhan, Bailloud and Brézillon 1962), provided a lot of details, including the relationship of the grave-goods to the burials. About 40 adults and 20 children had been inhumed there, although only about 20 had bones still connected, and in fact only 6 had not been displaced at all. The corpses had been placed in a supple shroud or bag not covering the head. This made it easier to move the bodies about at a later stage, the skulls being piled in corners. The arms were often folded on the chest. Burying a body thus bagged was a rapid operation, possibly not taking more than a minute.

The remarkable excavation of what was left of half the rock-cut hypogeum of Roaix, Vaucluse (Courtin 1974), gives a dramatic picture of the same sort of tomb for the south of France, also from a Chalcolithic culture (ill. 4). This site has not received the attention it deserves. In an upper layer one hundred corpses or so had been deposited or rather – extraordinarily – piled up one on top of the other, stretched out, sometimes with legs bent; the arms were folded over the chest, the feet often crossed, so that here again one can think of a bag or shroud. The bodies had clearly been buried all together at one moment, men, women and numerous children mixed up, often head to foot. Fierce fires had been lit on top of the last corpses. This massive burial may have been the result of some tragic event. A radiocarbon date of 2090 ± 140 BC is associated with this upper layer. The lower series, separated by a metre of sterile sand, was more normal, with the usual disorder of earlier skeletons. Some bones which still remained linked proved that the bodies had been placed in a crouched position, as was usual in the caves used as ossuaries in the south of France. Here the radiocarbon date is 2150 ± 140 BC.

A current theory is that the megalithic tombs of southern France were only secondary burial places, containing heaped bones from skeletons which had been discarnated elsewhere. No modern excavation has provided any evidence for this; on the contrary, convincing traces of at least parts of connected limbs survive. During the reshuffling to make room for new bodies, the skulls were usually stacked in corners or against the walls. A very precise excavation from this point of view has been conducted for six years in the dolmen of Les Peirières at Villedubert, Aude (Duday, forthcoming) (ill. 5). Sealed in and abandoned after the Beaker period, the monument offered an excellent opportunity to conduct a methodological test in an undisturbed deposit. Six yearly digging seasons have been devoted to the excavation of the upper level of burials of the Chalcolithic, and about forty groups of

5 The dolmen of Villedubert (Aude) during the excavation by H. Duday, in 1977: upper layer of Beaker period burials, with the lower limbs of an adult still joined together. (Photo H. Duday.)

bones have been discovered anatomically connected. This upper level was in use over quite a long period of time; the corpses were not strictly buried, but left on top of the sepulchral deposit. The dissection of the earlier level of burials under a pavement of stones will also probably be the scrupulous work of many years to come. The minuteness of this procedure, with the recording of the most infinitesimal details, is beyond description in a few words.

If we sum up these results, we see that except when bodies were dragged into a rock-cut tomb through a narrow aperture, corpses were generally deposited in a contracted position. In megalithic monuments with portholes we should also possibly expect the use of some kind of shroud.

Architectural Convergence

The best demonstration that there is something wrong in envisaging distant correlations between monuments of similar form baptized by the typologists with the same names, is given by a chronological comparison between some monuments in the British Isles or Ireland and those on the Continent. If we are to believe even the most recent textbooks (such as Megaw and Simpson 1979), the so-called 'passage graves' of Ireland or of Scotland came into existence some time after the building of 'passage graves' of more or less similar plan had been abandoned in Brittany. In the same way it is absurd to think that in calling the monuments of the Causses *dolmens à couloir* or 'passage graves' there is anything other than a purely verbal similitude.

It is more interesting to compare technologically monuments built out of the same sort of rocks, from stones with the same sort of characteristics, or in the same sort of topographical or morphological location. Similar conditions quite naturally tend to produce similarities in the solutions chosen by the different 'architects'. For instance, monuments made out of schist usually possess a whole host of detailed similarities. The number of obvious methods for solving techno-logical problems is limited. Perhaps quite a lot of similarities on a broader scale arise from such parallelisms.

The Complex Structure of the Great Cairns

Until recently both small and large cairns were con-sidered to have been created by the casual piling up of stones over and around monuments, with little or no method in the process. Certain excavators, such as Z. Le Rouzic in the Morbihan, had noticed traces of in-ternal walling in some cases. But the great lesson of Barnenez, twenty years ago, was that the outer walls were built to be seen. Also, that when a concentric series of walls existed, their tops were graduated so that the upper parts of all the internal walls would be partly visible, in a series of steps. The appearance of a heap of stones was only the result of collapse and time. In fact probably for hundreds of years cows at Barnenez had walked to the fields along a narrow lane, on one side of which was a large exposed part of the innermost original facing. It was not only the internal aspects of megalithic architecture that could be gran-diose – the façades were intended to be impressive as well.

Another practical lesson we learnt at Barnenez was that these facings could be excavated, exposed, strengthened and restored if necessary in the best preserved monuments. Everyone began hunting for façades in the large cairns of the Atlantic fringe.

Outer wallings at least have been found everywhere: for instance, in Normandy at La Hogue and at La Hoguette, Fontenay-le-Marmion. Concentric or suc-cessive walls, or walls with buttresses are known at Bougon (Mohen 1977), at Le Montiou (Germond and Joussaume 1978), at Les Mousseaux, Pornic (L'Helgouach 1977), at Dissignac, Saint-Nazaire (L'Helgouach 1976, 1977, 1979), at Larcuste I, Colpo (L'Helgouach and Lecornec 1976), at Kerleven, La Forêt-Fouesnant (Le Roux and L'Helgouach 1967), and at Carn (Giot 1980).

The large cairns containing more than two passage graves have quite often been built in a series of phases, by accretion and by modification. Clear cases are those of Barnenez, Carn, Guennoc III (Giot 1980), and on a different scale, Kerleven. The important cairn of Dissignac, with its two chambered tombs, has given a very clear and interesting case of remodelling, with lengthening of the passages. Good evidence for such a lengthening is also evident at least in the first phase at Barnenez, where the process may even have been quite general. Rebuilding of some kind may be suspected in many large megalithic tombs which have lost their cairns or barrows; the presence of dry-stone walling in a cairn helps one detect such reconstructions.

The re-use of stones and slabs from earlier stages of the same monument may have been more frequent than we tend to suspect. The abnormal position of or-namental stones, as at Barnenez and also at Gavrinis, is a good indication of this.

The closing in or the blocking of passages must have been a common practice. We found intact transversal walls in the passage of the central chamber at Carn, and large accumulations of stones blocking some of the passages at Barnenez. Evidence for the closing of the lateral cells of the monument of Larcuste II at Colpo has also been quite clear (L'Helgouach and Lecornec 1976). In some cases there were real doors of stone, such as between the chamber and the passage of the angled monument of Gâvres, Morbihan (L'Helgouach 1970), and a half-door at the entrance to the chamber of Barnenez A. Wooden doors are thus possible.

From many points of view, the outside of the monuments was quite as important as the inside. The Atlantic cairns do not present typical forecourts, but one can speak of a parvis. Recent excavations have shown that important events or ceremonies took place in front of the entrances to the tombs or on the lower buttress-like masses of stone-walling between them.

Often quite large quantities of sherds of pottery have been found there, coming sometimes from ceremonial sorts of pots.

Many other indications or hints have emerged from the more careful and methodical excavations of the large cairns. The ethical problem is sometimes to decide whether some parts should be completely stripped and taken down, or if it is more essential to preserve the maximum number of undisturbed structures. Archaeologists have a tendency to overdo investigation, and architects and contractors to overdo restoration!

Wooden Structures

The importance of associated wooden buildings for some later types of megalithic monument has been brilliantly demonstrated in Franche-Comté, especially for the site of Aillevans, where a trapezoidal house was set over the chamber (Pétrequin and Piningre 1976).

My personal impression is that the more frequent occurrence of these types of structure has been overlooked. Post-holes indicating structures of the same sort have been observed in the low long barrows of Brittany. The low barrows built around the later megalithic tombs of gallery-grave type are so similar to the low long barrows without a true megalithic structure that we would certainly expect wooden houses adjoining some of the western *allées couvertes*.

R. Joussaume (1977b) was obliged to postulate a covering of perishable materials for the curious megalithic tomb at Xanton-Chassenon in the Vendée.

Standing Stones

Menhirs have long been neglected and rather unpopular among professional archaeologists. A renewed interest is developing, however, quite apart from the problems and questions raised by the geometrical and astronomical theories.

Recent rescue excavations at Saint-Just, Ille-et-Vilaine (Le Roux 1979), on one of the small alignment sites, have shown the existence of post-holes interspersed with the stone menhirs. And beside the row of standing stones five post-holes seem to indicate the position of a small hut-like structure.

There were probably many more curious things in the megalithic world than we can ever imagine. Unhappily most of these types of sites are in places where the depth of soil is thin because of erosion, and only a very limited part of any one structure survives.

Megalithic Experimental Archaeology

The various popular media have demanded experiments in megalithic building for a long time. But they usually proposed that an authentic monument should be uprooted and then rebuilt, a procedure which could only be refused. At Bougon in July 1979, however, Dr J. P. Mohen was able to conduct a most interesting test. Amongst other achievements, a concrete block of 32 tons, equivalent to one of the capstones from the local monuments, was moved by about 200 people, 170 pulling ropes and 30 moving wooden rollers and using tree-trunks as levers to ease their efforts.

The experiment worked very well, and confirmed all the calculations which demonstrate that megalithic building was technically quite feasible for the types of society involved in it.

Many new facts have come to light and many theories have been proved or disproved during the last twenty years of work on the French megaliths. Undoubtedly during the next twenty years our information will improve at least as much, and many aspects of the subject which today seem 'mysterious' will have been explained rationally.

Bibliography

ABELANET, J. 1970 'Les dolmens du Roussillon', *Les civilisations néolithiques du Midi de la France*, Carcassonne, 74–9.

ARNAL, G.B. 1979 *Les mégalithes du Lodévois*, Lodève.

ARNAL, J. 1963 'Les dolmens du département de l'Hérault', *Préhistoire* XV.

AUDIBERT, J. 1958 'Les civilisations chalcolithiques du Gard', *Mémoires de la Société Préhistorique Française* V, 233–305.

1962 *La civilisation chalcolithique du Languedoc oriental*, Institut international d'études ligures, Bordighera-Montpellier.

BAILLOUD, G. 1964 'Le Néolithique dans le Bassin Parisien', *II° supplément à Gallia-Préhistoire* (2nd edn, 1974).

BURNEZ, C. 1976 'Le Neolithique et le Chalcolithique dans le Centre-Ouest de la France', *Mémoires de la Société Préhistorique Française* XII.

CAILLAUD, R. AND LAGNEL, E. 1972 'Le cairn et le crématoire néolithiques de la Hoguette à Fontenay-le-Marmion (Calvados)', *Gallia-Préhistoire* XV, 137–97.

CHAIGNEAU, P.R. 1966–7 'Les dolmens vendéens', *Société d'émulation de la Vendée*, 17–31.

CLOTTES, J. 1975 'Informations', *Gallia-Préhistoire* XVIII, 619.

1977 'Inventaire des mégalithes de la France, Lot', *I° supplément à Gallia-Préhistoire* V.

CORDIER, G. 1963 'Inventaire des mégalithes de la France, Indre-et-Loire', *I° supplément à Gallia-Préhistoire* I.

COURTIN, J. 1974 'Le Néolithique de la Provence', *Mémoires de la Société Préhistorique Française* XI.

DANIEL, G.E. 1941 'The Dual Nature of the Megalithic Colonisation of Prehistoric Europe', *Proc. Preh. Soc.* VII, 1–49.

1960 *The Prehistoric Chamber Tombs of France*, London.

1966 'The Megalith Builders of the SOM', *Palaeohistoria* XII, 199–208.

DESPRIEE, J. AND LEYMARIOS. C. 1974 'Inventaire des mégalithes de la France, Loir-et-Cher', *I° supplément à Gallia-Préhistoire* III.

GALTIER, J. 1971 'Les sépultures mégalithiques du Sud de l'Aveyron', Ph.D. Université de Paris I.

G.E.M.A. (BARBIER, L. et al.) 1973 'Répertoire préliminaire à un inventaire des monuments mégalithiques du Cantal, de la Haute-Loire et du Puy-de-Dôme', *Revue Archéologique du Centre* XII, 253–79.

GERMOND, G. 1980 'Inventaire des mégalithes de la France, Deux-Sèvres', *I° Supplément à Gallia-Préhistoire* VI.

GERMOND, G. AND JOUSSAUME, R. 1978 'Le tumulus du Montiou à Sainte-Soline (Deux-Sèvres)', *Bulletin de la Société historique et scientifique des Deux-Sèvres* (2), XI, 129–88.

GIOT, P.R. 1980 *Barnenez, Carn, Guennoc*, Rennes.

GIOT, P.R., L'HELGOUACH, J. AND MONNIER, J.L. 1979 *Préhistoire de la Bretagne*, Rennes.

GIOT, P.R. BRIARD, J. AND PAPE, L. 1979 *Protohistoire de la Bretagne*, Rennes.

GRUET, M. 1967 'Inventaire des mégalithes de la France, Maine-et-Loire', *I° supplément à Gallia-Préhistoire* II.

GUILAINE. J. 1972 *La nécropole mégalithique de la Clape (Aude)*, Carcassonne.

JOLY, J. 1965 'Les tombes mégalithiques du département de la Côte-d'Or', *Revue archéologique de l'Est et du Centre-Est* XVI, 57–74.

JOUSSAUME, R. 1972 'La préhistoire en Vendée, point des connaissances', *Société d'émulation de la Vendée* CXIX, 7–74.

1977a 'Les architectures mégalithiques particulières du Sud de la Vendée', *Bulletin de la Société Polymathique du Morbihan* CIV, 125–42.

1977b 'Le mégalithe de la Pierre-Virante à Xanton-Chassenon (Vendée)', *L'Anthropologie* LXXXI, 5–65.

LEROI-GOURHAN, A., BAILLOUD, G. AND BREZILLION, M. 1962 'L'hypogée II des Mournouards, Mesnil-sur-Oger, Marne', *Gallia-Préhistoire* V, 23–133.

LE ROUX, C.T. 1979 'Informations', *Gallia-Préhistoire* XXII, 526–30.

LE ROUX, C.T. AND LECERF, Y. 1977 'Le dolmen de Cruguelic en Ploemeur et les sépultures transeptées armoricaines', *Bulletin de la Société Polymathique du Morbihan* CIV, 143–60.

LE ROUX, C.T. AND L'HELGOUACH, J. 1966 'Le cairn mégalithique avec sépultures à chambre compartimentée de Kerleven, La Forêt-Fouesnant (Finistère)', *Annales de Bretagne* LXX, 7–52.

L'HELGOUACH, J. 1965 *Les sépultures mégalithiques en Armorique, dolmens à couloir et allées couvertes*, Rennes.

1970 'Le monument mégalithique du Goërem à Gâvres (Morbihan)', *Gallia-Préhistoire* XIII, 217–61.

1976 'Le tumulus de Dissignac à Saint-Nazaire (Loire-Atlantique)', *Dissertationes archaeologicae gandenses* XVI, 142–9.

1977 'Le cairn des Mousseaux à Pornic (Loire-Atlantique)', *Bulletin de la Société Polymathique du Morbihan* CIV, 161–72.

1979 'Informations', *Gallia-Préhistoire XXII*, 562–8.

L'HELGOUACH, J. AND LECORNEC, J. 1976 'Le site mégalithique Min Goh Ru près de Larcuste à Colpo (Morbihan)', *Bulletin de la Société Préhistorique Française* LXXIII, 370–97.

LORBLANCHET, M. 1965 'Contribution à l'étude du peuplement des Grands Causses', *Bulletin de la Société Préhistorique Française* LXII, 667–712.

MASSET, C. 1968 'Les incinérations du Néolithique ancien de Neuvy-en-Dunois (Eure-et-Loir)', *Gallia-Préhistoire* XI, 205–34.

1971 'Une sépulture collective mégalithique à la Chaussée-Tirancourt (Somme)', *Bulletin de la Société Préhistorique Française* LXVIII, 178–82.

1972 'The megalithic tomb of La Chaussée-Tirancourt', *Antiquity* XLVII, 297–300.

MAURY, J. 1967 *Les étapes du peuplement sur les Grands Causses*, Millau.

MEGAW, J.V.S. AND SIMPSON, D.D.A. 1979 *Introduction to British Prehistory*, Leicester.

MOHEN, J.P. 1977 'Les tumulus de Bougon', *Bulletin de la Société historique et scientifique des Deux-Sèvres* n° 2–3, 48.

PEEK, J. 1975 'Inventaire des mégalithes de la France,

Région parisienne', *I° supplément à Gallia-Préhistoire* IV.

PETREQUIN; P. AND PININGRE, J.F. 1976 'Les sépultures collectives mégalithiques de Franche-Comté', *Gallia-Préhistoire* XIX, 287–394.

PININGRE, J.F. 1980 'Dolmens et menhirs du Nord — Pas de Calais', *Atlas archéologique Nord — Pas de Calais* III.

SAUZADE, G. 1978 'Les sépultures du Vaucluse du Néolithique à l'Age du Bronze', Ph.D. Université d'Aix-en-Provence.

TANGUY, B. 1976 'Toponymie et peuplement', in Calvez, L. (ed.), *La presqu'ile de Crozon, Histoire, Art, Nature*, Paris, 61.

1979 'Toponyme et peuplement', in Dilasser, B. (ed.), *Un pays de Cornouaille, Locronan et sa région*, Paris, 70–2.

VAUFREY, R. 1943 'Projet d'Inventaire des monuments mégalithiques', *Bulletin de la Société normande d'Etudes préhistoriques* XXXII, 121–8.

VERRON, G. 1976 'Acculturation et continuité en Normandie durant le Néolithique et les âges des Métaux', *Dissertationes archaeologicae gandenses* XVI, 261–83.

1977 'Un type de monuments funéraires classique dans le Néolithique de Normandie', *Bulletin de la Société Polymathique du Morbihan* CIV, 187–219.

3 The Megalithic Tombs of Iberia

Robert W. Chapman

NEARLY A decade ago a reviewer of David Clarke's *Beaker Pottery of Great Britain and Ireland* gibed at Cambridge prehistorians, who, he claimed, believed that Africa began at the Pyrenees. Whatever the roots of this gibe, no such myopia can be attached to Glyn Daniel. Throughout his long career he has devoted consistent attention to the Iberian cultures and megalithic tombs which form the subject of this paper. Between hard covers there is his *Megalith Builders of Western Europe* (1963), which formed a worthy successor to earlier syntheses by James Fergusson (1872) and Eric Peet (1912) and gave due attention to the tombs from Spain and Portugal. Their position in the origins and development of Neolithic and Copper Age monumental tombs in western Europe and the Mediterranean was also discussed in a series of papers, ranging from the dual colonization model of his early career (1941) to the affirmation of multiple centres of megalithic genesis (e.g. 1966, 1967, 1970, 1973) in more recent years. This move from a predominantly diffusionist model to one of multilinear evolution nicely mirrors the thinking of European prehistorians in the last forty years. Debate over the origins of megalithic monuments depends fundamentally upon the adoption of different theoretical frameworks such as 'evolution' and 'diffusion', as Glyn Daniel also recognized in his contribution to the volume of the *Proceedings of the Prehistoric Society* dedicated to Grahame Clark (1971). Given the priority of theory in the successful pursuit of archaeology (a statement with which Professor Daniel may feel slightly less sympathy!), it seems appropriate to view the megalithic tombs of Spain and Portugal in terms of theory and approaches to culture change and to specify those dimensions of study which require close scrutiny.

Orientalists, Occidentalists and Culture Theory

The 'classic' theories of origins for Iberian megalithic tombs have been summarized too clearly elsewhere to require more than cursory repetition (see Daniel 1963; Almagro and Arribas 1963). The local development or 'occidentalist' position was formulated initially by Cartailhac (1886), who argued for an evolutionary sequence, beginning with the polygonal chambers in the upland areas of northern Portugal (Beira, Tras-os-Montes) and then spreading south and west, evolving into passage graves and 'tholoi'. This thesis was followed and developed by Wilke (1912), Leeds (1918–20), Obermaier (1919) and Aberg (1921) in the first two decades of the present century, although it should be noted that Wilke and Obermaier modified this position to allow for the introduction of corbelled passage graves into Iberia from the east Mediterranean.

29

But it was Bosch-Gimpera who built upon this foundation and integrated Iberian megalithic origins into a masterly synthesis of the peninsula's later prehistory (1932, 1944). He maintained this position throughout his career (e.g. 1967), defining stages in the evolution of megalithic architecture. But even at his most evolutionary he still acknowledged the existence of contact between Iberia and the central and eastern Mediterranean, with its implications for cultural development. Other prehistorians preferred to give this 'contact' greater weight and pursue an 'orientalist' argument (Forde 1929, 1930; Peake and Fleure 1930; Childe 1932), by which corbelled tombs and rock-cut tombs were introduced into Iberia and subsequently diffused and devolved into megalithic passage graves and single chambers. Glyn Daniel's paper on the dual nature of megalithic colonization in western Europe (1941) finds its context among the works of these orientalist proponents in the 1930s and 1940s. But it was the monumental syntheses of George and Vera Leisner which crystallized the debate over megalithic origins by providing the comprehensive treatment of the data which had been lacking in earlier analyses (1943, 1951, 1956; Leisner 1965; Márquez, Leisner and Leisner 1952). Now it would be rather facile to refer to them simply as orientalists or occidentalists, since their arguments for separate south-east and south-west Iberian origins for corbelled tombs and megalithic passage graves respectively were integrated within a context of wide Mediterranean contacts (e.g. 1943). In a similar vein one should also note the position adopted by Savory (e.g. 1968, 1977), who follows the Leisners' arguments regarding south-east and south-west Iberia, but finds an underlying unity of origin for megalithic culture(s) in the diffusion of communal burial from the east Mediterranean (cf. Blance 1960, 1961).

This East-West conflict was established before the development of radiometric dating techniques. So before we look in detail at the effects of radiocarbon and thermoluminescence dating on our knowledge of the chronology and genesis of Iberian megalithic tombs, let us pause to outline the basic assumptions and culture theory behind the debate. A good starting point here lies in Glyn Daniel's statement of the main questions asked by students of megalithic tombs (1963, 39):

> who were the builders, where did they come from, how and where did they live, why did they spread over western Europe and what contributions, if any, did they make to the future heritage of prehistoric Europe?

The basic unity of megalithic tombs and monuments is affirmed in terms of the defining characteristic of using large stones and, more particularly for the tombs, in terms of collective burial, which was 'a complicated and religious idea' (1963, 78). Given this unity we are witnessing 'the spread of styles of funerary architecture, with certain basic patterns on which regional and local variations are made' (1963, 45). This practice of communal burial in chamber tombs, attaining impressively monumental proportions (e.g. Cueva de Menga, Antequera – Leisner and Leisner 1943), seemed internally coherent and diverged from preceding mortuary practices in western Europe, which, where known, were characterized by individual inhumation. Thus the fundamental assumption made was that changes in mortuary practices of this kind reflected changes of culture and population. The pursuit of megalithic enquiries then became the pursuit of an area of origin and the plotting of the diffusion of the megalith builders through progressive changes in the form and dimensions of the individual tombs.

Whatever the favoured area of origins, it was assumed that formal similarities in mortuary practices reflected interaction between groups of megalith builders. Regular change in mortuary practices signified continuity, irregular change signified a break of population. Nuclear areas formed the focus of culture change, with diffusion as the process by which change was conveyed to increasingly wider areas. Now within the wider context of European prehistory and indeed of archaeology in the first half of this century, this approach and these assumptions were widespread. They reflect what has been called the normative and historical-distributional approaches to the study of culture (Binford 1965, 1971). Such assumptions were characteristic particularly of Iberian prehistorians. The identification of cultural assemblages with 'peoples' can be witnessed before Gordon Childe's work in the pioneering publications of Louis Siret in south-east Spain (1913). The seven successive chronological periods which he defined for the post-Pleistocene were argued to represent a series of separate 'couches ethniques'. Culture change was to be explained in terms of ethnic movement and survivals. The demonstration of movement and contact depended upon the formal comparison of cultural traits (e.g. Siret 1913, fig.3). With the subsequent development of models of Iberian prehistoric culture change based upon processes of diffusion, colonization or influence from the central and eastern Mediterranean, nuclear areas of contact and development were defined (e.g. south-east Spain, southern Portugal). The detailed discussion of this culture theory has already beeen presented elsewhere (Chapman 1975) and will be published (Chapman, forthcoming). Suffice it to say

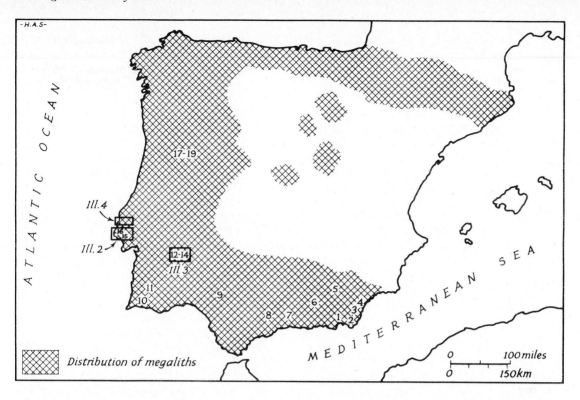

1 *Schematic distribution of megalithic tombs in Iberia. Main sites mentioned in text:* 1 *Los Millares* 2 *El Barranquete,* 3 *Cerro de Nieles,* 4 *Almizaraque,* 5 *Cerro de la Virgen,* 6 *Gorafe group,* 7 *Pantano de los Bermejales,* 8 *Antequera group,* 9 *Dolmen de Matarrubilla,* 10 *Alcala,* 11 *Anta dos Tassos 1,* 12 *Poço da Gateira,* 13 *Anta dos Gorginos,* 14 *Herdade de Farisoa,* 15 *Carenque,* 16 *Praia das Maças,* 17 *Carapito 1,* 18 *Orca dos Castenairos,* 19 *Seixas. Location of ills 2–4 is indicated.*

here that megalithic tombs represent just one type of cultural trait which was studied through normative theory and that the assumptions mentioned here applied to both orientalists and occidentalists (for an example of the latter, see Bosch-Gimpera 1932, 1944, 1967). My apologies to readers for this predominance of assertion over detailed argument, but time and space require brevity and we must move on rapidly to look at absolute chronology.

The Absolute Chronology of Iberian Megalithic Tombs

An independent chronology for Iberian megaliths was absent before the advent of radiocarbon and TL dating. Colin Renfrew has published a list of both radiocarbon and TL dates for the tombs (1976) and has discussed the implications of the new chronology in several publications (e.g. 1970, 1973), while the TL dates are published in full by Whittle and Arnaud (1975). What I wish to do here is to discuss these dates in more detail than has been attempted on previous occasions.

The dating of megalithic passage graves and single chambers in inland areas of northern Portugal now extends back to at least 3000 bc (c.3900 BC). From 1964 to 1967 Schubart, Ribeiro and Vera Leisner surveyed

and excavated tombs in the province of Beira Alta, between the rivers Mondego and Douro, over 600 m in altitude. Only the radiocarbon dates and the Carapito excavations have been published so far (Leisner and Ribeiro 1968). The dates come from three sites: Orca dos Castenairos – 3110 ± 50 bc (GrN 4924) from the bottom of the chamber fill overlying the natural weathered granite and 2660 ± 50 bc (GrN 4925) from a layer of black organic earth stratigraphically above the other sample in the chamber; Carapito 1 – 2900 ± 40 bc (GrN 5110) from the floor of the chamber, associated with microliths, flint blades, polished stone tools, callais and amphibolite beads, and 2640 ± 65 bc (GrN?) also from the chamber floor but nearer a gap in

31

the chamber wall where the entrance/passage may have been; and Orca de Seixas – 2950 ± 40 bc (GrN 5734) from wood charcoal from a lower level (no more precise information available). The last of these tombs is described as a 'dolmen', but although one may suppose that this refers to a single chamber, the Carapito sites (three passage graves and the dated tomb, which is now a single chamber) are referred to as 'die dolmen' by Leisner and Ribeiro (1968), thus creating confusion.

The single chambers and megalithic passage graves of Beira Alta have been included by Savory (1968, 105–7) within a group of such tombs in the northwest of Iberia supposedly later than, and derived from, the collective tombs of the Upper Alemtejo. This follows the views of the Leisners, Heleno and other Portuguese archaeologists as to the development of collective tombs in the south-west from earlier oblong or oval megalithic cists covered with circular mounds and initially containing single burials, axes, adzes and microlithic tools. Bosch-Gimpera, on the other hand, argued that the single round megalithic chambers of the north-west (Beira Alta, Tras-os-Montes) evolved first (c.4000 bc – period 1 of his Portuguese megalithic culture) and the passage graves of the Upper Alemtejo did not develop until his period 3, over a thousand years later (c.3000 bc – see Bosch-Gimpera 1967).

There are no radiocarbon dates from the Upper Alemtejo, but the programme of TL dating provided interesting results. The earliest dates come from the group of tombs studied by the Leisners around Reguengos de Monsaraz (Leisner and Leisner 1951). Poço da Gateira 1 has a polygonal chamber and a short passage and contained polished stone axes, adzes, flint blades, microliths and undecorated pottery which yielded a date of 4510 ± 360 bc (OxTL 169b). Anta dos Gorginos 2 is a similar type of tomb with similar grave goods and a date of 4440 ± 360 bc (OxTL 169c). Thus comparison of these dates with the calibrated radiocarbon dates given above from Beira Alta suggests that the tombs of the south-west in the Alemtejo evolved before those of the north-west. As Renfrew has pointed out, these dates also demonstrate that the Iberian tombs, with an origin by c.4500–4000 BC, begin before their alleged Aegean prototypes (1970, 1973, 1976).

The construction and use of passage graves with dry-stone walling and corbelled roofs seems to have begun by 2400 bc and continued in some areas until the middle of the second millennium bc. In calendar years this would be from before c.3000 BC down to c.2000 BC. There are eight dates from five sites in Almería and southern Portugal. From Los Millares 19 (Almagro and Arribas 1963) comes a date of 2430 ± 120 bc (KN

72) for one of a local series of tombs with side-chambers and a triple segmented passage, supposedly late in the evolution of the passage grave. Unfortunately the context of the charcoal sample is not known. A closely similar date (2345 ± 85 bc – H 204) was obtained from a sample at the inner foot of the settlement wall at Los Millares, but its position in relation to the duration of occupation on the site lacks clarity (Sangmeister, pers.comm., 1974). However, tomb 7 in the cemetery at El Barranquete (M.J. Almagro Gorbea 1973a), some thirty kilometres to the south-east of Los Millares, has also given comparable dates: 2330 ± 130 bc (CSIC 81) and 2350 ± 130 bc (CSIC 82) from wood samples from the central pillar in the chamber. Dates in the last quarter of the third millennium bc have also been obtained from contemporary settlements at Tabernas and Tarajal (M.Almagro Gorbea and Fernández-Miranda 1978).

In southern Portugal we have TL as well as radiocarbon dates (Whittle and Arnaud 1975; Arnaud 1978). Anta dos Tassos 1 (Alamo, Ourique, Bajo Alemtejo) has a dry-stone chamber and a short orthostatic passage (Viana, Veiga Ferreira and Freire de Andrades 1961, 9 – 12; Leisner 1965, 146) and two published dates – 1850 ± 200 bc (Sa?) and 1370 ± 200 bc (Sa 199) – though there are no details of their spatial/stratigraphical relationships to each other or to the period of construction. There has also been confusion as to the authenticity of the dates (M. Almagro Gorbea 1970, 20), both of which have been published as *the* date for the tomb (Leisner and Veiga Ferreira 1963, 364; Delibrias, Roche and Veiga Ferreira 1967). Savory (1968, 150) confuses the laboratory numbers. Clearly even the earliest of these dates is rather late compared with our expectations based on the Millares and Barranquete tombs. This is the case also with the TL date of 2675 ± 270 BC (OxTL 169j) from the 'tholos' of Herdade da Farisoa (Reguengos de Monsaraz, Leisner and Leisner 1951), which is almost indistinguishable from the date of 2405 ± 260 BC (OxTL 169i) from sherds in the primary passage grave at this site. Further north near Lisbon, there are radiocarbon dates from a primary rock-cut tomb – 2300 ± 60 bc (KN?) and BS 2210 ± 110 bc (H?) – and a secondary partly rock-cut passage grave with dry-stone walling and a corbelled vault – 1700 ± 100 bc (H?) and 1690 ± 60 bc (KN?) – at Praia das Maças (Sintra). On the basis of the grave goods Savory (1968, 122, 152) suggests that the dates for the primary tomb relate to disturbance when the secondary tomb was constructed and similarly that the dates for the secondary tomb are the result of later Beaker burials. This would mean in calendar years that the secondary tomb was built by c.3000 BC (in accordance with expectations) and the

32

primary tomb earlier. Support for this view may be derived from the TL date of 3930 ± 340 bc (OxTL 169h) from the rock-cut tomb Carenque 2, although this is much earlier than either of the two dates from the settlement nearby (Whittle and Arnaud 1975).

What conclusions may we draw about the absolute dating of Iberian megaliths? First the good news. The use and construction of collective tombs spans at least two thousand five hundred calendar years, from the middle fifth to the late third millennia bc, compared with a maximum of one thousand years allowed by the pre-radiocarbon and pre-TL chronology. There is now a basis for supporting the evolutionary development of tomb forms, with megalithic passage graves appearing by 4500–4000 bc in the north-west and south-west of the peninsula and the so-called 'tholoi' by 3000 bc in the south-east and the south-west. But what about the bad news? Unfortunately this comprises a lengthy bulletin. As the reader will notice there are pitifully few dates available given the numbers of tombs published for the peninsula. Leaving aside a small number of anomalous dates (M. Almagro Gorbea and Fernández-Miranda 1978), there are only twenty dates from twelve sites! This represents a very low coverage both temporally and spatially. For the south-east the dates given above are for two tombs out of over 350 in Almería (Leisner and Leisner 1943). We have no dates for tombs in the north and north-east of the peninsula. We have no dates for the primary *rundgräber* in the south-east nor the single chambers/cists excavated by Heleno (and still unpublished) in the south-west. For the dates that we do possess too many are either single dates or of ambiguous or unknown context. Given continued access to such tombs over at least a generation, if not several, then what phases of activity are being dated? Is a radiocarbon date from a charcoal sample on the floor of a chamber necessarily dating the construction or primary use of the tomb? A related point may be made about the dating of pottery sherds by TL – what relation do they bear to the lifespan of the tomb's use? It is noticeable also that the location of some of the sherd samples dated by TL (e.g. Carenque – Whittle and Arnaud 1975) was unknown. All these are important problems, but they are not insoluble. Much now depends upon the excavation of contemporary settlement sites, as has already begun in southern Portugal (see below). Given the highly variable stages of publication and destruction afflicting Iberian megaliths (as those of other areas of western Europe), excavation of settlements and the analysis of change through cultural sequences offers us a better means of organizing the data on megalith forms and grave goods. We may then begin to approach an understanding of regional variation in the construction

and use of tombs which is not solely dependent upon typology (e.g. Chapman in press, a).

Beyond Chronology: a Theoretical 'Knee-Jerk'

In spite of the bad news, we have seen that radiocarbon and TL dating have given us the basis of an independent chronology for megalithic tombs and cultural development within Iberia. This is also the case throughout western Europe (e.g. Renfrew 1973, 1976). With longer chronologies we lose the necessity for the 'catastrophic' explanations conditioned by pre-radiocarbon schemes (Clarke 1973). For megaliths in particular Glyn Daniel's writings witnessed a rapid change in his earlier views, now denying their unity within western Europe (1966, 201):

'I think it is fair to say nowadays that most archaeologists are prepared to accept several independent origins for megaliths and to realise that the phrase "megalith monument" does not mean specifically structures formally, constructionally and functionally identical and therefore historically connected.'

Iberia became one area of megalithic origins (cf. Daniel 1967, 1973; Renfrew 1973, 1976). However, among prehistorians concerned with Iberia reaction ranged from acceptance (e.g. Arnaud 1978) to cautious appraisal (e.g. M.J. Almagro Gorbea 1973b, 333; Balbín-Behrmann 1978) and disbelief. It is worthy of note that radiocarbon dating has been slower in its adoption in Iberia for all periods of prehistory than in other areas of western Europe.

Another reaction has been to accept broadly the new chronology but to maintain the mode of interpretation (e.g. Savory 1968, 1975, 1977; MacKie 1977). This reminds us that chronology does not constitute explanation. Time like space is but a dimension of archaeology. In order to explain we have to invoke a body of theory and move beyond chronology. Here I disagree with the assumptions underlying traditional culture theory in the discussion of megalithic origins. Formal similarities in mortuary practices do not necessarily reflect interaction between communities of builders. Indeed this would be a dubious assumption for any cultural studies, as Renfrew was arguing in his paper on supposed links between the eastern Mediterranean and prehistoric Iberia (1967) and has been discussed in other more recent case-studies (e.g. Hodder 1978). The sole identification of change within mortuary practices with religion or beliefs and hence with population change has also received criticism (e.g. Binford 1971; Chapman 1977, 1981 b; Chapman and Randsborg 1981). The social correlates of mortuary practices are now in the ascendant. Irregular change in mortuary practices, as in other cultural traits, does not necessarily imply any disjunction in human populations. Given periods of comparatively rapid social change, it is surely not surprising that our archaeological time-scales may be too coarse to plot the essentially continuous development. Changes in the form of mortuary practices may conceal continuity in the processes of social change.

Given assumptions such as these and a more anthropological approach to social change, more recent 'explanations' of megalithic origins are found wanting. The role of diffusion is central to the work of Savory (1968, 1975, 1977), Clark (1977) and MacKie (1977). For Savory it is the rite of collective burial which is the most important characteristic of megalithic tombs and which diffused westwards from the Levantine Near East (e.g. the Natufian culture *c.*8000 bc) to Iberia and then up the Atlantic façade (or 'corridor' as Savory refers to it) to the rest of western Europe. For Savory communal burial was 'more fundamental than tomb morphology'(1977, 162). But what is not explained is why communal burial should have been the result of monogenesis, what is symbolized that was different from individual or family burial and how it could diffuse through the length of the Mediterranean and up Atlantic Europe? In other words what is lacking is an explanation based on coherent, testable social theory. The unity of the megalith builders and their religious orientation is also assumed by Clark, who considers the role of fishermen in the exploration of 'remoter territories as well as helping to feed the builders and even themselves assisting in the new cult' (1977, 43). One wonders whether they were also 'fishers of men'! Certainly MacKie's megalith builders were (1977). Collective burial again forms the unifying factor, but MacKie is much more explicit about the nature of the diffusion process. In place of social evolution he presents an argument based upon ethnocentric attitude and genetic reductionism: following Darlington he claims that 'numerous recorded examples appear to show quite clearly that periods of innovation and rapid development in the past have coincided with hybridization between hitherto separate populations or classes' (1977, 139). The appearance of megalithic tombs in Iberia and western Europe is then reduced to the 'talents' and 'skills' of travelling 'theocrats'. With this untestable hypothesis based upon genetic rather than social theory MacKie then proceeds to a series of unwarranted assertions: for example 'the emergence of the rite of collective burial almost certainly means that a new class of dominant people had arrived or developed in Iberia' (1977, 158) and the existence of Copper Age water control in south-east Spain rein-

forces the existence of a 'well-organized governing class served by specialist professions' (1977, 161: for a contrary view, Chapman 1978).

In contrast there have been recent examples of testable theory which may be applied to megalithic tombs (Renfrew 1976, 1979; Chapman 1981 b). Elsewhere I have argued as follows (Chapman 1981 b):

> Interment in cemeteries or monuments will emerge in periods of imbalance between society and critical resources. Such imbalance may arise in many ways, but in all cases society perceives the spatial and/or temporal variation in important resources to have approached a critical level and devises new mechanisms to regulate access to these resources. The emergence of territorially based descent groups . . . is a response to this process and the new social order may be symbolized to the community at large by the use of formal disposal areas, through which a permanent claim to the use and control of critical resources is established by the presence of the ancestors.

The difference between cemeteries and monuments (whether megalithic or not) lies in the fact that the former are bounded in two dimensions while the latter are bounded in three dimensions. The emphasis here is upon processes of sociocultural change and their reflection in archaeologically discernible human behaviour. Furthermore the 'problem' of megalithic tombs dissolves and in each area where they occur attention is focussed upon patterns of variation within local cultural systems. The remaining sections of this paper consider Iberian megalithic tombs in this light.

Regional Distribution and Representation

We begin at the regional level and in subsequent sections move down to local areas, cemeteries and individual tombs. The aim here is to provoke thought on the regional distribution of tombs in Iberia and the degree to which it is fully representative of the original distribution in the fifth to third millennia BC. Such assessment is essential when analysing the intensity of prehistoric settlement and the relative importance of megalithic tombs in different regions of the peninsula. The map in ill 1 gives a schematic representation of tomb distribution. From this can be seen the overwhelming focus upon the northern, western and southern edges of the peninsula, with the central and eastern areas containing few, if any, tombs (for more detailed maps, see Savory 1968, Figs. 23, 32, 37, 41 and 44). Corpus volumes have been published for the tombs of Andalucia and the south-east (Leisner and

Leisner 1943), Huelva (Márquez, Leisner and Leisner 1952), Reguengos de Monsaraz (Leisner and Leisner 1951), southern Portugal (Leisner and Leisner 1956; Leisner 1965) and Catalonia and the Pyrenees (Pericot 1950). Further publications are awaited, for example on Beira Alta, while in the north-west publication has been supplemented by the volumes of the *Corpus de Sepulcros Megaliticos* and by distribution maps and a corpus of tombs for the province of Alava (Apellániz 1973; Ciprés, Galilea and Lopez 1978).

Work on a number of areas of southern Iberia encourages the conclusion that the main distribution of tombs as published by the Leisners is an accurate reflection of the survival of tombs, although there are one or two interesting exceptions. In the south-east there have been two cemeteries published since the 1940s, at El Barranquete (at least thirty tombs – M.J. Almagro Gorbea 1973a) and Cerro de Nieles, La Huelga (again at least thirty tombs – Algorra Esteban 1953). Elsewhere there have only been three further tombs published in lowland Almeria. Moving over into Granada, in the east there have been occasional finds of single or small numbers of tombs (e.g. Cerro de la Virgen – Schüle and Pellicer 1966), while the main change in our knowledge occurred within the confines of an already existing group at Gorafe, where García Sánchez and Spanhi (1959) increased by a quarter the number of tombs excavated by the Sirets. To the west the only sizeable number of recently published tombs occurred at Pantano de los Bermejales (Arenas del Rey – e.g. Arribas and Sánchez de Corral 1970). Moving into Seville and Huelva provinces the basic frequency and distribution of tombs has remained unaltered in the last thirty years.

The estimation of tomb destruction, even in modern times, is a difficult process. For the present century García Sánchez and Spanhi (1959) calculated that some forty tombs in the Gorafe area has been destroyed. This amounts to a quarter of those excavated by the Sirets and one-sixth of the total number known.

The central plateau, the Meseta, presents problems of interpretation when looking at prehistoric human occupation in any period, especially when one considers the nature of the environment and the low density of the contemporary human population. The main concentration of tombs is to be found on the western side (e.g. around Salamanca: Losada 1976) and seems to represent the extension of settlement and megalith building up the valleys of the main rivers (Guadiana, Tagus and Duero). More isolated tombs extend to the east to Guadalajara and through the provinces of Burgos, Palencia and Logrono (discussion in Savory 1975). The north-western and south-eastern Meseta

are devoid of tombs. How do we interpret these distributions? Savory (1977) suggests that we do not know the extent of tomb destruction and that fieldwork may yet change our knowledge of tomb distribution. In this light it is certainly true that new tombs have been discovered in the last two decades, as Savory discusses elsewhere (1975). New sites have been discovered for other prehistoric periods. For the Lower Palaeolithic the need for more systematic survey was highlighted by the concentration of new sites found on the southern Meseta around Calatrava (Santonja Gómez 1976). The same point was made by the distribution of Bronze Age 'motilla' sites on the south-east Meseta: recent publication shows just how many of these highly visible sites had escaped previous attention (Molina and Najera 1978). On the other hand the low density of occupation on the north-west and south-east Meseta is noted even in the Lower Palaeolithic and is repeated in the Upper Palaeolithic (Davidson 1980) and in the distribution of Beaker culture material (Delibes de Castro 1977; Harrison 1977). In one area where fairly intensive survey has been undertaken recently, in the north of Burgos, no new tomb finds were noted (Clark 1979). What is interesting here is that the authors concluded that the main human exploitation of this area did not begin until the second and first millennia bc. Prior to this there was a low population density and a mainly pastoral exploitation is favoured. Given the severe climatic extremes and higher altitudes of the Meseta, it is a logical hypothesis that the main initial centres of prehistoric populations in the peninsula were around the lower coastal fringes and that the last two millennia bc represented periods of more substantial colonization (e.g. the period of the Beaker finds, including grave goods in megalithic tombs, and of the 'motillas' in the south-east) of the plateau. However, this should not be taken as support for the proposition that the distribution of megalithic tombs in the Meseta and in the peninsula as a whole could be accounted for by the pattern of medieval and modern transhumance (e.g. the Mesta – Higgs 1976). The distribution of tombs is not identical to that of the transhumance routes and the medieval flock movements were directed and determined by political and economic pressures (Chapman 1979).

Groups, Cemeteries and Settlement: the Spatial Dimension

Moving down from the broad regional level, we must now focus on the spatial patterning of tombs and groups of tombs within the settlement landscape. What patterns can be defined? How do they relate to

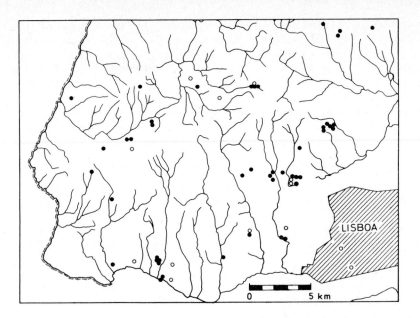

2 Tombs and Copper Age settlements in the Lisbon peninsula. Closed circles: all tombs (megalithic, rock-cut etc.). Open circles: settlements. (After Leisner 1965.)

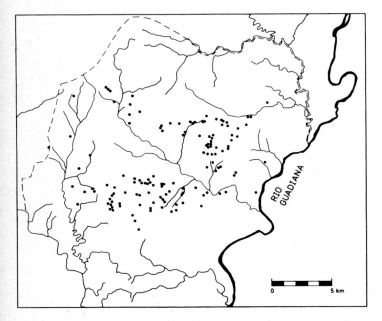

3 Megalithic tombs in Reguengos de Monsaraz. (After Leisner and Leisner 1951.)

settlements and resource distribution? Ultimately our interest here lies in the relationship between the settlement landscape of the living and the funerary landscape of the dead (Chapman and Randsborg in press). To put it another way, what factors govern the spatial location of megalithic tombs in relation to the everyday activities of the surviving members of the local community? On this level the archaeologist can approach the question of territorial definition and resource control raised in recent theoretical discussions (Renfrew 1976; Chapman in press, b).

Our knowledge of spatial patterning for megalithic tombs is rather poor for south-east Spain. The tombs published by the Leisners (1943) for Almeria are divided into groups 1–40, but no large-scale plans of their locations have been published, with the exception of the tombs at Almizaraque (Leisner and Leisner 1943, taf. 165, top; also M.J. Almagro Gorbea 1965) and Mojácar (Leisner and Leisner 1943, taf. 165; cf. Arribas 1955–6). More recently we have seen the plans of the cemeteries from Los Millares (Almagro and Arribas 1963) and El Barranquete (M.J. Almagro Gorbea 1973a). It is a matter of debate whether the Leisners' groups represent coherent cemeteries as opposed to more dispersed arrangements: certainly their groups 32 (Tabernas) and 20 (Nijar) do not form single cemeteries. We also have a poor knowledge of the internal chronology of the cemeteries of the Copper Age (Chapman in press, a) and of the association of all the tombs with settlements (although note the exceptions of Los Millares, El Barranquete (M.J. Almagro Gorbea 1977), Cerro de la Virgen (Schüle and Pellicer 1966), Almizaraque and Mojácar.

36

Further to the west in Granada there are plans of the groups at Gorafe and Alicún (García Sánchez and Spanhi 1959), Laborcillas and Fonelas (Leisner and Leisner 1943, tafs. 167–8), with the latter examples showing more localized, nucleated patterns.

In the south-west of the peninsula there are more maps of megalith distributions (e.g. Leisner and Leisner 1951, 1956; Leisner 1965). For the Alto Alemtejo and the Lisbon peninsula there is a much surer basis for analysis of spatial patterning. In addition more Neolithic and Copper Age settlement locations have been published. Ill. 2 shows the distribution of megalithic tombs and rock-cut tombs in relation to Copper Age settlements in the Lisbon peninsula. For Alto Alemtejo Arnaud (1971) has published a list of a dozen Neolithic-Copper Age settlements which were known from surface collections and has subsequently excavated at Castelo do Giraldo, from which a date of *c.*3100 BC was obtained on pottery (Whittle and Arnaud 1975). To the south, in the Algarve, excavation has begun on the settlement located within 200 m of the famous group of tombs at Alcalar (Arnaud and Gamito 1978).

The nature of spatial patterning in the south-east and the south-west has aroused interest. It has been suggested that there is an important contrast between the nucleated cemeteries of the south-east and the dispersed examples of the south-west. The distribution of tombs at Reguengos de Monsaraz (ill. 3) and near Torres Vedras (ill. 4) (to the north of Lisbon) could be contrasted with that in the cemetery at Los Millares (ill. 5). It is certainly true that a dispersed pattern of tomb distribution is visible in the south-west and there is no cemetery like Los Millares. On the other hand Millares is exceptional in the south-east, with its eighty to one hundred tombs. With the exception of the Gorafe tombs as well, only two other

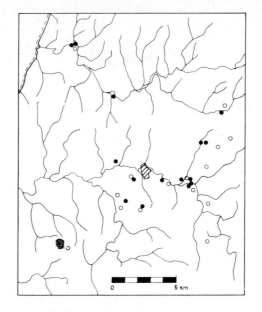

4 Tombs (closed circles) and Copper Age settlements (open circles) near Torres Vedras (shaded). (After Leisner 1965.)

5 Cemetery of tombs at Los Millares (Almeria).

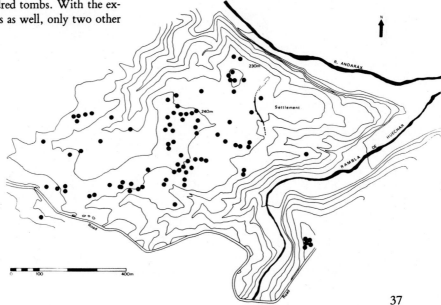

37

cemeteries or groups have at least thirty tombs and the overwhelming majority only have between one and five tombs in each group. Thus it can be argued that the contrast between the large, nucleated cemeteries of the south-east and the smaller or dispersed groups of the south-west has been overemphasized. Which all goes to raise further questions about the conditions under which nucleated cemeteries appear, in particular the parts played by social development and increased settlement hierarchization and the control of critical resources (Chapman, 1981 b; Renfrew 1979).

Tombs, Formation Processes and 'Megalithometry'

The last level of analysis relates the form, dimensions, internal division and contents of individual tombs to their design and the sequence of activities which took place within them. As with other levels it has its difficulties: if the analysis of spatial patterning is affected by tomb destruction, then individual tombs are subject to robbing and many an indecent assault in the name of excavation! In most cases we have to work with tombs through such filters (e.g. Chapman, 1981 c). Basically all tombs share the common factor of providing an enclosed space for a series of activities relating to the disposal of the dead, or rather, to follow Kinnes (in press) the preservation and utilization of the dead. Their morphology may be seen as the result of what Fleming has referred to as 'a process of problem-solving' (1973). Both Fleming (1972, 1973) and Kinnes (1975, in press) have focussed upon the factors which lie behind tomb morphology, with (in Fleming's case) the use of metrical indices to distinguish the

6 Examples of structural differentiation within megalithic tombs in Iberia. Top left, Fonelas 10. Top right, Fonelas 9 Bottom left, Los Rurialillos 2. Bottom right, Los Millares 17. (All after Leisner and Leisner 1943.) Scale 1:100.

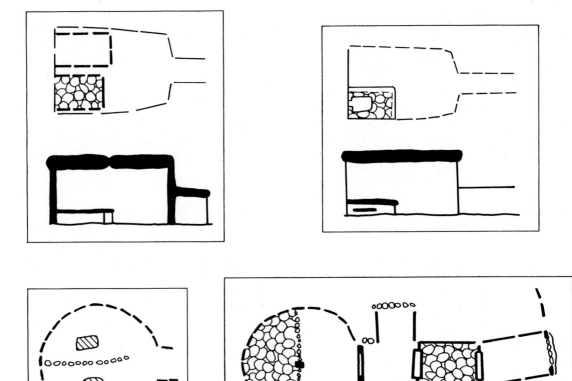

relative importance of tomb and mound. This study of 'megalithometry' has yet to be pursued for Iberian tombs, although an initial attempt was published by Ruiz (1973). Note might also be made of the relationship between the increased enclosed space provided by later tombs in some areas and the increase in the range and frequency of activities carried out within them. This would reflect the distinction between earlier burial 'crypts' and later 'charnel houses', as discussed by James Brown (nd) for the middle Woodland period in the Eastern United States.

Given differential preservation and destruction, one cannot be sure that a sufficient sample of tombs with internal structural differentiation is available. In the Leisners (1943) publication one can find examples of tombs with segmented passages and others with divisions of the chamber area, including stone slab divisions, walls, stone paving, and slab compartments (e.g. ill. 6). In some cases (e.g. the Fonelas tombs) there are even details of the presence of skeletal material and grave goods associated with these divisions. But as a whole there are only a few tombs in Almería and Granada for which we have any knowledge of the spatial distribution of skeletal parts, and grave goods. For the cemetery of Los Millares we only have the plan of tomb XXI (Almagro and Arribas 1963), with its evidence for the differential treatment and arrangement of crania, long bones and vertebrae. With the exception of an old sketch of Luis Siret's of the Encantada I tomb at Almizaraque, the only other plans from Almería come from the more recent excavations at El Barranquete: the excavator noted clusters of crania, piles or bundles of bones and in a few cases more completely articulated skeletons, as well as distinct layers of deposits (M.J. Almagro Gorbea 1973a). In addition it should be noted that further evidence was found which supported the conclusion that the size of such tombs was not simply determined by the number of individuals to be accorded final interment within them. In the Guadalquivir valley, tombs such as the Cueva del Vaquero, Cañada Honda and the Dolmen de Matarrubilla have preserved evidence for depositional sequences and spatial arrangements of skeletal remains and grave goods (Leisner and Leisner 1943; Collantes de Teran 1969). The best evidence from southern Portugal comes from Praia das Maças (Leisner 1965), while in the north we may note the Carapito tombs (Leisner and Ribeiro 1968). It is upon such few tombs as these that attention will have to be focussed, as well as any future excavations.

Conclusion

In 1970 Glyn Daniel wrote that 'the question now before earnest megalithic enquirers is this: what ancient peoples built megalithic tombs in which ancient places in Europe, and why?' (1970, 267). In this paper I have considered Iberian megalithic tombs and have argued that the 'ancient peoples' were indigenous to the peninsula. How do we explain the tomb development? The answer lies in the development of coherent theory which links change in mortuary practices to the wider sociocultural setting. Above all else we now seek to understand these tombs in a context and not as isolated entities. As a contribution towards this aim I have considered three levels of analysis which might be pursued: the regional level, the local settlement landscape level and the individual tomb level. At each level we are concerned with different problems and scales of analysis. If this paper serves no other purpose than to demonstrate the inadequacy and futility of pursuing the megalithic 'problem', then a step will have been taken in the right direction.

Acknowledgments

I would like to thank Jan Chapman for typing this paper, and for her general support during the writing of it. Ills 2–4 and 6 were kindly prepared by Averil Martin-Hoogewerf.

Bibliography

ABERG, N. 1921 *La Civilisation Enéolithique dans la Péninsule Ibérique,* Leipzig.

ALGARRA ESTEBAN, R. 1953 'Cerro de Nieles', *Noticiario Arqueológico Hispánico* I, 37.

ALMAGRO, M. AND ARRIBAS, A. 1963 *El poblado y la necropólis megalíticos de Los Millares,* Madrid.

ALMAGRO GORBEA, M. 1970 'Las Fechas del C–14 para la Prehistoria y la Arqueología Peninsular', *Trabajos de Prehistoria* XXVII, 9–44.

ALMAGRO GORBEA, M. AND FERNÁNDEZ-MIRANDA, M. (eds.) 1978 *C–14 y Prehistoria de la Península Ibérica, Reunión* 1978, Madrid.

ALMAGRO GORBEA, M.J. 1965 *Las Tres Tumbas Megalíticas de Almizaraque*, Madrid.

1973a *El Poblado y la necrópolis de El Barranquete (Almeria)*, Madrid.

1973b *Los Idolos del Bronce I Hispano*, Madrid.

1977 'El recientemente destruido poblado de El Tarajal', *XIV Congreso Nacional de Arqueologia*, 305–18.

APELLÁNIZ, J.M. 1973 'Corpus de materiales de las culturas prehistoricas con ceramica de la poblacion de cavernas del Pais Vasco meridional', *Munibe* suplemento 1, 7–366.

ARNAUD, J.M. 1971 'Os povoados "Neo-Eneoliticos" de Famao e Aboboreira (Ciladas, Vila Viçosa)'. Noticia Preliminar, *II Congreso Nacional de Arqueologia*, 199–221.

1978 'O Megalitismo en Portugal: Problemas e Perspectivas'. *Actas das III Jornadas Arqueológicas*, 91–112.

ARNAUD, J.M. AND GAMITO, T.J. 1978 'Povoãdo Calcolítico de Alcalar. Notícia de sua identificaçao', *Anais do Município* VIII, 3–10.

ARRIBAS, A. 1955–6 'El sepulcro megalítico del Cabecico de Aguilar de Cuartillas (Mojácar, Almería)', *Ampurias* XVII–XVIII, 210–14.

ARRIBAS, A. AND SANCHEZ DEL CORRAL, J.M. 1970 'La necrópolis megalitica del Pantano de los Bermejales (Arenas del Rey, Granada)', *XI Congreso Nacional de Arqueologia*, 284–91.

BALBÍN-BEHRMANN, R. DE 1978 'Problematica actual de la cronologia radioactiva en relacion con la tradicional durante el megalitismo y el eneolítico', in Almagro Gorbea, M. and Fernãndez-Miranda M. (eds), *C-14 y Prehistoria de la Península Ibérica, Reunión 1978*, Madrid.

BINFORD, L.R. 1965 'Archaeological systematics and the study of culture process', *American Antiquity* XXXI, 203–10.

1971 Mortuary practices: their study and potential, in Brown, J.A. (ed.), *Approaches to the social dimensions of mortuary practices*, Memoirs of the Society for American Archaeology no.25.

BLANCE, B.M. 1960 *The Origins and Development of the Early Bronze Age in the Iberian Peninsula*, Ph.D. dissertation, University of Edinburgh.

1961 'Early Bronze Age colonists in Iberia', *Antiquity* XXXV, 192–202.

BOSCH-GIMPERA, P. 1932 *Etnologia de la Península Ibérica*, Barcelona.

1944 *El poblamiento antiguo y la formación de los pueblos de España*, Mexico.

1967 'Civilisation mégalithique portugaise et civilisations espagnoles', *L'Anthropologie* LXXI, 1–48.

BROWN, J.A. n.d. 'Charnel houses and mortuary crypts: disposal of the dead in the Middle Woodland Period.'

CARTAILHAC, E. 1886 *Les âges préhistoriques de l'Espagne et du Portugal*, Paris.

CHAPMAN, R.W. 1975 *Economy and society within later prehistoric Iberia: a new framework*, Ph.D. dissertation, University of Cambridge.

1977 'Burial practices – an area of mutual interest', in Spriggs, M. (ed.) *Archaeology and Anthropology. Areas of Mutual Interest*, Oxford.

1978 'The evidence for prehistoric water control in south-east Spain', *Journal of Arid Environments* I, 261–74.

1979 'Transhumance and megalithic tombs in Iberia', *Antiquity* LIII, 150–2.

1981 (a) 'Los Millares and the relative chronology of the Copper Age in south-east Spain', *Trabajos de Prehistoria* XXXVII.

1981 (b) 'The emergence of formal disposal areas and the 'problem' of megalithic tombs in prehistoric Europe', in Chapman, R.W., Kinnes, I.A. and Randsborg, K. *The Archaeology of Death*, Cambridge.

1981 (c) 'Archaeological theory and communal burial in prehistoric Europe', in Hodder, I., Isaac, G. and Hammond N. (eds) *Pattern of the Past: studies in honour of David Clarke*, Cambridge.

forthcoming *Autonomy and Social Evolution: the later prehistory of the Iberian peninsula*, Cambridge.

CHAPMAN, R.W. AND RANDSBORG, K. 1981 'Approaches to the archaeology of death', in Chapman, R.W., Kinnes, I.A. and Randsborg, K. (eds) *The Archaeology of Death*, Cambridge.

CHILDE, V.G. 1932 'Scottish megalithic tombs and their affinities', *Transactions of the Glasgow Archaeological Society*, 120–3.

CIPRÉS, A., GALILEA, F. AND LÓPEZ, L. 1978 'Dolmenes y tumulos de las Sierras de Guibijo y Badaya. Plantamiento para su estudio a la vista de los ultimos descubrimientos', *Estudios de Arqueologia Alavesa* IX, 65–125.

CLARK, G. (ed.) 1979 *The North Burgos Archaeological Survey. Bronze and Iron Age Archaeology on the Meseta del Norte (Province of Burgos, North-Central Spain)*, Arizona.

CLARK, J.G.D. 1977 'The economic context of dolmens and passage graves in Sweden', in Markotic, V. (ed.), *Ancient Europe and the Mediterranean*, Warminster.

CLARKE, D.L. 1973 'Archaeology: the loss of innocence', *Antiquity* XLVII, 6–18.

COLLANTES DE TERÁN, F. 1969 'El Dolmen de Matarrubilla', in *Tartessos y sus problemas, V Symposium*

Internacional de Prehistoria Peninsular, Barcelona.

DANIEL, G.E. 1941 'The Dual Nature of the Megalithic Colonisation of Prehistoric Europe', *Proc. Preh. Soc.* VII, 1–49.

1963 *The Megalith Builders of Western Europe*, 2nd edn, London.

1966 'Megalith builders of the SOM', *Palaeohistoria* XII, 199–208.

1967 'Northmen and Southmen', *Antiquity* XLI, 313–17.

1970 'Megalithic Answers', *Antiquity* XLIV, 260–9.

1971 'From Worsaae to Childe: the models of prehistory', *Proc. Preh. Soc.* XXXVII, part II, 140–53.

1973 'Spain and the problem of European megalithic origins', in *Estudios dedicados al Prof. Dr. Luis Pericot*, Barcelona, 209–14.

DAVIDSON, I. 1980 'Transhumance, Spain and ethnoarchaeology', *Antiquity* LIV, 144–7.

DELIBES DE CASTRO, G. 1977 *El Vaso Campaniforme en la Meseta Norte Española*, Valladolid.

DELIBRIAS, J., ROCHE, J. AND VEIGA FERREIRA, O.da 1967 'Chronologie absolue d'un monument énéolithique du Bas Alentejo (Portugal) par la méthode du carbone 14', *Comptes Rendus Academie des Sciences de Paris* 265, serie D, 245–6.

FERGUSSON, J. 1872 *Rude Stone Monuments in all Countries, Their Age and Uses*, London.

FLEMING, A. 1972 'Vision and design: approaches to ceremonial monument typology', *Man* VII, 57–73.

1973 'Tombs for the living', *Man* VIII, 177–93.

FORDE, C.D. 1929 'The Megalithic culture sequence in Iberia', *Liverpool Annals of Archaeology and Anthropology* XVI, 37–46.

1930 'Early Cultures of Atlantic Europe', *American Anthropologist* XXXII, 19–100.

GARCÍA SÁNCHEZ, M. AND SPANHI, J.-C 1959 'Sepulcros megalíticos de la región de Gorafe (Granada)', *Archivo de Prehistoria Levantina* VIII, 43–113.

HARRISON, R.J. 1977 *The Bell Beaker cultures of Spain and Portugal*, Cambridge, Mass.

HIGGS, E.S. 1976 'The history of European agriculture: the uplands', *Philosophical Transactions of the Royal Society of London*, B, 275, 159–73.

HODDER, I. (ed.) 1978 *The Spatial Organisation of Culture*, London.

KINNES, I. 1975 'Monumental function in British neolithic burial practices', *World Arch.* VII, 16–29.

in press 'Dialogues with death', in Chapman, R.W., Kinnes, I.A. and Randsborg, K. (eds) *The Archaeology of Death*, Cambridge.

LEEDS, E.T. 1918–20 'The Dolmens and Megalithic Tombs of Spain and Portugal', *Archaeologia* LXX, 201–32.

LEISNER, G. AND LEISNER, V. 1943 *Die Megalithgräber der Iberischen Halbinsel: Der Süden*, Berlin.

1951 *Antas do Concelho de Reguëngos de Monsaraz*, Lisbon.

1956 *Die Megalithgräber der Iberischen Halbinsel: Der Westen*, Berlin.

LEISNER, V. 1965 *Die Megalithgräber der Iberischen Halbinsel: Der Westen*, Berlin.

LEISNER, V. AND RIBEIRO, C. 1968 'Die Dolmen von Carapito', *Madrider Mitteilungen* IX, 11–62.

LEISNER, V. AND VEIGA FERREIRA, O. DA 1963 'Primeiras datas de rádiocarbono 14 para a cultura megalítica portuguesa', *Revista de Guimaraes* LXXIII, 358–66.

LOSADA, H. 1976 'El Dolmen de Entreterminos (Madrid)', *Trabajos de Prehistoria*, XXXIII, 209–26.

MACKIE, E.W. 1977 *The Megalith Builders*, Oxford.

MÁRQUEZ, C.C., LEISNER, G. AND LEISNER, V. 1952 *Los Sepulcros Megalíticos de Huelva*, Madrid.

MOLINA, F. AND NAJERA, T. 1978 'Die Motillas von Azuer und Los Palacios (Prov. Ciudad Real)', *Madrider Mitteilungen* XIX, 52–74.

OBERMAIER, H. 1919 *El Dolmen de Matarrubilla*, Madrid.

PEAKE, H.J.E. AND FLEURE, H.J. 1930 'Megaliths and Beakers', *Journal of the Royal Anthropological Institute* IX, 47–72.

PEET, T.E. 1912 *Rough Stone Monuments and their Builders*, London.

PERICOT, L. 1950 *Los Sepulcros Megalíticos Catalanes y la Cultura Pirenaica*, Barcelona.

RENFREW, C. 1967 'Colonialism and megalithismus', *Antiquity* XLI, 276–88.

1970 'The tree-ring calibration of radiocarbon: an archaeological evaluation', *Proc. Preh. Soc.* XXXVI, 280–311.

1973 *Before Civilisation*, London.

1976 'Megaliths, territories and populations', in De Laet, S.J. (ed.), *Acculturation and continuity in Atlantic Europe*, Bruges.

1979 *Investigations in Orkney*, London.

RUIZ SOLANES, J. 1973 'Para el estudio estadistico de los sepulcros megalíticos', *XII Congreso Nacional de Arqueologia*, 201–10.

SANTONJA GÓMEZ, M. 1976 'Industrias del Paleolítico Inferior en la Meseta Española', *Trabajos de Prehistoria* XXXIII, 121–64.

SAVORY, H.N. 1968 *Spain and Portugal*, London.

1975 'The role of the Upper Duero and Ebro basins in megalithic diffusion', *Boletin del Seminario de Estudios de Arte y Arqueologia* XL–XLI, 159–74.

1977 'The role of Iberian communal tombs in Mediterranean and Atlantic prehistory', in Markotic, V. (ed.), *Ancient Europe and the Mediterranean*, Warminster.

SCHÜLE, W. AND PELLICER, M. 1966 *El Cerro de la Virgen, Orce (Granada)*, Madrid.

SIRET, L. 1913 *Questions de Chronologie et D'Ethnographie Ibériques*, Paris.

VIANA, A., VEIGA FERREIRA, O. DA AND FREIRE DE ANDRADE, R. 1961 'Descoberta de dois monumentos de falsa cúpula na regaio de Ourique', *Revista de Guimarães* LXXI, 5–12.

WHITTLE, E.H. AND ARNAUD, J.M. 1975 'Thermoluminescent dating of neolithic and chalcolithic pottery from sites in central Portugal', *Archaeometry* XVII, 5–24.

WILKE, G. 1912 'Sudwesteuropäische Megalithkultur', in *Mannus Bibliothek* VII.

4 Megaliths of the Central Mediterranean

Ruth Whitehouse

THIS ESSAY discusses the peninsula and island zones of the central Mediterranean, excepting only Malta which is the subject of a separate article by David Trump. The main regions covered are peninsular Italy, Sicily, Sardinia and Corsica. In this region we find a great variety of monuments: rock-cut tombs, megalithic chamber tombs, menhirs and statue–menhirs, and tower-like structures of cyclopean masonry (*nuraghi* and *torri*). All these diverse monuments have at times been labelled megaliths and have been considered part of a megalithic complex or movement. Work in the last twenty years has done much to establish the dates and relationships of the various groups of monuments of all these types. However, not all the information has yet percolated through to the general literature and much misunderstanding persists. I feel, therefore, that the most useful thing I can do in this paper is to devote most of it to a straightforward description of what we can establish about the distribution, function and dates of these monuments. I shall deal with all the funerary monuments and the menhirs and statue-menhirs, but shall not consider the *nuraghi* or *torri*, which are beyond the scope of this discussion. I shall make no attempt to present a full bibliography, which would be truly vast, but under each heading I shall list a few important references. Almost all these themselves contain a useful bibliography.

Rock-cut Tombs

Of all the monuments described in this paper, the rock-cut tombs are the most widespread in the central Mediterranean; they also start earliest and last longest. Moreover they demonstrate no obvious connection with any of the other types of monuments: although there is *some* chronological and geographical overlap, the rock-cut tombs occurred initially before any of the other monuments existed and they occurred in areas where the other types of monuments were never built. In 1972 I published a paper in which I drew attention to these facts and argued that rock-cut tombs developed independently in the central Mediterranean and were not part of an intrusive megalithic complex (Whitehouse 1972). Indeed there is no reason to see them as part of a megalithic complex of any kind, whether indigenous or intrusive. I do not wish to rehearse all the arguments here, but shall outline briefly the salient facts about the tombs.

Distribution (ill. 1) Rock-cut tombs occur throughout the central and southern part of the Italian peninsula, in Sicily and in Sardinia. They are not found in Corsica or in Italy north of Tuscany.

Typology (ill. 2) On Sicily and the Italian mainland the most common tomb form in use in the early phases was the *a forno* or oven-shaped type, entered usually from a shaft, sometimes from a cliff face, occasionally through a hole in the roof. Most commonly these tombs have a single chamber, though two- and even three-chambered examples occur. In the Bronze Age there was a tendency to more regularly-made tombs, often rectangular in plan. Other forms also occur, for example a tomb with a kidney-shaped chamber and bulbous passage at Altamura in south-east Italy (late Copper Age/Early Bronze Age); or the tomb with a long passage and lateral niches on the island of Ognina, in south-east Sicily (Middle Bronze Age). In Sicily

tombs on the Early Bronze Age site of Castelluccio have blocking slabs decorated with carved spirals (once compared to those of Mycenae). In the Middle Bronze Age Thapsos culture some tombs with more elaborate architecture occur, including one with a four-pillared ante-chamber and another with a façade with sham pillars.

By far the most elaborate tombs in our area, however, are found on the island of Sardinia. Here more than 1,100 tombs have been recorded. These are entered either directly from a cliff face or through long entrance passages descending from the surface. The chambers are oval or rectangular, or, occasionally, round, and there may be many of them, often clustering round a large central chamber. Skeuomorphic wooden architectural features, such as beams, lintels and gables, are characteristic of these tombs. Other decoration occurs quite commonly: schematic bulls'

heads and other stylized designs executed in red paint or sculpted in relief.

Burial Rite It has generally been assumed that rock-cut tombs are invariably associated with the practice of collective burial, but this is not the case in the central Mediterranean. In the earliest tombs, both in Italy and Sicily, single or double burials only occur. Good examples are Final Neolithic tombs at Serra d'Alto and Arnesano in south-east Italy and thirty-three out of thirty-six tombs in the Copper Age cemetery at Sciacca (prov. Agrigento) in southern Sicily. In this cemetery the other three tombs had been used for collective burial and these were, on the basis of the pot-

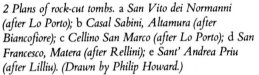

2 Plans of rock-cut tombs. a San Vito dei Normanni (after Lo Porto); b Casal Sabini, Altamura (after Biancofiore); c Cellino San Marco (after Lo Porto); d San Francesco, Matera (after Rellini); e Sant' Andrea Priu (after Lilliu). (Drawn by Philip Howard.)

tery they contained, later in date. On this site at least single burial was the rule initially, with collective burial coming in at a later stage. In the third millennium BC and later collective burial seems to have been the general rule everywhere. Skeletons are often found disarticulated, with only the last interment complete. Pottery, flint and metal weapons and ornaments commonly occur as grave goods.

Chronology There is some controversy over the date of the earliest rock-cut tombs in the central Mediterranean. The earliest dates actually from rock-cut tombs occur in the south-west Italian cemetery at Buccino, in association with artifacts of the Copper Age Gaudo group. A series of six radiocarbon dates from this site fall between 2580 and 1970 bc, correcting to c. 3350–2500 BC (all radiocarbon dates are listed with full details in the Appendix). However, the earliest tombs are certainly earlier than this. In 1972 I claimed that rock-cut tombs were used first in Italy not in the Copper Age, as had always been claimed, but in the Neolithic (Whitehouse 1972, 276). In support of this claim I quoted two damaged examples of probable fifth millennium BC (Middle Neolithic) date

– Fonteviva on the Tavoliere plain and Pizzone near Taranto – and an undamaged example of early fourth millennium BC (Final Neolithic) date at Serra d' Alto near Matera. At a conference held in Foggia in April 1973 (Tinè 1975), my view came under attack from David Trump and Santo Tinè, both of whom claimed that the structure at Fonteviva was not a true rock-cut tomb and that the date and nature of the Pizzone example were not established. These criticisms I accept to some extent. The Pizzone example is certainly unsatisfactory and there are also some problems about the Fonteviva structure. However, this latter structure *was* Neolithic, *was* cut in the rock (though apparently from the side of a village ditch) and *was* used for burial. If not a true cut tomb, it makes a good prototype for the real thing. There has been no challenge to the validity of my third Neolithic example: the tomb excavated by Rellini at Serra d'Alto. Moreover, since then another rock-cut tomb of indisputably Final Neolithic date, at Arnesano near Lecce, has been published (Lo Porto 1973). This tomb, of the *a forno* type, was used for the burial of a single individual, who was interred with pottery of Bellavista type (Whitehouse 1969, 300–3). This tomb should be approximately contemporary with the Serra d'Alto one, dating to c. 3950–3750 BC (C14 dates 3200–2900 bc; Whitehouse 1978, 81). It is clear that rock-cut tombs were in use in the first half of the fourth millennium BC in Italy; they may have begun in the fifth millennium BC.

Some of the Sardinian rock-cut tombs may be almost as early. We have no radiocarbon dates from the tombs themselves, but we have dates for the Ozieri culture, with which many of the tombs are associated, from the Grotta del Guano and from Bonu Ighinu of 3140-2880 bc (3950-3650 BC)

In the peninsula rock-cut tombs became common in the Copper Age, c. 3300–2300 BC (Whitehouse 1978, 84–5), and it is to the same period that we should probably assign many of the rock-cut tombs in Sardinia and Sicily; tombs on both islands have yielded sherds and occasional complete vessels of Beaker pottery, in keeping with the chronology just suggested. The main cultural groups of the Copper Age with which rock-cut tombs are associated are: Rinaldone, Gaudo and Laterza in peninsular Italy (Whitehouse and Renfrew 1975), Ozieri in Sardinia, Conca d'Oro, San Cono and Malpasso in Sicily.

After the third millennium BC rock-cut tombs went out of fashion in most of peninsular Italy; they continued in use, however, in south-east Italy, in Sicily and in Sardinia. In Sicily indeed they continued to be the main tomb form throughout the Bronze Age and into the Iron Age, and until and beyond the Greek col-

3 Distribution of megalithic tombs in the central Mediterranean.

Legend:
- Bari-Taranto tombs
- Otranto tombs
- Corsican and Sardinian cists
- Corsican and Sardinian dolmens
- *tombe di giganti*

onization of the island. Huge cemeteries of thousands of tombs characterize the Sicilian Iron Age, e.g. the Pantalica North and Caltagirone cemeteries. Late Bronze Age and Iron Age examples are found also in south-east Italy and in the extreme south-west (southern Calabria). In Sardinia they continued in use well into the Nuragic period, in the second millennium BC. In central Italy their use was reintroduced by the Etruscans in the seventh century BC.

Relationships In the central Mediterranean, rock-cut tombs are not generally associated with megalithic chamber tombs as they are in Portugal. Megalithic tombs indeed are not found at all in Sicily or in much of peninsular Italy. In those areas where rock-cut and megalithic tombs *are* both found – south-east Italy and Sardinia – the rock-cut tombs begin earlier, though they continue in use alongside the megaliths.

In both areas also some rock-cut tombs (including examples of both early and late types) are associated with menhirs.

In 1972 I expressed the view that there was no reason to believe that the rock-cut tombs of the central Mediterranean represented an intrusive feature. I based this on the fact that central Mediterranean tombs are at least as early as, and perhaps earlier than, hypothetical prototypes in the east Mediterranean (Cyprus and the Cyclades). Moreover the earliest tombs in mainland Italy and Sicily are simple in form and were used for single or double burial only. They appear in the context of local Neolithic cultures and cannot be seen as part of an intrusive Copper Age complex. The

45

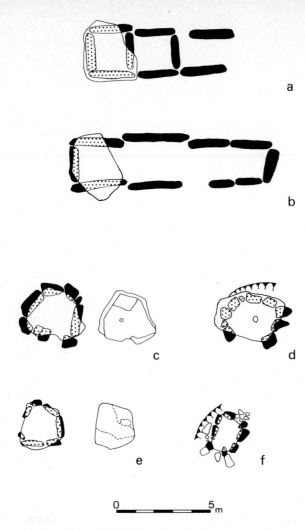

4 Plans of megalithic tombs in Italy. a Corato (after Gervasio); b Bisceglie (after Gervasio); c Quattromacine; d Scusi; e Placa; f Gurgulante. (Drawn by Philip Howard.)

simplest explanation is to see a local development within the central Mediterranean from the simple Neolithic tombs to the more elaborate Copper Age and later ones.

References Bernabò Brea 1957, Chapter III; Bray 1963: Guido 1963, Chapter II; Lilliu 1975, Chapter IVa, 2; Whitehouse 1972.

Megalithic Chamber Tombs (ill. 3)

True megalithic chamber tombs occur in three separate areas within our region: south-east Italy, Corsica and Sardinia. 'Sub-megalithic' tombs such as small stone cists also occur, both within these areas and else-

where, but I shall exclude these in general from the present discussion. I shall deal, however, with those examples that have been claimed as ancestors of the true megalithic tombs: the stone cists of southern Corsica and northern Sardinia and the group at Pian Sultano on the Tyrrhenian coast of mainland Italy just north of Rome.

I shall deal separately with the three main areas in which megalithic tombs occur.

South-east Italian Megalithic Tombs

The south-east Italian megalithic tombs, always known as dolmens, fall into two clearly defined groups, to which Evans gave the names Bari-Taranto and Otranto groups (Evans 1956, 85). I employed these names in my account of the Apulian megaliths in 1967 (Whitehouse 1967).

Distribution The Bari-Taranto tombs number ten, all found within 15 km of the sea, seven near the Adriatic coast, three near the Ionian Gulf. There is also a possible megalithic tomb near Vieste on the northern coast of the Gargano promontory. The Otranto group consisted formerly of at least sixteen tombs (of which only five were extant in 1965 when I visited them); they are concentrated on the eastern side of the Terra d'Otranto (the 'heel' of Italy) and eleven of them are clustered round the village of Giurdignano.

Typology (ill. 4) The Bari-Taranto tombs are either simple rectangular chambers (e.g. Acetulla, Taviano and Trani) or larger gallery graves. They vary in length from *c*.3 to *c*. 17 m. They are built of stone (usually limestone) slabs, supplemented at Giovinazzo by a stretch of drystone walling. The tombs at Corato and Giovinazzo were subdivided into segments. Two other tombs –Bisceglie and Leucaspide – were closed at both ends and were also divided into a distinct chamber or *cella* at one end, separated from the main gallery. The exceptional Giovinazzo tomb has a damaged circular structure at one end, which appears to be original and is interpreted by the excavator as an *anticella* or lobby. This tomb was also unusually long and the passage/chamber was divided into several segments. Traces of a 'port-hole' can be seen in one slab, but this appears not to be in its original position. Six capstones survive at Giovinazzo; elsewhere only one or none at all survive. Most of the tombs have, or had when discovered, traces at least of earth or earth and stone mounds, oval or rectangular with rounded corners, sometimes revetted with drystone walls. Many tombs are aligned east-west, with the entrance facing east.

The Otranto tombs are quite different from those of the northern group. They are much smaller and lack the rectangular form and regular slab construction that characterize the Bari-Taranto group. Instead they are oval, polygonal or sub-rectangular in plan and are built in what I have called the *block-and-boulder* style. The supports for the capstones vary in number from two to eight and may be rough slabs, monolithic blocks, pillars made of several superimposed stones, projecting blocks of bedrock or even, in one case, a section of dry-stone walling. Several tombs were built over shallow hollows in the bedrock. The tombs are rarely more than 1 m high and vary from *c.* 2 to 4 m in length. Unlike the Bari-Taranto tombs, they lack any regular orientation; they also lack any surviving traces of mounds (though this may be an accident of preservation). Interesting features of these tombs are various markings on the upper surfaces of the capstones; two tombs had perforated capstones and another three had shallower holes, while two tombs had incised grooves.

Burial Rite No finds – neither skeletal material nor artifacts – have ever been recorded from tombs of the Otranto group, which are generally open and have often been used as tool stores or pigsties by the local *contadini*. Indeed, we have no direct evidence that these monuments were tombs at all, though their similarity to definite funerary structures elsewhere (see below) makes it likely that they were.

The Bari-Taranto monuments were certainly tombs. Many of these too had been robbed along ago, but several have yielded both human remains and artifacts. The Bisceglie tomb contained the remains of at least thirteen individuals; most of the skeletons were disarticulated, but a few survived intact and these had been buried in the contracted position. In the Giovinazzo tomb human bones were found only in one section, marked off by septal slabs; the bones, fragmentary and in a state of complete disorder, represented the remains of at least nine adults, two youths and two children.

Chronology We have no radiocarbon dates for any south Italian megalithic tomb, so for discussion of dating we are dependent on the typology of artifacts found within them or – with due caution – on the typology of the tombs themselves.

Until 1967 it was customary to date the Bari-Taranto tombs to the Middle or Late Bronze Age or even the Early Iron Age (Puglisi 1959,43; Trump 1966, 145–8). Certainly material of the Apennine culture of the later second millennium and early first millennium BC has been found in several tombs (Bisceglie, Albarosa). However, in 1967 I pointed out that some of the material from one tomb – Leucaspide – belongs to the very beginning of the Bronze Age, to

the phase sometimes called Proto-Apennine (Lo Porto's Protoappenninico B (Lo Porto 1963, 363)). Moreover, the material from Giovinazzo, published in the same year, also belongs to the Proto-Apennine B phase (Lo Porto 1967). There is also full Apennine pottery from Giovinazzo and one sherd of painted ware, which may come from an imported vessel of Late Helladic I/II type, suggesting that the tomb was still in use in the sixteenth century BC. We have no radiocarbon dates for Proto-Apennine material, but we should expect this phase to fall in the range 1800-1400 bc, between the Copper Age and the full Apennine culture (Whitehouse 1978, 84–7). This chronology, corresponding to *c.* 2300–1750 BC in calendar years, is consistent with the discovery of imported sherds of Middle Helladic type (datable to *c.* 2000–1600 BC) in Proto-Apennine levels at Porto Perone, Leporano (Lo Porto 1963). If the Bari-Taranto tombs *were* built during this period, they would overlap the main period of megalith construction elsewhere in the Mediterranean, rather than being very much later.

The Otranto tombs can only be dated – very speculatively – by comparative typology. Evans pointed out in 1956 that the Otranto tombs were very similar to those of Malta, which share the hollows beneath the tombs, the holes and grooves in the capstones, as well as the general block-and-boulder style of building. The Maltese dolmens are associated with the Tarxien Cemetery Culture, which has radiocarbon dates ranging from *c.* 1900 to 1350 bc (*c.* 2400-1650 BC). The evidence is flimsy, but as far as it goes it suggests a late third-early second millennium BC date for the initial construction of monuments of both groups.

Relationships South-east Italy has, as well as megalithic tombs, both menhirs and statue-menhirs (see below). The distribution of the menhirs is very similar to that of the chamber tombs. In the Terra d'Otranto there seems to be a specific association between menhirs and some megalithic tombs (as well as rock-cut tombs): two tombs – Scusi and Chiancuse – have in their immediate vicinity small rectangular holes in the rock, exactly like those in which surviving menhirs stand. It seems likely that these originally held menhirs, which were used as stelae marking tomb positions.

The relationship between the two groups of tombs themselves has been a matter of controversy in the past. Whereas most Italian archaeologists have always regarded them as closely related (e.g. Puglisi 1959, 43 and, by implication, Peroni 1967, 85, fig. 18), the English archaeologists Evans (1966, 90–3) and Trump (1966, 87–9, 145–7) have regarded them as entirely separate. This arose from the divergent dating for the two groups (Copper or Early Bronze Age for the Otranto group, Late Bronze or Early Iron Age for the Bari-Taranto group) and, in view of the apparent contemporaneity of the two groups on recent evidence, now seems less likely. In 1967 I regarded the two groups as related, with the Otranto tombs as derivatives of the – intrusive – Bari-Taranto group. Now I think of them as varying manifestations of the same phenomenon, much as the Italian scholars do (though I favour an earlier date and a different origin).

Parallels for both types of tombs have been sought in other parts of the central and west Mediterranean. Evans pointed out the similarities between the Otranto dolmens and those of Malta (Evans 1956), while other scholars (e.g. Guido 1963, 82–8) have pointed to similarities also with some of the Sardinian dolmens. In the case of the Bari-Taranto tombs, the best parallels are to be found in the southern French gallery graves, especially those of the Aude group (Daniel 1960, 146–54), though similar tombs occur elsewhere in France and in Iberia. The Sardinian gallery graves (tombe di giganti) discussed below, also have some features in common with the Bari-Taranto tombs.

The parallels for both groups of Apulian tombs are to the south or west: indeed the Apulian tombs represent the easternmost occurrence of a west European phenomenon. As the tombs are also relatively late compared to those of west and north-west Europe, it seems reasonable to look for a western origin for the Italian tombs. However, I do not believe in the route proposed by Puglisi (1959, 43), which brings them first to the Tyrrhenian coast at Pian Sultano (where there is a group of small megalithic cists), then across the Apennines (where there is nothing) to the Gargano promontory (where there is a monument of doubtful type and function). Nor indeed do I now feel convinced, as I did in 1967, that there was an actual intrusion of French megalith builders by sea to southern Italy (Whitehouse 1967, 360–4). When all is said and done, the Italian tombs are of very simple forms; it may simply have been the idea of megalithic tombs that spread, through maritime trade and other contacts, within the central Mediterranean in the third millennium BC. This will be discussed further in the final section.

References Evans 1956; Gervasio 1913; Jatta 1914; Lo Porto 1967; Palumbo 1956; Whitehouse 1967.

Corsican Megalithic Tombs

There are two types of megalithic tomb in Corsica: slab cists set into the ground, known as coffres, and above ground chamber tombs, known as dolmens.

Distribution The stone cists occur singly, in small groups and in larger cemeteries. Grosjean (1966, 24–5) lists six major groups, all in the south of the island, but isolated examples are found in other regions also. Grosjean claims there are 'tens' of these cists known, presumably fewer than one hundred. The dolmens occur all over the island, but the greatest concentration is in the south. About one hundred are known.

Typology The stone cists measure up to 3 m in length and are built of large stone slabs, often of granite. They are set into the ground, sometimes up to 2 m deep. They are frequently surrounded by stone circles, which mark the perimeter of a low mound. No coffres have been found with surviving capstones; it is not known whether they were originally roofed or not.

The dolmens are either simple rectangular chambers or, rarely, have a chamber approached by a separate short passage. The Corsican tombs are all built of large slabs and not in the block-and-boulder style sometimes found in south-east Italy, Malta and Sardinia. Three tombs – Settiva (Petreto-Bicchisano), Cardiccia (Giunchetu) and Taravu (Sollacaro) – have 'portholes' in the upper part of the entrance slab. Two other tombs – Capu-di-Logu (Campo Moro) and Pagliaiu (Sartène) – have simple incised decoration. Traces of mounds survive in a few cases. The Settiva dolmen has a 'horned' facade like the Sardinian tombe di giganti (see below).

Burial Rite Neither the stone cists nor the dolmens are normally found intact: as in Italy and in other areas legends that they contain treasure have made them the objects of clandestini or chercheurs de la nuit. However, fragments of bone and artifacts sometimes survive. Grosjean believes that the cists were used for individual burial, but claims also that they were reused for centuries. They may, perhaps, never have held more than one body at any one time. The artifacts found include tools of Sardinian obsidian, ground stone axes, stone beads and, in one case, a perforated stone macehead. Most of the dolmens have been robbed, but one – Settiva (Petreto-Bicchisano) – has yielded the remains of at least five individuals, indicating that collective burial was practised.

Chronology Grosjean assigns the stone cists to his Megalithic I period, which he believes began in the late fourth or early third millennium BC and lasted through much of the third millennium. The only direct evidence comes from one cist at Pagliaiu (or Palaggiu), which had only been partially robbed; this yielded material of Beaker type (Peretti 1966), which suggests a third millennium BC date. The only other – indirect

– dating evidence is the similarity to the cemetery of circular tombs excavated at Li Muri (Arzachena) in north-east Sardinia. If this parallel is valid, it may indicate a date as early as the early fourth millennium BC (see below).

The above-ground megalithic chamber tombs – the dolmens – are assigned by Grosjean to his Megalithic II period, on the grounds of their association with menhirs of this phase. This period he dates from late third to late second millennium BC. There is a radiocarbon date for this period, not from a dolmen, but from a presumed cult site at Castello d'Alo (Bilia). This date, which belongs to the middle phase – IIB – of the period, is *c*. 1870 bc, which corrects to *c*. 2350 BC. The dolmen of Settiva (Petreto-Bicchisano) produced in its primary level twenty single-handed conical cups, for which Grosjean has sought parallels in Copper and Bronze Age material from elsewhere in the central Mediterranean; this would fit with a late third or early second millennium BC date (Grosjean 1974).

Relationships There is a close association in Corsica between megalithic tombs and menhirs of all kinds. The coffres are associated with small menhirs of Grosjean's stage 1 (see below), which are found in the immediate vicinity of the tombs. The dolmens are associated with the menhirs and statue-menhirs of Grosjean's stages 2–5; these are often found in alignments or in other groupings and may be a few metres or tens of metres away from the tombs. Grosjean believes that the dolmens developed out of the earlier coffres and indeed that they represent simply above-ground versions of the same tomb type. This is difficult to demonstrate, but seems plausible and there are some tombs, which are partly sunk into the ground, which would make a plausible half-way stage in this hypothetical sequence.

For external relationships, the closest parallels for the stone cists are the ones at Li Muri (Arzachena) already mentioned, and others in the same area of northern Sardinia. However, rather similar monuments are found in many parts of the Mediterranean and parallels have been claimed, both to the west (e.g. the round tombs of Almeria) and to the east (e.g. the cemetery of cist tombs excavated by Dörpfeld on the island of Levkas).

For the dolmens parallels can be found among the simpler tombs in most areas where megaliths occur; they are particularly common in southern France, in the Pyrenees and in Catalonia. They are also like some of the Sardinian dolmens (those not built in the block-and-boulder style).

References Grosjean 1966a, 1966b, 1967, 1974; Jehasse and Grosjean 1976.

Sardinian Megalithic Tombs

Sardinia has three main varieties of megalithic tomb: stone cists, known as *circoli megalitici* or *dolmenici*; simple rectangular chambers known as *dolmens;* and large and elaborate gallery graves known as *tombe di giganti*. There are also a number of long cists, some of which are built in a megalithic manner; these are known as *tombe a poliandro,* because of the large number of bodies they contain.

Distribution The fifty or so known stone cists occur only in the Gallura, the north-east part of Sardinia, close to Corsica. The dolmens are found in the northern half of the island; about forty are known. The *tombe di giganti* are found all over the island. Lilliu (1975) claims 321 of these monuments, but Castaldi regards only 219 of these as true *tombe di giganti,* characterized by forecourts and stelae (Castaldi 1969, 251–6, Appendix I). She regards the other 102 monuments as megaliths of simpler type. There certainly are in Sardinia megalithic tombs that do not fit very comfortably into either the dolmen or the *tombe di giganti* category; these include some of the *tombe a poliandro.*

Typology (ill. 5) The stone cists of the Gallura (Lilliu's *circoli dolmenici*) take the form of a cist of stone slabs in the centre of a round mound made of earth and stone, which is surrounded by a peristalith of stone slabs set on end. The cists themselves measure from 1.2 x 1.6 m to 2 x 2 m; three sides are made of large slabs, while the fourth, usually that facing south or south-west, either has no slab or one much smaller than the others. The diameters of the mounds range from 5.3 to 8.5 m. Associated with the mounds, but outside them, are smaller cists perhaps used to hold funerary offerings, and vertical stone menhirs, used as stelae.

Lilliu divides the dolmens into two groups. The first group have a mound and surrounding peristalith, usually elliptical in shape; the second group has neither. Many dolmens have simple rectangular chambers 3–4 m long, e.g. Elcomis (Buddoso) or a larger chamber, divided into two, e.g. Perdalonga (Austis). One dolmen at Motorra (Dorgali) has a polygonal chamber approached by a short passage – a true passage grave in fact. As well as regular slab-built dolmens, there are also tombs consisting of a rectangular, oval or polygonal chamber, roofed by a large capstone which is supported on a number of uprights, varying from three to seven (or perhaps even more originally). In this respect these dolmens resemble the block-and-boulder-style dolmens of Apulia and Malta, though other features of these, e.g. pillars made of superimposed stones or pierced or decorated capstones, do not occur in Sardinia.

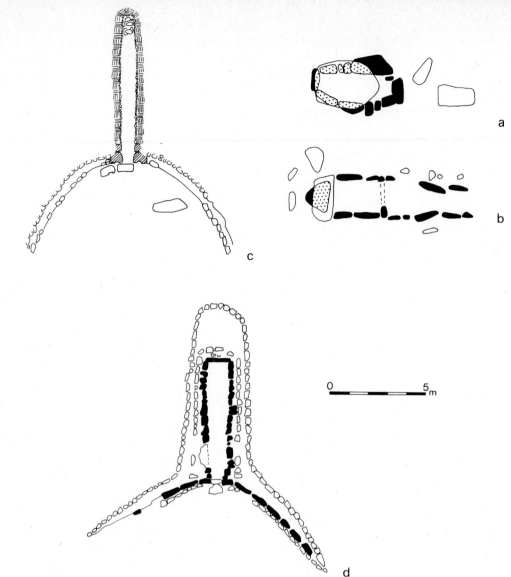

5 *Plans of Sardinian megalithic tombs.* a *Maone (after Guido)*; b *Perdalonga (after Guido)*; c *Oridda (after Castaldi)*; d *Li Mizzani (after Castaldi). (Drawn by Philip Howard.)*

The *tombe di giganti* are the most elaborate of all the megalithic tombs in the central Mediterranean. The distinguishing features of these tombs are their long chambers, entered through the centre of a façade, which frames an apsidal, semi-circular or occasionally almost circular forecourt. The chambers may have walls of orthostats roofed with slabs or be made of coursed masonry, inclining inwards to form the roof.

The mounds that cover these chambers, sometimes surrounded by a peristalith, are long, rounded at the far end and often expand out in two long 'horns' behind the wings of the façade at the entrance end. This feature has in the past provoked some inappropriate comparison with the 'horned cairns' of the Irish Carlingford group. The chambers range from a few metres to *c.* 15 m in length and the monuments as a whole may exceed 20 m (the longest, Li Lolghi near Arzachena, is *c.*27 m long). In the centre of the façade, closing the entrance to the chamber, is often a tall carved slab – described as a stele – which has a small arch-shaped opening at the base, often no more than 50 cm high, giving access to the chamber.

Recent meticulous work on four *tombe di giganti* in

the province of Sassari has demonstrated that, like many British tombs, they were rebuilt many times and used over a very long period. The final plans are sometimes complex with double chambers, changes in level and other features. Interesting connections with the rock-cut tombs are evident. Both Lilliu (1975, 311) and Castaldi (1969, 242–50) believe that the stelae of the *tombe di giganti* copy the carved features found above the entrances to earlier rock-cut tombs in the Sassari area, e.g. one at Molafa. The chronology of the finds from the tombs favours this view, rather than that of Guido (1963, 91) who believes that the rock-cut tomb carvings copy the *tombe di giganti*. 'Hybrid' tombs also occur. One, at Oridda, is actually a rock-cut tomb, but the rock-cut chamber is long, narrow and rectangular, like that of the *tombe di giganti*, and the entrance is flanked by stone 'horns', enclosing a semi-circular forecourt. The entrance itself is closed by a stele, shorter than that commonly closing the *tombe di giganti*, but otherwise very similar and with the customary small opening in the bottom.

Yet another kind of megalithic tomb is the long stone cist, of which examples have been found in many parts of the island. These tombs are sunken, rectangular, trapezoid or boat-shaped, lined with slabs or drystone walling, and may be several metres long. Some had one or more capstones.

Burial Rite Lilliu suggests that only some of the fifty or so circular structures were used for burial: others may have been used for cult purposes. Indeed only three tombs have actually yielded skeletal material: one of the tombs at Li Muri, Li Muracci and San Pantaleo. The first two tombs had a single burial each; the third contained two skeletons, an adult and a child.

Most of the dolmens, long exposed to the elements and to man, have yielded neither skeletal remains nor artifacts, though occasionally fragmentary material survives. We do not know whether the dolmens were intended for single or collective burial.

The *tombe di giganti* have fared a little better than the dolmens; although undisturbed tombs are rarely found, many have yielded material. These tombs were undoubtedly used for collective burial. The tomb of Preganti (Gergei) produced remains of about fifty individuals, that of Las Plassas about sixty, while the hybrid tomb of Oridda (Sennori) produced remains of at least twenty-seven bodies. Pottery, stone and metal artifacts have been retrieved from some of these tombs, presumably representing original grave goods.

The long cists were also used for collective burial, from which they derive the name *tombe a poliandro*. One tomb at Ena' e Muros (Ossi) had more than thirty skeletons, while one at San Giuliano (Alghero) contained some fifty-four. Pottery and other artifacts also occur in these tombs.

Chronology We have no radiocarbon dates for the construction of Sardinian megalithic tombs, any more than for Apulian or Corsican ones, but we do have some chronological information from the artifacts found in the tombs, and one radiocarbon date for later material from one.

For the circular tombs with their cists the best information comes from the goods found at Li Muri. As well as flint and obsidian flakes and sherds of coarse pottery these cists yielded a number of polished stone objects: axes, perforated maceheads, beads and a carinated cup with spool handles, made of steatite. Parallels for this vessel have been sought in third millennium BC Egypt and Crete, but the form is very close to that found in pottery in the Final Neolithic Diana culture of Lipari. As already mentioned, the Diana Culture has radiocarbon dates which correct to calendrical dates of *c.* 3950-3750 BC. So, if we accept this geographically much closer parallel, we should perhaps think of a date much earlier than usually envisaged for the Sardinian stone cists, and perhaps for the Corsican ones as well.

Some information about the date of the dolmens comes from the one at Motorra (Dorgali), which has produced a stone wristguard, stone beads, flint and bone flakes and potsherds which apparently have parallels in the Ferrières-Fontbouisse cultures of the south French Chalcolithic. These cultures, traditionally dated to the early second millennium BC, should now, in the light of the tree-ring calibration, be dated to the first half of the third millennium BC.

The *tombe di giganti* have long been recognized as the main burial places of the people of the Nuragic culture, producing characteristic Nuragic pottery and metal artifacts. Radiocarbon dates for this culture run from *c.* 1500 bc to *c.* 700 bc (*c.* 1900–900 BC) and we know that *nuraghi* continued to be built and used still later, indeed into the third century BC in the northern part of the island (outside the area of Carthaginian domination). The beginning of the culture must go back into the third millennium BC: the 'protonuraghe' of Brunku Madugui has yielded a radiocarbon date of *c.* 1820 bc (2300 BC). The earliest *tombe di giganti* may even be earlier than this. Castaldi suggests that the tomb of Coddu Vecchiu was built in the Early Bronze Age, which she dates to *c.* 1800 BC, but which should now be pushed back into the third millennium BC. Earlier still is the 'hybrid' tomb at Oridda, which has produced Copper Age and Early Bronze Age material, suggesting a date early in the third millennium BC. The *tombe di giganti* were used over very long periods of

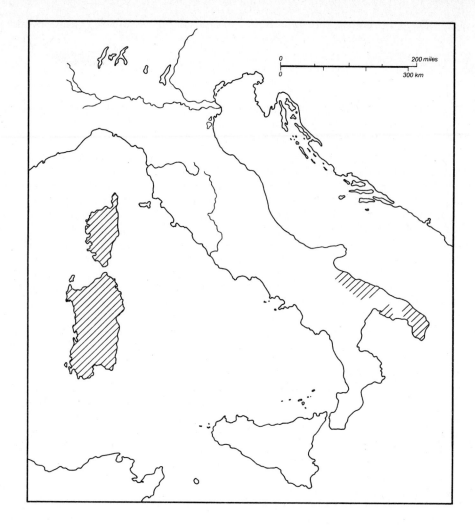

6 Distribution of menhirs.

time: Li Lolghi was still in use in the Late Iron Age, having been built in the Middle Bronze Age (indicating use for more than a thousand years). Some tombs have even yielded Roman sherds, suggesting use into the third century BC.

The long stone cists also seem to have a long date range. San Giuliano (Alghero) is attributed by Lilliu to the Early Bronze Age Bunnanaro culture and others are attributed to the succeeding Monte Claro culture (late third to early second millennium BC). Others belong to the full Nuragic culture.

To summarize, it seems that the earliest 'megaliths' in Sardinia, the slab cists, may have been fourth millennium BC in date, perhaps contemporary with the earliest rock-cut tombs. To the early third millennium BC may belong the dolmens, as well as many of the

rock-cut tombs. The more elaborate megaliths, the *tombe di giganti*, as well as the long stone cists were probably first built in the later third millennium BC and continued to be constructed and used throughout the second millennium BC and much of the first also.

Relationships Menhirs are found in association with most of the types of tombs (see below). As far as relationships between the different groups of tombs themselves are concerned, the circular tombs with their slab cists seem to be separate, but it is difficult to make hard and fast distinctions between the other groups: tombs intermediate between simple dolmens and *tombe di giganti* exist, as do forms intermediate between *tombe di giganti* and rock-cut tombs. Also, as we have seen, there is probably considerable chronological overlap in the use of the different types of monuments.

As far as external relationships are concerned, for the slab cists and the dolmens, similar parallels are sought

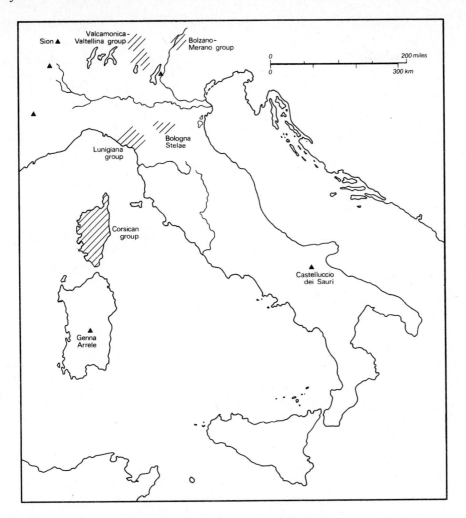

as for the Corsican tombs. For the slab cists, the similarities with the Corsican *coffres* themselves are close, other parallels (whether eastern or western) more remote. Among the dolmens, some are very like those found on Corsica; others more closely resemble the block-and-boulder-style dolmens of Malta and the Otranto group in southern Italy.

For the *tombe di giganti* there are no plausible parallels outside the island. The most reasonable hypothesis derives them from the dolmens by a process of local evolution.

References Castaldi 1969; Guido 1963, Chapter III; Lilliu 1975, 98–105, 319–16; Puglisi 1941–2.

Menhirs and Statue-Menhirs (ills 6 and 7)

In the central Mediterranean standing stones, both unadorned examples known as menhirs and an-

7 Distribution of statue-menhirs.

thropomorphic ones called statue-menhirs are found in all the areas where megalithic tombs occur and also in parts of northern Italy. The area in which this particular form of megalithism was most highly developed was undoubtedly the island of Corsica. I shall describe the different groups separately.

Southern Italy (ill. 8)

There is a single group of statue-menhirs in southern Italy, found at Castelluccio dei Sauri on the southern edge of the Tavoliere plain. Three small stone slabs (none more than 1 m high), one very fragmentary, were carved to indicate breasts, necklaces and other features. The breasts are in relief with an incised outline, the rest incised. A fragment of a possible

53

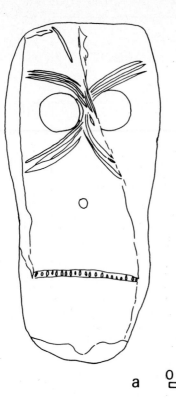

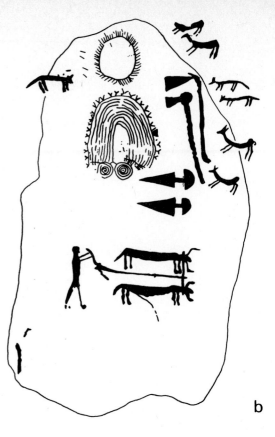

8 *Italian statue-menhirs. a* Castelluccio dei Sauri; b *Bagnolo II, Val Camonica (after Anati). (Drawn by Philip Howard.)*

fourth statue-menhir shows a dagger with a triangular blade and rounded pommel. This group of menhirs is isolated and there is no associated dating evidence. On typological grounds they are usually assigned to the Copper Age.

The undecorated menhirs occur in much the same areas as the megalithic tombs of Apulia. A sparse group of twenty-eight known menhirs (not all surviving) occur in the province of Bari. Most of these are isolated but two groups at Sovereto, one of four stones and one of three, are said to form alignments, the first *c.* 2 km long, the other much shorter. A much larger group of menhirs, numbering about sixty today, but formerly at least 101, occurs in the Terra d'Otranto. These menhirs, known locally as *pietrefitte*, are narrow stone pillars of rectangular section, ranging in height from *c.* 2 m to more than 4 m. They are made of soft local limestone, carefully shaped and tend to be aligned north-south (i.e. with the longer sides facing east and west). Alignments are not recorded in this group.

These *menhirs* are sometimes found in association with tombs. These may be rock-cut tombs, both early (Copper or Early Bronze Age) and late (Iron Age) examples; there is some evidence that they may be associated with *dolmens* of the Otranto group also (see above).

References Gervasio 1913; Ornella Acanfora 1960; Palumbo 1955; Whitehouse 1967.

Northern Italy (ill. 8)

In northern Italy undecorated menhirs do not occur, but several groups of statue-menhirs are known. One group is found in various parts of the central Alps: at least seven in the upper Adige valley, about ten in the Val Camonica (famous for its rock carvings) and another seven in the neighbouring valley of Valtellina. Most of these menhirs have no clear heads and are identifiable as human figures through the depiction of collars and belts and, in one case, breasts. These figures are sometimes provided with incised axes and daggers (triangular with crescentic pommels) and some have carts or ploughs pulled by oxen. These are all like

54

similar artifacts depicted in the Val Camonica rock carvings and assigned to the Copper or Early Bronze Age. The best dating evidence, however, comes from the site of Sion, over the border in Switzerland. Here a very similar statue-menhir with a dagger had been reused in the side of a Bell Beaker cist burial (suggesting a date no later than the early third millennium BC for the menhir).

Another numerous group of statue-menhirs occurs in north-west Tuscany and is known as the Lunigiana group. Trump (1966, 98, 166) suggests a two-fold division of this group. The first sub-group is named after the site of Pontevecchio. Menhirs of this group have faces indicated schematically and arms more clearly; some have breasts and no weapons; other have no breasts indicated, but are provided with triangular daggers with crescentric pommels like the Alpine examples. This group Trump regards as Copper or Early Bronze Age like the Alpine statue-menhirs. The other component of the Lunigiana group is named after the site of Filetto. These are more elaborate. They appear to be male figures, with face, arms and legs all shown clearly and equipped with weapons which include long swords, spade-shaped axes and lances. Trump suggests a Late Bronze Age or Early Iron Age date for this group and believes that a long gap intervened between the Pontevecchio group and the Filetto group. To me this seems unlikely; there may have been a continuous and very long-lived tradition of erecting statue-menhirs of increasing complexity in this area, just as there was in Corsica (see below). None of the statue-menhirs of the Lunigiana group is associated with a tomb. Nor are alignments recorded.

The last group in northern Italy is of the same period as the Filetto group – Late Bronze Age to Early Iron Age – but these *are* associated with tombs. They are the stelae set over late Villanovan and Etruscan tombs in the Bologna area, which are carved to suggest the head and shoulders of a human form.

References Anati 1973; Barfield 1971, 65–7; Formentini 1972; Ornella Acanfora 1952–5; Trump 1966, 98–100, 166–7.

Sardinia

About fifty menhirs survive in Sardinia, distributed all over the island. These are usually made of basalt or granite and vary both in height (from less than 1 to 6.5 m) and in the amount of dressing they have received. Only one true statue-menhir has been published. This figure, at Genna Arrele (Laconi), is 1.45 m high.

It appears to be a male, with facial features indicated schematically by a T-shape in relief; he is equipped with a dagger below the waist and a trident-shaped object on his chest, both in relief also. The dagger is like Copper Age examples and suggests a fourth or third millennium date. A few other menhirs have simple decoration, which may be anthropomorphic in intention. Perda Fitta (Serramanna) has a vertical row of ten carved hollows down one side and several have multiple breast-like protuberances, e.g. Is Araus (S. Vero Milis), which has four.

The Sardinian menhirs are often associated with tombs: rock-cut tombs, the slab cists of the Gallura, dolmens in the same area, and also *tombe di giganti*. No alignments are recorded, but the menhirs are often found in groups; thirteen pairs have been recorded and six groups of three. To judge by the dates of associated tombs, it seems likely that the Sardinian menhirs were erected from the Copper Age (fourth millennium BC), right through the Bronze Age and into the Iron Age (mid-first millennium BC).

We should perhaps consider here the marble statuette, of the type often labelled 'Cycladic' (though now widely thought to be of local origin) from Senorbi. This female figure, 44 cm high, had been set into the ground; while hardly monumental, this figure is larger than the smaller idols of similar type found in the rock-cut tombs of the Ozieri culture.

References Atzeni 1972; Guido 1963, Chapter III: Lilliu 1957, 20–5, 92–5; Lilliu 1975, 129–36.

Corsica (ill. 9)

While Corsica cannot compete with its neighbouring island Sardinia in the number or splendour of its megalithic tombs or its cyclopean towers, in the production of menhirs and statue-menhirs the northern island is undisputed leader. Some 450 menhirs and statue-menhirs are known in Corsica, most of them in the south of the island. Alignments and groups of various sorts are the rule rather than the exception in Corsica and the largest group at Pagliaiu (or Palaggiu) consisted originally of no fewer than 258 menhirs in seven distinct groups. Groups of this size do not occur elsewhere in the Mediterranean and are reminiscent of the great alignments of Brittany.

All but five of the Corsican menhirs are made of granite, and they vary in form from small undecorated stones less than 1 m in height to elaborately ornamented statues several metres high. On typological grounds Grosjean has divided the Corsican menhirs and statue-menhirs into six stages which he believes represent a real sequence of development.

55

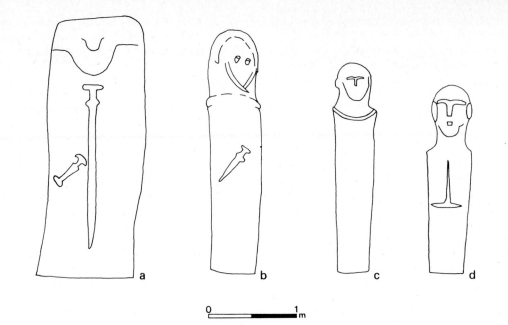

9 Corsican statue-menhirs. a Filitosa V; b Nativu, Barbaggiu; c Tavera; d Filitosa IV. (Drawn by Philip Howard.)

Stage 1 consists of small stones, normally associated with tombs. They are usually less than 1 m high and may be triangular, round or oval in section.

Stage 2 menhirs are described by Grosjean as 'proto-anthropomorphic', by which he means that the sculptors intended to indicate the human form (though sometimes very schematically). These menhirs are 2–5 m high, well shaped, thin and rectangular, semi-circular or oval in section.

Stage 3 has anthropomorphic menhirs with the head clearly separated from the body. No features are shown on these menhirs, which are rarely more than 2 m high. Sections may be rectangular, semi-circular or oval.

Stage 4 consists of statue-menhirs with facial features shown. These menhirs have no weapons. They are 2–3 m high, rectangular, oval or semi-circular in section. They occur only in the south of the island.

Stage 5 consists of statue-menhirs with weapons. Twenty-three of these are known, all from the south of the island and many of them from Filitosa. They are of similar height and shape to those of Stage 4. On most of the statue-menhirs the weapons are shown in bas relief, but on three examples from Pagliaiu and one from Rinaiu they are engraved. The weapons shown include daggers, long swords, corselets and helmets of various sorts (including ones that Grosjean thinks were originally equipped with horns).

Stage 6 consists of statue-menhirs found only in the north of the island (north of the area in which the Torrean culture is found). These statue-menhirs have no weapons; they are thinner and narrower than those of the other stages.

Grosjean's interpretation of the development is as follows. The sequence begins with the introduction from further east of the 'megalithic idea', which included the erection of small menhirs, associated with the slab cists. After this the whole development was a local phenomenon. Grosjean believes that all the menhirs, including the undecorated ones, represent dead individuals and all represent males (certainly there are no specifically female figures in Corsica: breasts are never shown). Grosjean's interpretation of the armed figures of his Stage 5 is particularly interesting: he sees these as portraits of dead enemies, who invaded Corsica at this time. He claims that the people of the megalithic culture were not metal-using and that the undoubtedly metal weapons portrayed on the statues are closely comparable with those of the 'Peoples of the Sea', especially the Shardana, as portrayed in particular on the famous reliefs on the Temple of Medinet Habu, Thebes, of the early twelfth century BC. He believes that the Shardana invaded Corsica at about this time, destroyed the megalithic culture and established the culture of the Torri in the south of the island. The statue-menhirs of Stage 6 represent the phase following the establishment of the Torrean culture in the

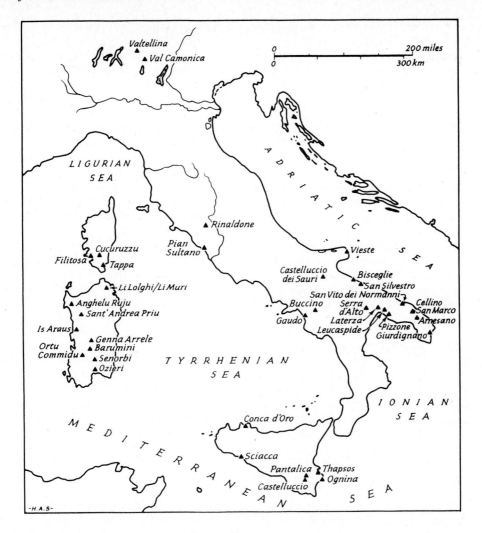

LIGURIAN
SEA

ADRIATIC SEA

▲ Valtellina
▲ Val Camonica

200 miles
300 km

▲ Rinaldone

Pian
Sultano ▲

▲ Cucuruzzu
Filitosa▲ ▲ Tappa

▲–Li Lolghi/Li Muri

▲ Anghelu Ruju
▲ Sant'Andrea Priu

Is Araus▲

Ortu
Commidu▲ ▲ Genna Arrele
▲ Barumini
▲ Senorbi
▲ Ozieri

TYRRHENIAN
SEA

▲ Vieste

Castelluccio
dei Sauri ▲   ▲ Bisceglie
▲ San Silvestro
San Vito dei Normanni
Buccino ▲   Serra   ▲ Cellino
d'Alto   ▲ San Marco
Gaudo ▲   Laterza   ▲ Amesano
Leucaspide▲   ▲ Pizzone
Giurdignano ▲

IONIAN
SEA

Conca d'Oro ▲

MEDITERRANEAN

▲ Sciacca

Pantalica ▲ ▲ Thapsos
▲ Ognina
Castelluccio ▲

SEA

-H.A.S-

south, when the defeated megalith builders fled to the north of the island.

Such independent chronological evidence as there is does not entirely support Grosjean's interpretation. There is one early radiocarbon date associated with menhirs – *c.* 1870 bc (*c.* 2400 BC) – from the cult site of Castello d'Alo (Bilia), which is associated with fragmentary menhirs of Stage 2 type. Other evidence comes from Filitosa, where statue-menhirs of several stages, including Stage 5, had been broken transversely and the fragments incorporated into the construction of the Torrean period, which has radiocarbon dates of *c.* 1430 and 1200 bc (*c.* 1750–1500 BC), as well as some later ones. If Grosjean is right, this date should represent a *terminus ante quem* for the main development of the megalithic culture on the island, only those menhirs of Stage 6 being later. However, there are dates later than this associated with two alignments of

10 Important sites mentioned in the text.

statue-menhirs of earlier stages (Stantare: dates of *c.* 1000, 170 and 130 BC; Pagliaiu, or Palaggiu: 730 and 700 BC). The second-century dates presumably represent later activity on the site and the other dates *may* not represent primary use either; this must remain an open question at the moment.

On the oft-debated subject of the Shardana I do not wish to say much except that radiocarbon dates indicate that both the Torrean and the Nuragic cultures were in existence by *c.* 1800 BC; moreover proto-nuragic structures were being built before 2000 BC. These dates are far too early to allow either of these cultures to be the work of Sea People warriors fleeing to the central Mediterranean after their defeat by the

Egyptians. The alternative hypothesis – that Sardinia and/or Corsica was the original *homeland* of the Shardana – remains possible at least on chronological grounds, but further discussion of this topic is beyond the scope of the present paper.

References Grosjean 1966a, 1966b, 1967; Jehasse and Grosjean 1976.

Discussion

I do not feel qualified, nor have I space here, to discuss the origins and relationships of the various monuments described in this chapter in any detail. I shall confine myself to taking a quick look at how the evidence from the central Mediterranean relates to some of the major topics of discussion about megaliths, both current and perennial. The topics I shall look at are the existence or otherwise of a 'megalithic complex'; diffusion or independent invention, and the 'mother-goddess'.

The Megalithic Complex It has been customary to regard rock-cut tombs, megalithic tombs, menhirs and statue-menhirs, circles and alignments and, often enough, also stone temples, as part of a total megalithic complex (e.g. Daniel 1963, 27). In the central Mediterranean, as we have already seen, it seems unjustified to regard the rock-cut tombs as part of such a complex. They begin earlier than the other types of monument and they occur in many areas where no megalithic tombs or standing stones are found; moreover they may well have been developed locally by indigenous Neolithic groups (Whitehouse 1972). It is true that in the central Mediterranean rock-cut tombs are sometimes associated with menhirs, but these may represent a feature which was added later in some areas only.

As for the other types of monuments, within our area they *do* on the whole seem to belong together. All areas with megalithic tombs also have menhirs and there are many examples of specific associations between menhirs and tombs. In Corsica the statue-menhirs are equally clearly associated with megalithic tombs, though this is not the case with any of the statue-menhirs on the Italian mainland, with the exception of the stelae from the Bologna cemeteries.

Diffusion or Independent Invention?
Traditional views derived the whole megalithic complex of Europe from the east Mediterranean. In this interpretation it would have been logical if scholars had regarded the central Mediterranean as crucial in the transmission of megalithism from east to west. In

practice, although rock-cut tombs were sometimes claimed as evidence for such a role (e.g. Childe 1957, 234–42; Daniel 1963, 81), there were always chronological difficulties to contend with in pursuing such an interpretation. In the case of the megalithic tombs and standing stones, the chronological problems were greater still and it was always difficult to claim that the central Mediterranean monuments could have been ancestral to those of west and north-west Europe. In 1963 Glyn Daniel recognized (89–94) that the Italian and Sardinian tombs must be later than those of France and Iberia. This fact has been made crystal clear by the subsequent publication of the early radiocarbon dates for north-west European megaliths, which are now so well known.

It is certainly impossible to see the central Mediterranean megaliths as transitional between hypothetical east Mediterranean ones and well known west European ones. However, an external origin for the central Mediterranean megaliths remains a possible interpretation and indeed the one favoured by most scholars working within the area, such as Puglisi, Lilliu and Grosjean. There is no agreement, however, about the source of the megalithic inspiration, with parallels being chased round almost the entire shoreline of the Mediterranean basin!

Both Lilliu (1975, 100) and Grosjean (1966a, 23–8) believe that it was only the simplest forms of megaliths (the slab-cists, perhaps simple dolmens and small plain menhirs) that were introduced to their respective islands. The more complex monuments – the Sardinian *tombe di giganti* and the elaborately decorated statue-menhirs of Corsica – are seen as the products of long processes of local development on the islands. In the case of the Apulian megaliths there is general agreement that these must have been introduced from the west, for the simple reason that there are no megalithic tombs further east.

Whether one accepts the view that megaliths were introduced from outside or believes that they developed locally is largely a matter of personal prejudice, since it is impossible to demonstrate conclusively on chronological or other grounds, that either of these views is untenable. I cannot resist taking the opportunity here, in an article that has otherwise been devoted largely to description, of airing – briefly – my own prejudices on this issue. I tend to favour a local origin, for the following reason. If the complex monuments are demonstrably the result of local development, we are left with small and unimpressive monuments – simple stone chambers, small undecorated standing stones – as the 'introduced' megaliths. And yet these are just the types of monument that might well have developed locally, particularly in the geological regions in question, where stone was an easily available building material and natural outcrops might suggest the form of chamber or standing stone.

Having said that, it seems to me unlikely that the various areas with megaliths in the central and west Mediterrranean were completely unconnected. We know from analyses of obsidian that trade, both maritime and overland, had been established since the sixth millennium BC in the central Mediterranean (at least between Sardinia and Corsica) and we have evidence for increasing connections in the subsequent millennia. I imagine the spread of megalithic ideas taking place in this context of increasing contact, but without significant movements of people. In any case, all the more remarkable manifestations of megalithism in Sardinia and Corsica, as in the case of the Maltese temples, seem to be the products of largely isolated insular traditions.

The Mother Goddess The 'mother goddess' can be disposed of more quickly. Fleming (1969) has argued cogently against the interpretation of all megalithic art (and indeed of anything decorated that comes out of a megalith) in terms of a universal mother goddess cult. The case for a female deity in the area we have been considering is particularly thin. Only a handful of all the hundreds of statue-menhirs in this region have breasts and many carry weapons and these in all probability represent males (unless we have an Amazon mother goddess!). The whole complex of decorated statue-menhirs of Corsica does not include one single example that is clearly, or even probably, female. The only clearly female figures are the few statue-menhirs with breasts from the Italian mainland and the Senorbi 'Cycladic' type statuette in Sardinia, as well as the related small idols from the rock-cut tombs. They are certainly female but none the less may not represent a mother goddess; there are other possibilities, as Ucko has pointed out in the case of figurines from Egypt, western Asia and Greece (Ucko 1968, 427–44).

The central Mediterranean megaliths when looked at from afar and as a whole, as through the wrong end of a telescope, appear as a clear-cut and coherent group. When the telescope is reversed and the monuments looked at in detail, the group dissolves into a number of separate elements, with differing typologies, differing dates, differing associated artifactual material and, in some cases, possibly different functions as well. The apparent coherence is the product of generalization. Such generalizations may, of course, be both valid and helpful, but in the case of megalithic monuments, they have dominated interpretation too long. The detailed analysis of individual monuments and groups of monuments in their local context should now be the aim of research in the central Mediterranean. Much valuable work of this kind has already been done; more work in the future will, I hope, bring to this region the kind of enlightenment that recent studies have brought to the megaliths of the north and north-west.

Bibliography

BPI   *Bullettino di Paletnologia italiana*
BSPF   *Bulletin de la Société préhistorique française*
NSc   *Notizie degli scavi di antichità*
PPS   *Proceedings of the Prehistoric Society*
RSP   *Rivista di Scienze preistoriche*

ANATI, E. 1973 'Le Statue Stele di Bagnolo', *Origini* VII, 229–83.

ATZENI, E. 1972 'Notiziario', *RSP* XXVII, 476.

BARFIELD, L. 1971 *Northern Italy before Rome*, London.

BERNARBÒ BREA, L. 1957 *Sicily before the Greeks*, London.

BRAY, W. 1963 'The Ozieri Culture of Sardinia', *RSP* XVIII, 155 ff.

1964 'Sardinian Beakers', *PPS* XXX, 75–98.

CASTALDI, E. 1969 'Tombe di Giganti nel Sassarese', *Origini* III, 119–274.

CHILDE, V. G. 1957 *The Dawn of European Civilization*, 6th edn, London.

DANIEL, G. 1960 *The Chambered Tombs of France*, London.

1963 *The Megalith Builders of Western Europe*, Harmondsworth.

DRAGO, C. 1947 'Sepolcreto del Pizzone', *RSP* XI, 333.

EVANS, J. D. 1956 'The 'dolmens' of Malta and the origins of the Tarxien cemetery culture', *PPS* XXII, 85–101.

FLEMING, A. 1969 'The myth of the mother-goddess', *World Archaeology* I, 247–61.

FORMENTINI, U. 1927 'Statue stele della Lunigiana', *Studi etruschi* I, 61.

GERVASIO, M. 1913 *I dolmen e la civiltà del bronzo nelle Puglie*, Bari.

GIORGI, C. DE, 1912 'Censimento dei dolmens di Terra d'Otranto', *Apulia* III, 99.

GROSJEAN, R. AND LIEGEOIS, J. 1964 'Les coffres mégalithiques de la region de Porto-Vecchio', *l'Anthropologie* LXVIII, 527–48.

1966a *La Corse avant l'Histoire*, Paris.

1966b 'Recent Work in Corsica', *Antiquity* XL, 190–8.

1967 'Classification descriptive du Mégalithique Corse, *BSPF* XLIV, 707–42.

1974 'Le complexe dolmenique de Settiva', *Gallia préhistoire XVII*, 707–9.

GUIDO, M. 1963 *Sardinia*, London.

JATTA, A. 1914 *La Puglia preistorica*, Bari.

JEHASSE, J. AND GROSJEAN, R. 1976 *Sites préhistoriques et protohistoriques de l'Ile de Corse*, UISS IX Congress, Nice 1976. Livret-guide de l'Excursion C4.

LILLIU, G. 1957 'Religione della Sardegna prenuragica', *BPI* LXVI, 7–96.

1968a II Dolmen di Motorra (Dorgali-Nuoro)', *Studi Sardi* XX, 74–128.

1968b 'Rapporti tra la cultura 'torreana' e aspetti pre e **protonuragici della Sardegna', *Studi Sardi* XX, 3–47.**

1975 *La Civiltà dei Sardi*, 2nd edn. Turin.

LO PORTO, F. G. 1961 'Notizie', *RSP* XVI, 270.

1963 'Leporano (Taranto) – la stazione preistorica di Porto Perone', *NSc*, Ser. 8, 17, 280–380.

1967 'Il "dolmen a galleria" di Giovinazzo', *BPI*. LXXVI, 137–80.

1972 'La tomba neolitica con idolo in pietra di Arnesano (Lecce)', *RSP* XXXVII, 357–72.

ORNELLA ACANFORA, M. 1952–5 'Le Statue Antropomorfe dell'Alto Adige', *Cultura Atestina* VI, 1952–5.

1960 'Le stele antropomorfe di Castelluccio dei Sauri', *RSP* XV, 95–123.

PALUMBO, G. 1955 'Inventario delle pietrefitte Salentine', *RSP* X, 86–147.

1956 'Inventario dei dolmen di Terra d'Otranto', *RSP* XI, 84–108.

PERETTI, G: 1966 'Une sepulture campaniforme en rapport avec l'alignement des menhirs de Palaggiu (Sartène, Corse)', *Actes du XVIIIe congrès préhistorique de France*, Ajaccio 1966, 230–42.

PERONI, R. 1967 *Archeologia della Puglia preistorica*, Florence.

PUGLISI, S. M. 1941–2 'Villaggi sotto roccia e sepolcri megalitici nella Gallura', *BPI* V–VI, 123–41.

1950 'Le culture dei capannicoli sul promontorio Gargano', *Atti Accad. naz. Lincei. Memorie*, ser. 8, 3–57.

1959 *La civiltà appenninica*, Florence.

RELLINI, U. 1925 'Scavi preistorici a Serra d'Alto', *NSc*, ser. 6, 1, 257–95.

TINÈ, S, (ed.) 1975 *Cilità Preistoriche e Protostoriche della Daunia*, Atti del Colloquio Internazionale di Preistoria e Protostoria della Daunia, Foggia 1973, Florence

TRUMP, D. H. 1966 *Central and Southern Italy before Rome*, London.

UCKO, P. J. 1968 *Anthropomorphic Figurines of Predynastic Egypt and Neolithic Crete*, London.

WHITEHOUSE, R. 1967 'The megalithic monuments of south-east Italy', *Man* II, 347–65.

1969 'The Neolithic Pottery Sequence in Southern Italy', *PPS* XXXV, 267–310.

1972 'The rock-cut tombs of the central Mediterranean', *Antiquity* XLVI, 275–81.

1978 'Italian Prehistory, Carbon 14 and the Tree-ring Calibration', in H. Mck. Blake, Potter, T. W. and Whitehouse, D. B. (eds), *Papers in Italian Archaeology I: the Lancaster Seminar*, Brit. Arch. Reports, S 41, 71–91.

WHITEHOUSE, R. AND RENFREW, C. 1975 'The Copper Age in Peninsular Italy and the Aegean', *Annual of the British School in Athens* LXIX, 343–90.

Appendix

List of relevant C14 dates

Site	Culture	Lab. no.	C14 date 5568 half-life bc	Corrected date BC, to nearest 50 years
MAINLAND ITALY				
Grotta della Madonna, Praia a Mare, prov. Cosenza	Diana	R–283	3160 ± 70	3950 ± 110
Lipari acropolis prov. Messina	Diana	R–180	3050 ± 200	3850 ± 210
Contrada Diana, Lipari, prov. Messina	Diana	R–182	2935 ± 55	3750 ± 110
Buccino, prov. Salerno	Gaudo	St–3627	2580 ± 100	3350 ± 115
	Gaudo	St–3620	2370 ± 120	
	Gaudo	St–3632	2155 ± 120	
	Gaudo	St–3628	2075 ± 100	
	Gaudo	St–3634	2060 ± 100	2600 ± 115
	Gaudo	St–3631	1970 ± 360	2500 ± 365
Riparo La Romita, Asciano, prov. Pisa	Rinaldone	Pi–100	2298 ± 115	2950 ± 130
Grotta dei Piccioni, Bolognano, prov. Pescara	Rinaldone	Pi–50	2356 ± 105	3050 ± 120
Luni sul Mignone, prov. Viterbo	Rinaldone	St–2043	2075 ± 100	2650 ± 115
	Rinaldone	St–2042	2005 ± 200	
	Rinaldone	St–1343	1850 ± 80	2350 ± 110
Grotta del Pertusello, Val Pennavaira, prov. Savona	Beakers	R–155	2440 ± 70	3150 ± 110
Monte Covolo, prov. Brescia	Beakers	Birm–471	2000 ± 320	2550 ± 325
	Beakers	Birm–470	1860 ± 210	2350 ± 215
Riparo Arma di Nasino, prov. Savona	Beakers	R–309	2270 ± 70	2950 ± 110
	Beakers	R–311	1815 ± 70	2300 ± 110
MALTA				
Tarxien	Tarxien Cemetery	BM–141	1930 ± 150	2400 ± 160
	Tarxien Cemetery	BM–711	1404 ± 76	
	Tarxien Cemetery	BM–710	1336 ± 72	1600 ± 110

Site	Culture	Lab. no.	C14 date 5568 half-life bc	Corrected date to nearest 50 y
SARDINIA				
Grotta di Sa 'Ucca de	Bonu Ighinu	R–882	3730 ± 160	4550 ± 170
su Tintirriolu, Bonu Ighinu,	Ozieri	R–884	3140 ± 50	3950 ± 110
prov. Sassari	Ozieri	R–883a	2980 ± 50	3800 ± 110
	Ozieri and Bonu Ighinu	R–879	2900 ± 50	3700 ± 110
Grotta del Guano	Ozieri	R–609a	2950 ± 50	3750 ± 110
or Gonagosula, Oliena, prov. Nuoro	Ozieri	R–609	2880 ± 50	3700 ± 110
Sa Turricula, Muros, prov. Sassari	Bunnannaro	R–963a	1510 ± 50	1850 ± 110
Brunku Madugui, Gesturi, prov. Cagliari	Monte Claro	Gif–243	1820 ± 250	2300 ± 255
Grotta d'Acqua Calda, Nuxis, prov. Cagliari	Monte Claro	R–677	1740 ± 60	2150 ± 110
Barumini, prov. Cagliari	Nuragic	K–151	1470 ± 200	1800 ± 210
Albucciu, prov. Sassari	Nuragic	Gif–242	1220 ± 250	1500 ± 110
Oridda, Sennori, prov. Sassari	Nuragic	R–1060	1220 ± 50	1500 ± 110
Ortu Commidu,	Nuragic	P–2401	1130 ± 60	1450 ± 110
Sardara, prov.	Nuragic	P–2402	1020 ± 50	1300 ± 110
Cagliari	Nuragic	P–2400	960 ± 250	1150 ± 255
	Nuragic	P–2399	960 ± 220	1150 ± 230
Genna Maria, Villanovaforru, prov. Cagliari	Nuragic	P–2403	970 ± 50	1150 ± 110
Sa Mandra 'e Sa	Nuragic	R–1094a	1100 ± 50	1400 ± 110
Giua, Ossi, prov	Nuragic	R–1096	860 ± 50	
Sassari	Nuragic	R–1097	850 ± 50	
	Nuragic	R–1092a	790 ± 50	
	Nuragic	R–1093a	740 ± 50	
	Nuragic	R–1098	720 ± 50	
	Nuragic	R–1095a	640 ± 50	850 ± 70
Su foxi 'e S'Abba,	Nuragic	R–1074a	960 ± 50	1150 ± 110
Lecorci, prov.	Nuragic	R–1065a	720 ± 50	
Nuoro	Nuragic	R–1065	700 ± 50	900 ± 70
Grotta A.S.I. or	Nuragic	R–492	820 ± 60	1000 ± 110
Piroso, Santadi, prov. Cagliari	Nuragic	R–492a	730 ± 60	900 ± 80

Site	Culture	Lab. no.	C14 date 5568 half-life bc	Corrected date BC, to nearest 50 years
CORSICA				
Basi, Serra-di-Ferro	Basien 'Chalcolithic'	Gif–1849	3300 ± 120	4100 ± 135
		Gif–1850	3250 ± 120	4050 ± 135
		Gif–1848	3250 ± 120	4050 ± 135
Curacchiaghiu, Lévie	'Late Neolithic'	Gif–1960	2980 ± 140	3800 ± 150
Araguina-Sennola, Bonifacio	'Late Neolithic'	Gif–779	2030 ± 140	2550 ± 150
	'EBA'	Gif–778	1600 ± 120	2000 ± 135
	'MBA'	Gif–777	1350 ± 120	1650 ± 135
	'LBA'	Gif–776	1090 ± 110	1350 ± 125
Curacchiaghiu, Lévie	'BA'	Gif–1959	1280 ± 130	1550 ± 145
	'IA'	Gif–1958	660 ± 110	850 ± 120
Basi, Serra-di-Ferro	Torrean	Gif–1847	1620 ± 110	2000 ± 125
	Torrean	Gif–1846	1400 ± 110	1750 ± 125
Tappa II, Porto-Vecchio	perhaps pre-Torrean	Gsy–94B	1915 ± 125	2450 ± 140
Tappa I, Porto-Vecchio	Torrean	Gsy–94A	680 ± 200	850 ± 205
Castello d' Alo, Bilia	pre-Torrean	Gif–480	1870 ± 200	2350 ± 210
		Gif–479	1550 ± 120	1900 ± 135
		Gif–478	1150 ± 110	1450 ± 125
Castello de Caccia 3, Porto-Vecchio	Torrean	Gsy–120	1345 ± 110	1650 ± 125
Filitosa, Sollacaro	Torrean	Gif–2399	1430 ± 110	1750 ± 125
	Torrean	Gsy–58	1200 ± 150	
	Torrean	Gif-2398	1130 ± 110	
	Torrean	Gif–150	600 ± 170	800 ± 175
Cucuruzzu 3, Lévie	Torrean	Gif–241	880 ± 150	1050 ± 160
Cucuruzzu 1, Lévie	Torrean	Gif–239	600 ± 150	800 ± 160
Stantare alignment, Sartène	?	Gif–1396	1000 ± 110	1250 ± 125
	?	Gif–1397	170 ± 110	170 ± 120
	?	Gif–2103	130 ± 110	130 ± 120
Palaggiu, Sartène, funeral chest A	?	Gif–476	700 ± 150	900 ± 160
Palaggiu alignment, Sartène	?	Gif–477	730 ± 150	950 ± 160

5 Megalithic Architecture in Malta

David Trump

COMPARED WITH the other regions of Europe being considered–Iberia, Scandinavia, even the British Isles–the Maltese islands are minute and would hardly seem to merit a chapter to themselves in a work such as this. The evidence which has survived there, however, is out of all proportion to the islands' size, and no study of megalithic architecture, particularly as regards origin and function, would be complete without them. Further, it gives me the opportunity to contribute to this volume, and to record my profound thanks to Glyn Daniel for directing my interest towards both the Mediterranean and megaliths many happy years ago.

Malta and Gozo together have a surface area of only 320 sq. km and lie nearly 100 km from the nearest other land, Cape Passero in south-east Sicily. There is unequivocal archaeological evidence throughout prehistory for contact with the larger island and beyond in the form of imported raw materials, notably a good brown flint from the Monti Iblei and obsidian, from Lipari and, to a lesser extent, Pantelleria (Cann and Renfrew 1964). But equally clear is the minimal extent of cultural dependence during the period of the temples, 4000–2500 bc; the number of sherds of foreign manufacture so far recovered in Malta is barely a score, against many millions in local wares.

1 Skorba, the 'shrines' of c.4000 BC, possible ancestors of the Maltese temples. Lengths 8.40 and 5.60 m.

Although overseas influences on temple architecture cannot be excluded, there is little to suggest that they in any way explain its introduction to the islands. Closer study reinforces the argument by failing to reveal any but a few superficial details of similarity with architecture elsewhere. Some of these details are too generalized to carry much weight, others lose all significance when radiocarbon dating places them substantially earlier than their suggested prototypes.

Megalithic architecture in Malta, then, is an indigenous phenomenon, and its origins and function must be sought in the purely local context. The account given here follows closely that suggested by J. D. Evans (1959, 84-134), expanded but not materially altered by details discovered subsequently. I would freely admit that it is not the only possible interpretation of the recorded facts, but it seems easily the most convincing, given the evidence at present available.

The use of stone masonry in Malta is attested from the time of the earliest known inhabitants, immigrant farmers of the Ghar Dalam phase (Trump 1966, amending and dating Evans 1953, 1959), deriving immediately from Sicily and bringing a variant of that island's Stentinello culture with them. Associated radiocarbon dates at Skorba gave readings of 4190 ± 160 bc (BM 378) and 3810 ± 200 bc (BM 216). Unfortunately, a single 11 m length of straight stone wall, a footing for one of mudbrick, is the only structure that has yet been located (Trump 1966, 10), so nothing can be said of building plans. By the end of this first cycle of cultural development in the Red Skorba phase, 3225 ± 150 bc (BM 148), a building of two oval chambers, 5.60 and 8.40 m long, had appeared nearby (ill. 1). It had much more substantial walls, still for upward continuation in mudbrick. The absence of a reasonable floor surface, easy access or any hearth, and the presence of a number of figurines, tentatively suggested that the rooms were shrines, but this cannot be pressed. The masonry was of uncoursed but in no sense megalithic stonework.

The immigrants who initiated the second cycle of cultural development c. 3200 bc brought with them, in the Zebbug phase, a material culture recognizably related to that of the San Cono-Piano Notaro culture

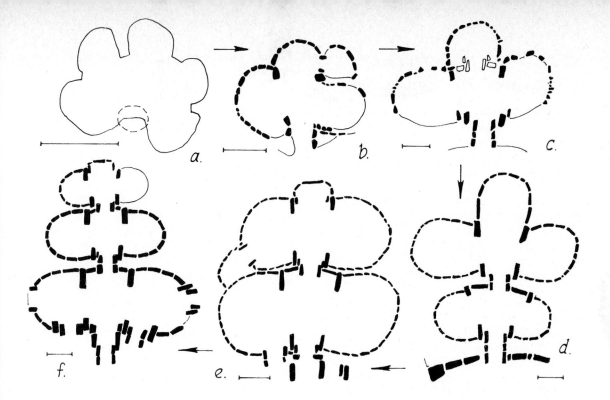

2 The evolution of the Maltese temples. a rock-cut tomb, Xemxija 5; b lobed temple, Mgarr East; c trefoil temple, with later cross-wall, Skorba West; d 5-apse temple, Ggantija South; e 4-apse temple, Mnajdra Central; f 6-apse temple, Tarxien Central. The scale measures 3 m.

of Sicily, probably including the practice of excavating rock-cut tombs for their dead (Whitehouse 1972). This seems more likely than that they invented this burial rite in the islands independently.

The rock-cut tombs call for a digression, the relevance of which will become apparent shortly. Though they are not themselves megalithic, it has long been recognized that, at least in western Europe, there is some sort of relationship with megalithic tombs, if only one of parallel development. There would be some truth in the view that both are artificial substitutes for natural caves, and could arise wherever caves are found inadequate as chambers to accommodate collective burials (Whitehouse 1972). I leave it to colleagues writing on other areas to explore possible relationships there, and look forward to seeing the results of their latest thinking, but must myself confine my attention to the Maltese temples.

The earliest of these known are the group of five at Ta Trapna, Zebbug (Baldacchino and Evans 1954; Evans 1971, 166), which are, however, of little relevance here since their orignial form is unclear. At the time of discovery they consisted of no more than oval depressions in the rock, but whether these were the surviving remains of chambers entered from a shaft, or of simple shafts, or are exactly as first constructed cannot now be determined. With one very notable exception, the other tombs are of the more characteristic

shaft-and-chamber form, the latter simple oval or kidney shaped (Nadur, Xaghra, Xemxija tombs 3, 4 and 6), or more elaborately lobed (Xemxija 1, 2 and particularly 5). All contained material of the Ggantija and later phases, Xemxija having in addition a little going back to Zebbug. It seems, then, that rock-cut tombs were coming into use in Malta early in the fourth millennium BC.

It was early in the Ggantija phase of pottery development in Malta, around 2800 bc (3500 BC) that the islanders began to build massive stone monuments of Cyclopean or orthostatic masonry, the famous prehistoric temples. They can best be explained as the result of a decision to build a copy of a lobed rock-cut tomb of the Xemxija 5 type above ground. Some change of function is also implied, and it could well have been this, elaboration of ceremonies before the tomb, which produced the need for a more appropriate setting than the shaft in bare rock offered. The small eastern temples at Kordin III and Mgarr show the sort of structures that would result, though excavation at the latter in 1960 (Trump 1966, 17-19) showed that this building probably belonged in the succeeding Saflieni phase. If the lobed temple/rock-cut tomb link is not accepted, the similarity of plan must be explained as later convergent development of the two classes of monument, or else complete coincidence. This would make the trefoil temples, to be considered next, the earliest form, with no antecedents since the Red Skorba 'shrines' five centuries earlier. Apart from traces of simple huts at the Skorba site, no above-ground buildings dating to the Zebbug and Mgarr phases have been located. A derivation of the lobed temples from the tombs, already a considerable intellectual leap, must surely appear more likely.

Perhaps before proceeding further, we should justify the use of the term 'temple'. There is fortunately strong supporting evidence. The complete absence from the built structures of contemporary burials excludes a funerary function, the internal chambers would seem too small for assembly, and though a domestic use cannot be quite so categorically denied, it is hardly more convincing. Their interpretation as places of worship, temples, does not depend solely on negative evidence. In the ceramic repertoire, one vessel shape which occurs in extraordinary numbers and often in both enormous and minute sizes, equally clearly non-functional, has been plausibly recognized as an offering bowl. Handsome decorated blocks in the temples seem better fitted to serve as altars than tables. Numerous statues, again one at least greater than lifesize, look like cult figures. Holes far too small for passages connecting separate chambers have been interpreted as oracle holes, though the exact nature of their use cannot now be recovered. All these indentifications are clearly matters of assumption rather than proof, but all are reasonable and mutually consistent.

In the trefoil temples we see the first formalized plan, and can recognize the prototype of the later forms. Already present are the concave and monumental façade, trilithon entrance passage, paired lateral and single terminal chambers (somewhat misleadingly described in the literature as 'apses'), and the use of both orthostatic and megalithic blocks. Surviving examples include the western temples in the Mgarr, Kordin III and Skorba groups. If we do not need to look outside the islands for the form of the temples, nor do we have to for the constructional techniques. With stone so readily available in Malta, as is immediately apparent to any visitor, its use, even in exceptionally large blocks, occasions no surprise. There can be few areas in the world where the incentives to megalithic building were greater.

Subsequently the trefoil temples were all altered by having the large central chamber closed off with a substantial cross wall, apart from a central lintelled doorway. There are perforations in the jambs apparently to support some form of door or screen of wood or leather, and bar holes by which it could be secured. It was investigations at Skorba which proved this cross wall to be a later addition, as is very probably the case at the other two sites.

This stage of development, with its division between an inner area which could be securely closed off and the more public outer chambers, can be convincingly recognized again in those temples with five apses. The same result is achieved here by the addition of an extra pair of apses between the façade and the lateral apses of the trefoil plan. Seating for a door is again provided in the central passage between the two pairs, and serves the same purpose as the closing wall across the terminal apse, which is therefore not needed. The five-apse plan is represented at the Ggantija South, Hagar Qim North and, probably, Ta Marziena. All these temples, note, were shown by material in their floors to be still of the Ggantija phase. In other words, we are dealing so far with a typological seriation. It must be frankly admitted that this sequence is unsupported by (though in only one, possibly unimportant, respect (at Mgarr East, referred to above) contradicted by) the evidence of associated pottery. Further, there are a number of sites, or elements of compound sites, which do not fit into the classification, either because they do not follow a regular apsed plan, or because they have been too damaged for their original form and affiliation to be determined.

The final stage, excepting the six-apse temple of Tarxien Central, includes all the temples whose underfloor and wall deposits include material of the Tarxien phase, a terminus post quem for their construction. Their distinguishing feature is the reduction in size of the central apse of the five-apse plan to a mere niche. Perhaps the three-apse-with-closed-terminal chamber was felt to be clumsy, and the five-apse-with-three-closed too roomy in its inner parts. Be that as it may, all Tarxien phase temples in the main line of development are of this four-apse-and-niche form. One example, the Ggantija North, yielded only material of the Ggantija phase in the areas sampled, but since this gives, as already mentioned, only a terminus post quem, it is possible that it could fall in the later phase, making the correlation lobed/three/five apses – Ggantija phase, four apse – Tarxien phase, complete. Tarxien Central is unique, though clearly only a variant on the four-apse plan, in having an additional pair of apses making six in all. Associated pottery places it in an advanced stage of the Tarxien phase and so later than the four-apse temples on either side of it at this complex site.

The description of this sequence may seem a little laboured, but is designed to stress the progressive advances made by the designers of these buildings. This shows in many other ways. All the early temples were built of rubble masonry, and were probably originally plastered to a smooth surface internally and painted. Only at the Ggantija and Skorba could this be demonstrated. In these, only the external walls and the doorways and passages were of truly megalithic construction, of carefully selected or well-tooled orthostatic blocks. Later, all walls were so constructed, giving a much more impressive result. For one thing, tooled blocks, meeting along the whole of their adjacent faces, gave much greater stability, and successive courses could be over-sailed as horizontal arches, allowing the roof opening to be appreciably narrowed before it was closed with a beam and thatch ceiling. At Mnajdra South (ill. 8), Hagar Qim and Tarxien Central, this over-sailing is shown in the surviving walls, together with the inward slope of the blocks which proves the horizontal arch – as opposed to the corbel – principle of construction. Nowhere outside Malta is this principle known at such an early date, probably well before 2500 BC: indeed the horizontal arch has rarely been used elsewhere at any period.

Unfortunately, though fragments of wall plaster covered in red paint were found at both the Ggantija and Skorba, we do not know if this was applied in patterns or as an all-over wash. The walls of the Hypogeum demonstrate both. Certainly altar blocks and other internal fittings within the temples had their surfaces decoratively carved in three successive styles. In the first flat surfaces were relieved by being sparsely pitted. Then the pitting, by either pecking or drilling, was much more closely spaced and framed within a relief border. Later still, spiral designs were carved in relief like the borders, the pitting being relegated to the background or suppressed altogether. A fragment from Wiel Filep suggests that this background was painted red, the relief designs being reserved, and this may well have been general practice. More ambitious designs were occasionally attempted, particularly at Tarxien (animal friezes, repeat curves; see ill. 4), and there is a notable piece from Bugibba portraying two fish. This could be contemporary with the third style or constitute a fourth: we do not have chronological evidence as we certainly do for the earlier ones. For example, the central altar in Tarxien South shows a fragment of a style 2 panel left as a result of the floor level having been raised when the rest was cut away to take style 3 relief spirals. Artistically too, then, there is evidence for progress and innovation, paralleled in the case of the spirals in the decoration of the pottery.

Technically the remains testify to the introduction

3 The Hypogeum, the rock-cut temple at the heart of the site. Height of doorway 1 m.

4 Altar in Tarxien South. Note the relief spirals and D-shaped plug. Height of altar block 1.15 m.

67

of two constructional aids, one probably very generally spread, though rarely so clearly demonstrated as here, the other apparently unknown outside Malta. Many orthostats show a prominent notch in the middle of a long side, the clearest examples being visible in Tarxien East. This notch must have been deliberately cut to take the tip of a sizeable lever with which the final adjustment of the block into position could be effected. The value of such an aid is obvious when one remembers that individual blocks could reach a weight of 19 tonnes. A stone roller beneath a massive threshold slab in Tarxien Central demonstrates the use of cannon-ball-like spheroids frequently found on temple sites. Timber rollers have long been postulated as aids to the moving of megalithic blocks, but we have no other records of 'ball-bearings' until several thousand years later.

All this builds up to an impressive record of the highly ingenious designers, engineers, architects even, who were responsible for the development of the Maltese temples (Trump 1980). The title 'architect' perhaps needs further substantiation, but this is not far to seek. There are a number of well-known contemporary illustrations of temples, both two-dimensional engravings and three-dimensional models. With many of them, we cannot demonstrate that they were other than artists' views of buildings already erected. For example, though the temple façade beautifully carved on a limestone slab from Tarxien (ill. 5) strongly suggests an architect's elevation, prepared in advance to show what was required, this is now unprovable.

But the terracotta model from Hagar Qim (ill. 6) shows a five-apse temple in the form of wall stumps, a form in which no temple could have physically appeared even during the course of construction. It is an abstract plan, presumably drawn up before building (of Hagar Qim North?) was commenced. Even more intriguing is the stone fragment from Tarxien (ill. 7) showing a complex building of rectangular rooms on an ashlar podium, intriguing because no building remotely like this is known in Malta of that period. It would seem that a plan was prepared but never put into effect – the Planning Committee turned down so revolutionary a design, and the architect was required to submit a more traditional, and more acceptable, scheme in keeping with the apsed structures already

5 The limestone façade model from Tarxien. Width as restored 39 cm.

6 The terracotta temple plan from Hagar Qim. Width of larger fragment c.12 cm.

7 The limestone rectilinear building model from Tarxien. Length surviving 29 cm.

standing on the site. It is very difficult here not to speculate beyond the material finds, to reach out to the people behind the objects. Even if we regard the Planning Committee and its decisions as too hypothetical to be taken seriously, we certainly seem to have an individual, the architect, inherent in that physical evidence.

We need to remind ourselves of the antiquity of the period we are talking about. The span of the Maltese temple development covered 2800–2000 bc, *c.* 3600 –2500 BC. In comparison with Mesopotamia, it began about the same time as the mudbrick temples of Eridu and Uruk, though Tepe Gawra is older, and it ended around the time of the Royal Cemetery at Ur. As regards Egypt, its end overlapped by only a century or so the building of the pyramids (Renfrew 1972). Imhotep, who is honoured as the world's first architect for his introduction of stone masonry in the Step Pyramid of Sakkara, could have been a contemporary of that other nameless architect who worked on

8 Mnajdra South, interior of the first apse. Note the trilithon doorway, porthole slab, two oracle holes, and the over-sailing and inward slope of the upper blocks in the wall. Width of apse 6.20 m.

Tarxien Central. He in turn was a thousand years later than his predecessor who had designed and built the first of the Maltese temples.

This might be a suitable moment to return to the subject of the Hypogeum (ill. 3) (Evans 1971, 44). We suggested that the temples began with an imaginative leap, surely by an individual – let us build a copy of a rock-cut tomb above ground, where it will be so much more conveniently accessible for us to carry out communally the associated rites and ceremonies. Long after, it was asked why, when the underground cemetery of interconnecting rock-cut tomb chambers under what is now Hal Saflieni had grown so large, a temple along the lines of those being built at the time

9 *The giant statue in Tarxien. Width of skirt as restored c.1.60 m.*

was not carved out of the solid rock as part of that site. The suggestion was acted on. At the centre of the Hypogeum can still be seen the chambers carved in close imitation of the above-ground architecture, with such details as trilithon door-frames, pierced door slabs ('porthole' entrances), wall courses projecting in order to narrow roof openings, together with ochred spirals and wash decoration, all preserved by being cut and painted deep below ground. This part of the site, if we interpret the often inadequate excavation reports aright, did not contain burials, so was probably in function as well as form more closely related to the temples than to the rock-cut tombs from which the Hypogeum sprang. The great water cistern at one end of the site would seem also to fit better into a religious context than a funerary one. The revolutionary decision to construct, or rather excavate, a temple below ground must once more imply an individual initiative, even if it was effected by that individual's society.

The contrast between this and the situation with all other ancient megalithic architecture, indeed prehistoric architecture of any kind, hardly needs spelling out. Elsewhere, the great majority of monuments are so firmly rooted in the tradition of the society that erected them that there seems no room for individual architects, rather a long line of architects, each trying *not* to make innovations. Even where a particular structure stands out as a masterpiece – the Cueva de Romeral, Gavr'inis and Maes Howe might be instanced – our only evidence on the designer is what can be read directly from his architecture, and that is usually but little. It is not surprising that study, if it extends beyond the monuments themselves, does so in the direction of the societies they were meant to serve, or in the efforts of the labourers who raised them, but very rarely, and then often controversially, to the designers, the architects. Thanks to their technical innovations, and above all their models, we can approach much more closely to those of Maltese temples.

Such a discussion leads us on naturally to a consideration of the role these temples played among the communities who built them. The evidence that they really were places of worship has been already briefly

70

reviewed, though a little more should be said on what can be recovered of the religious beliefs and practices of the time. There is here little to imply connection with megalithic sites elsewhere, whether funerary, astronomical or religious, unless the Maltese 'mother goddess' of fertility and death can, as an act of faith rather than proof, be equated with the much more shadowy 'dolmen deity' of western Europe. The evidence is as follows.

The deity of the temples is presumably to be recognized in the above-lifesized statue in Tarxien (ill. 9). Despite the loss of its upper half, this can be equated iconographically with similar standing figures, though of smaller size, from Hagar Qim (ill. 10) and Ta Silg, and seated ones from Tarxien and, in a slightly different posture, Hagar Qim. All these represent a grossly corpulent figure, skirted or nude, on which, however, sexual characteristics are noticeably lacking. That should immediately advise caution in the use of terms like 'mother goddess' or, less flattering, 'fat lady'. When figures of the same proportions are clearly female, as with the 'sleeping lady' from the Hypogeum, they are on a much smaller scale and no longer necessarily divine. Another terracotta from Hagar Qim is a delightful female figure with none of the grossness of the others, but again not necessarily a goddess.

But despite that hesitation, the underlying idea of fertility symbolism remains probable, and receives unequivocal support from other finds, particularly from Tarxien. There a wall relief shows a very male bull and a very female sow, with no less than fourteen piglets at suck, immediately adjacent. This site has, too, produced several indubitable carved phalli.

Suggestive but less explicit is the link between the temple deity and death, probably implied by the tomb-to-temple development, more certainly by the funerary temple within the Hypogeum.

Practices should be more easily recoverable by archaeology than beliefs. Animal sacrifice is well attested. The flint knife and goat horn core from the 'cupboard' in the decorated altar in Tarxien South, and the dove skeleton in the central niche of Skorba East, are but two examples. Animal bone was frequent on many sites, and the rows of animals carved in relief at Tarxien hint at the same. The forecourts so apparent at most sites must have been designed for open-air ceremonies before the shrines, but the content of those ceremonies is now quite irrecoverable.

Two pieces of evidence suggest the presence of a priesthood of some kind – and I do not include the so-called 'priest' figurine from Tarxien, whose sex and calling are alike matters of conjecture only. The distinction in the temples between 'public' outer parts, in which the decorated blocks are concentrated, and 'private' inner parts, with doors which could be barred only from the inside, indicates that access to those inner parts was restricted to a small and in some way privileged group of people. Whatever passed through the 'oracle holes', they too imply two classes of person, one positioned in the inner, even secret, chamber in contrast to the other in the outer or public part of the building. The 'oracular' reverberation of a deep voice in one chamber of the Hypogeum cannot be considered conclusive unless it can be shown to have been deliberately planned, which seems unlikely. It is tantalizing how far the evidence will take us before it gives out, with so many questions still unanswered.

But if the specific functions and even more beliefs are so difficult to recover, the general ones of displaying and stressing a community's existence and separateness from other communities are much more readily apparent. Renfrew broke new ground when he pointed out (1973, 147–67) that the distribution of the temples could be interpreted as mirroring a social or political grouping of the population of Malta at the time. While his criterion for the 'really big' temples was both somewhat arbitrary and inconsistently applied, the pattern changes little when all known buildings of the temple period are added in. The only danger comes

10 Limestone seated figure from Hagar Qim. Height 23.5 cm.

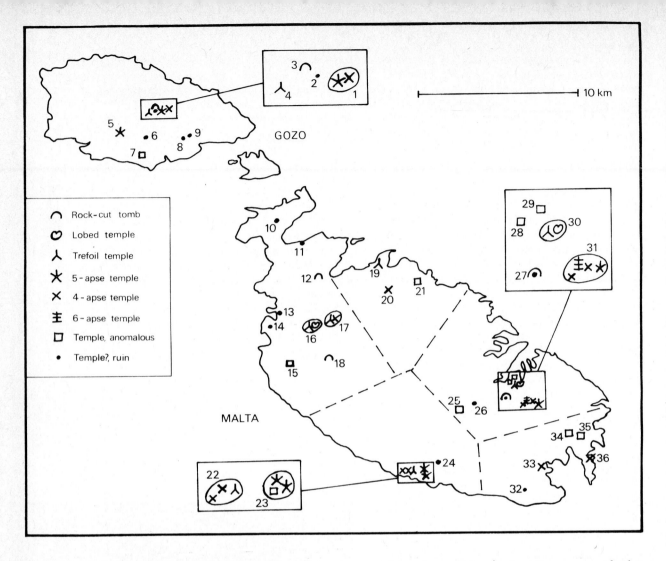

11 The distribution of the Maltese temples, with suggested territories. (After Renfrew 1973, with additions.) 1 Ggantija, 2 Ghar ta Ghejzu, 3 Xaghra tomb, 4 Santa Verna, 5 Ta Marziena, 6 Xewkija, 7 Borg li Mramma, 8 Li Mrejsbiet, 9 Borg il Gharib, 10 Armier, 11 Ghajn Zejtuna, 12 Xemxija 1–5, 13 Ta Lippija, 14 Ras il Pellegrin, 15 Li Mdawwar, 16 Ta Hagrat, Mgarr, 17 Li Skorba, 18 Bengemma, 19 Bugibba, 20 Tal Qadi, 21 Il Maghtab, 22 Mnajdra, 23 Hagar Qim, 24 Sqaq il Bal, Qrendi, 25 Debdieba, 26 It Tumbata, 27 Hal Saflieni, 28 Kordin I, 29 Kordin II, 30 Kordin III, 31 Tarxien, 32 Hal Far, 33 Borg in Nadur, 34 Hal Ginwi, 35 Ta Silg, 36 Xrobb il Ghagin.

from the possible complete disappearance of other temples of which we know nothing, and against this we have no defence. But using what evidence has come down to us, we could reasonably argue for six 'tribal' territories in the islands, each responsible for the erection and maintenance of the major and minor temple sites therein contained (ill. 11).

The new map might suggest a further possibility, that the pattern is of three territories rather than six. There is, of course, no reason why territories of human groups should necessarily be of equal size, like those of a single pair of nesting birds, since the numbers within the groups could vary. The gap across central Malta, despite just as appropriate areas as elsewhere in the island for the survival of monuments, around Naxxar and Rabat in particular, remains very clear, whereas the boundaries between Renfrew's three eastern territories have become rather more blurred. In either case, the monuments presumably served as foci for the ceremonies which marked off tribe from tribe. What we cannot explain is the multiplication of temple sites within each group, but this is hardly more of a problem than that long recognized, the reason for the multiplication of temples on each site.

One crucial piece of evidence seems to have been consistently undervalued. The stone trough in Kordin III (ill. 12) was, as recognized by Evans (1971, 73), an integral part of the temple into which it was built, though he had doubts whether the grooves worn into it were contemporary with the temple occupation. The fact that it is the only block of coralline limestone to be used on the site, having been transported at least a kilometre for the purpose, implies that it was chosen for some particular need, surely the grinding that was undoubtedly carried out on it. The substance ground, therefore, is likely to have been grain, as Ashby (Ashby *et al.* 1913, 42) originally suggested. The number and depth of the grooves, seven and at least 18 cm deep, in turn suggest a very considerable quantity of grain, probably over a long period of time. It would be interesting to speculate what proportion of limestone grit in the flour was considered acceptable. To me the implication seems clear that it was the community's grain being brought into the temple to be ground

under the immediate protection of the community's deity. There was almost certainly also a strong social element in this communal grinding of the daily flour. While the case would be greatly strengthened if every temple, or at least one in each territory, had its public quern, no other explanation seems to explain the facts from Kordin III so satisfactorily.

On the matter of the political organization of temple-period Malta, and the likelihood of some sort of chieftainship, I can add nothing useful to those points Renfrew has already advanced, and refer readers to his work *(op. cit.)*.

A consequence of this patent link between the temples and the society which produced them is that the collapse of the one around 2400 BC can be regarded as prime evidence for the breakdown of the other. Despite the considerable body of information which has been recovered on these events, however (Trump 1978), its interpretation has so far produced no clear answers. The end of the temples is even more mysterious than their beginning. There is a hint of decline

12 The communal quern of coralline limestone in the Kordin III temple. Length 2.66 m.

13 The Wied Znuber dolmen. Length 3.70 m.

at Skorba, where the east temple went out of use before the west temple, to be used for rubbish dumping. Otherwise the collapse seems to have been sudden and complete, as if the whole population of Malta and Gozo had abandoned everything and fled the islands. So far, none of the many possible explanations, singly or collectively, is clearly preferred by the recovered evidence. It remains only to be hoped that future research, probably environmental and not necessarily within the temples themselves, will eventually allow us to suggest what really happened to destroy such remarkable buildings, their culture and their people.

It could be argued that Malta and Gozo's very isolation, giving us almost laboratory conditions so little affected by extraneous influences, automatically reduces their value for comparative purposes. This is not so, since no claim is being made, or can be made, that any one set of circumstances will provide answers for application elsewhere. On the contrary, although the islands allow us to advance a powerful argument for Maltese temple architecture being the result of a remarkable indigenous development, the product of not only a human community but of a few gifted individuals within that community, we have already noted in the appearance of agriculture in the Ghar

Dalam phase, and of new pottery styles and tomb forms in the Zebbug phase, equally clear examples of cultural diffusion, invasion even, however unfashionable that term now is.

Following the temple period, we have another example of massive overseas influence on the Maltese islands, which must represent an immigrant population. The use of megalithic architecture again comes into the story, though in a very different form. The culture of the Tarxien Cemetery demonstrates a total break with the tradition built up over the preceding millennium and a half. It owed nothing to the earlier inhabitants of its new home, its antecedents all lying elsewhere (Evans 1956). Only one of its cultural elements need be pursued here, that of building with large blocks of stone.

Some sixteen dolmens have been recorded from the Maltese islands, though the exact number is uncertain by reason of their often ruinous state. One at least, at Ta Hammut near the north coast, has produced an archaeological deposit of the Tarxien Cemetery phase, *c.*2500–1500 BC. Several of them are distinctive, if not exactly distinguished, monuments, Wied Znuber (ill. 13), Safi, the Misrah Sinjura and Wied Filep, to name only the four finest. These share characteristics in general and in detail with the Otranto group in the Salentine peninsula, the heel of Italy. They consist of a slab of limestone up to 4.40 x 3.80 m poised on stone

74

supports. The Misrah Sinjura has a groove cut around its margin on the upper surface, and this and the Safi and Bidni dolmens have vertical perforations through the slab. The suggestion that both are connected with libation rites is tempting, if speculative. Both these features can be paralleled in the Otranto area, implying some meaningful connection. Admittedly this takes us very little further in explaining how either group is affiliated to the mainstream of western European megalithic tombs. There is effectively nothing to suggest that they appeared independently in either of these areas, but hardly more to indicate how they could have reached either from further west.

Even the function they served amongst the Maltese communities which raised them is uncertain. The associated material at Ta Hammut included broken pottery but no bone, and the small size of the chamber implied that any interment there may once have been must have been by cremation, as in the Tarxien Cemetery itself. All other dolmens had been stripped bare before discovery, so it is only an assumption, based on evidence from other parts of Europe, that the dolmens of Malta were burial chambers at all. In consequence, they offer us little help in the wider enquiry we are here pursuing.

Several menhirs have been recorded from the islands (Evans 1971, 198–9), but only two seem to be rightly so called. These are the well-squared pillars at Kirkop and Kercem. Being without association of any kind,

they are undatable, and one can only note that similar pillars are known around Otranto, in the area which yields the best parallels for the Maltese dolmens. Other examples from Malta are unshaped and have scatters of temple-period pottery around them. They are probably, as that at Skorba was demonstrated to be, surviving blocks of temple-like buildings otherwise destroyed.

Malta and Gozo, then, have offered us excellent examples of both local evolution and diffusion from an external source in their megalithic architecture, their geography allowing us to trace both processes more clearly than is possible in many other areas. They serve to remind us that if a coin falls head-side-up on one occasion, or even on many consecutive occasions, that does not in the least alter the chances of its falling heads or tails on the next toss, provided only that the coin has not been mischievously given two heads. The origins of any group of megalithic monuments, or indeed of any other cultural trait, will be determined only when all the available evidence is assembled and weighed dispassionately.

Acknowledgments

All objects illustrated are in the National Museum of Malta, Valletta. Ill. 10 is by courtesy of the Malta Government Tourist Board; all other illustrations are by the author.

Bibliography

ASHBY, T., BRADLEY, R. N., PEET, T. E., TAGLIA-FERRO, N. 1913 'Excavations in 1908–11 in various megalithic buildings in Malta and Gozo', *BSR* VI, 1.

BALDACCHINO J.G. AND EVANS, J.D. 1954 'Prehistoric Tombs near Zebbug', *BSR* XXII, n.s.IX, 1.

CANN, J. R. AND RENFREW, C. 1964, The Characterization of Obsidian and its application to the Mediterranean Region', *Proc. Preh. Soc.* XXX, 111.

EVANS, J. D. 1953 'The Prehistoric Culture Sequence in the Maltese Archipelago', *Proc. Preh. Soc.* XIX, 41.

1956 'The "Dolmens" of Malta and the Origins of the Tarxien Cemetery Culture', *Proc. Preh. Soc.* XXII, 80.

1959 *Malta*, London and New York.

1971 *The Prehistoric Antiquities of the Maltese Islands*, London.

RENFREW, C. 1972 'Malta and the calibrated radiocarbon chronology', *Antiquity* XLVI, no. 184, 141–5.

1973 *Before Civilization*, London.

TRUMP, D. H. 1966 *Skorba*, Oxford.

1972 *Malta, an archaeological guide*, London.

1978 'The collapse of the Maltese temples', in Sieveking, G. de G., Longworth, I.H. and Wilson, K. E. (eds), *Problems in Economic and Social Archaeology*, London.

1980 'I primi architetti del mondo, i costruttori dei templi maltesi', in Fontana, M. J., Piraino, M. T. and Rizzo, F. P. (eds), *Miscellanea di Studi Classici in Onore di Eugenio Manni*, Rome.

Appendix

Catalogue of Temples and Rock-Cut Tombs

No. on map	Site	Form	Length (m)	Breadth (m)	Earliest material	Orientation
1	Ggantija North	4-apse	18.75	17.50	Ggantija?	133°
	South	5-apse	26.25	23.75	Ggantija	128°
2	Ghar ta Ghejzu	ruinous			Ggantija	
3	Xaghra tomb	r.c.t.	1.73		Ggantija?	
4	Santa Verna	3-apse?	16.90?	16.15?	Ggantija	120°?
5	Ta Marziena	5-apse	17?	16.80?	Ggantija	180°?
6	Xewkija	destroyed				
7	Borg li Mramma	anomalous		37.50 max.		
8	Li Mrejsbiet	ruinous				
9	Borg il Gharib	ruinous				
10	Armier	ruinous				
11	Ghajn Zejtuna	destroyed				
12	Xemxija 1–5	r.c.t.'s		5.65 max.	Zebbug	
13	Ta Lippija	ruinous				
14	Ras il Pellegrin	ruinous			Tarxien	
15	Li Mdawwar	anomalous			Tarxien	
16	Ta Hagrat, Mgarr W.	3-a	14	12.55	Ggantija	135°
	E.	lobed	7.25	8.90	Saflieni?	176°
17	Li Skorba West	3-apse	14.20	18.30	Ggantija	139°
	East	4-apse	16.15	14.20	Tarxien	170°
18	Bengemma	r.c.t.			Ggantija	
19	Bugibba	3-apse?	?	13.45?	Tarxien	200°
20	Tal Qadi	3-apse?	10.50?	18.30	Tarxien?	78°
21	Il Maghtab	anomalous				
22	Mnajdra South	4-apse	15.15	13.65	Tarxien	103°
	Central	4-apse	18.05	16.60	Tarxien	148°
	East	3-apse	7.05	9.25	Ggantija	218°
23	Hagar Qim Central	4-apse, anom.	17.10	20	Ggantija	132°
	North	5-apse	16	7.30	Ggantija	184°
24	Sqaq il Bal, Qrendi	ruinous				
25	Debdieba	anomalous	23 max.		Tarxien?	
26	It Tumbata	ruinous				
27	Hal Saflieni	r.c.cem. ruinous	29.40 max.	22.50 max.	Zebbug	
28	Kordin I	anomalous	20			
29	II	anomalous	25.50			
30	III West	3-apse	15.45	13.65	Ggantija	149°
	East	lobed	9.10	12.25	Ggantija	203°?
31	Tarxien West	4-apse	22.80	18.30	Early Tarxien	204°
	Central	6-apse	23.10	18.60	Tarxien	230°
	East	4-apse	15.60	12.60	Early Tarxien	200°
	Far East	5-apse	12	6?	Ggantija	176°
32	Hal Far	destroyed				
33	Borg in Nadur	4-apse	8.45?	8.45	Tarxien	108°
34	Hal Ginwi	anomalous	10.60 max.		Ggantija	
35	Ta Silg	anomalous	15.50			106°
36	Xrobb il Ghagin	4-apse	13.50	9.10?	Ggantija	135°

6 Megaliths of the Funnel Beaker Culture in Germany and Scandinavia

Lili Kaelas

SINCE THE Second World War, Professor Glyn Daniel has been the vanguard figure in megalithic tomb research. His field of studies has covered major areas of Atlantic Europe. To collaborate in a work of tribute to my colleague Glyn is like continuing a dialogue, both one which took place at a personal level and one which sprang from the reading of his many investigations and surveys. Nothing could be more inviting.

Fifteen years ago I wrote a survey of megalithic tombs in southern Scandinavia. In this survey I discussed their architecture and building technique as well as their functions as graves and cult-centres. I concentrated on chronology, migration and cultural influences. This approach was in no way unique to Scandinavian research. Similar questions were regarded as central by scholars in other parts of Europe where megalithic tomb research has been done.

Since this study was published (1966/67) I have been mainly involved with administrative work. A great deal has happened in megalithic research since then. The evidence is more solid now. When my article was written, few monuments in Scandinavia had been totally examined by modern field-methods. During the 1960s and 1970s many such examinations were conducted in Denmark and southern Sweden (Scania). However, the most comprehensive ever to be carried out were those in Mecklenburg, East Germany. Under the guidance of Evald Schuldt, 106 megalithic tombs were investigated and the results recorded in the course of six and a half years. As a result, Mecklenburg is the best-recorded area in Europe. But in West Germany (Lower Saxony) too, new investigations and findings have extended the evidence for theoretical judgment.

What can we learn from Recent Investigations?

First and foremost we have gained increased knowledge of the architecture and techniques of tomb-building in these areas. The finds and observations made during the numerous investigations have partly substantiated previous conclusions, and also provided new information about ritual and cult observances. It is now for example possible to compare the Mecklenburg tombs with the southern Scandinavian ones in terms of age with much greater certainty, and to include them in the chronological scheme used by Scandinavian scholars.

In addition, the new evidence provides a better basis for understanding the megalithic-tomb society's economic structure, a problem which has now become more relevant than when I wrote my earlier paper.

I shall first give a survey of some of the new evidence of the architecture of the tombs and related problems.

The Tomb Monuments

Dolmens Interest in the origin of Nordic dolmens has not slackened. It has kept scholars busy almost continuously for over a hundred years, since the time of Montelius. The simple rectangular dolmens, the so-called 'urdolmens', and their development have always attracted the greatest attention and still do. I shall not dwell on the details of design and construction of different local dolmen types since the evidence is well known, but briefly compare differences and similarities.

German and Scandinavian scholars had long regarded the rectangular and polygonal dolmens as generically connected forms. The polygonal were treated as a development via several typologically related links from the 'urdolmens'. Becker's interpretation (1947, 266–9) of the small rectangular southern Danish dolmens was therefore welcomed as a turning point in the discussion. He characterized these as a local counterpart of the subterranean human-length stone cists found in the continental Funnel Beaker Culture, i.e. similar to the Funnel Beaker Culture people's characteristic early stone tombs. This view rests on the assumption that some of the oldest southern Danish dolmens are subterranean, which is not proven. His view is still accepted, especially in Denmark.

However, some objections have been raised (Kaelas 1956, 11). The dating of these subterranean southern Danish dolmens presents difficulties. According to known finds they are from the beginning of the Middle Neolithic. New arguments have recently emerged which dispute Becker's interpretation.

The subterranean stone cists are single graves. The small dolmens have also been regarded as such up till now. Recent German research, however, has begun to question the plausibility of this theory. It has been possible to establish that also in the small rectangular dolmens, with a few exceptions, skeletal fragments from more than one individual as primary interments can be found and consequently they cannot be considered as single graves (Raddatz 1979, 130). The question of the origin of the rectangular dolmens has therefore become more complicated.

Long barrows without stone chambers

Rectangular dolmens *in* long barrows (ill.1) are typical of southern Scandinavia. Rectangular dolmens *without* long barrows appear for example in France, Scotland and Portugal. Some of these are very like the Nordic 'urdolmens'. In addition, long barrows *without stone chambers* exist both in Scandinavia and elsewhere.

The fact remains that the Nordic rectangular dolmens in long barrows have no counterpart anywhere, as has been previously maintained (Kaelas 1966/67, 229). Long barrows without stone chambers appear in the west of France, mainly in the Department of Morbihan in Brittany. In southern England, they occur between Portland and Eastbourne and on the coastline of Lincolnshire and Yorkshire. Within the cultural area of the Funnel Beaker

Culture – that is, in Denmark, northern Germany and Poland – they are to be found in Jutland and Schleswig-Holstein, western Mecklenburg, western Pomerania and in Kujavia (north-western Poland) (ill.2).

Within this large area the long barrows are not uniform either in shape or chronology. Within the Funnel Beaker Culture area rectangular long barrows dominate up to the Oder, but are not found east of the river (although a few trapezoid long barrows occur in western Pomerania). In Kujavia at Weichsel Knie, triangular barrows with a blunt end, often very extended, predominate (see ills 3–4). The River Oder forms a border in another sense as well: east of the river there appear no megalithic tombs proper within the Funnel Beaker Culture groups. All the passage graves found in barrows there are secondary and built within already existing barrows (Jazdzewski 1973, 65 with references). In western Europe trapezoid long barrows predominate.

In all the above areas long barrows appear sometimes in groups, sometimes singly, usually in areas without megalithic tombs. In Jutland and Mecklenburg, however, single long barrows are found within groups of megalithic tombs.

There are great similarities between the Funnel Beaker Culture 'chamberless' earthen long barrows and long barrows with stone chambers (= dolmens). There are also similarities between the Funnel Beaker Culture and western European 'chamberless' long barrows. What is common to both types of long barrow is that they are usually surrounded by a frame of erratic

1 View from the west of long barrow (22 x 8 m) at Araslöv in Vinslöv, Scania, surrounded by megalithic blocks. The gaps between the boulders were originally sealed with slab-shaped stones and similar material in a dry-masonry technique, enclosing the barrow with a continuous wall. There are two rectangular dolmens within the 'wall'. (Photo Skanes Hembygsförbund/Carin Bunte.)

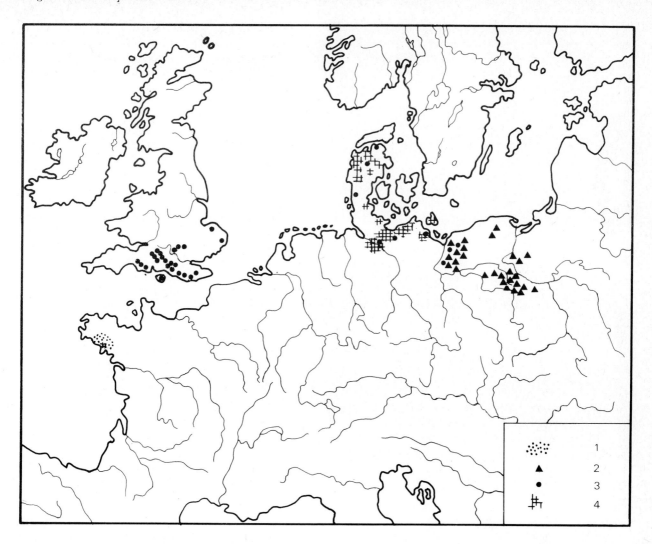

2 *'Chamberless' earthen long barrows in Europe: 1 and 3 barrows of general trapezoid shape; 2 triangular barrows (i.e. Kujavian barrows); 4 rectangular barrows. (Poland, England and Brittany after Jazdzewski 1972, with revisions; northern Germany after Schuldt 1972; Denmark after Madsen 1979, with revisions.)*

boulders (ills 1 and 3–4) and with dry masonry between the stones (– a closed stone wall). In Britain and Poland ditches are usually found along the barrows – that is to say, quarries from which the earth was taken for the barrow. In both Britain and Denmark traces of a timber façade in the eastern end of the barrow have been discovered. In both areas there are palisade enclosures and transverse rows of poles sectioning the barrows (probably remainders of hurdle fences, according to Madsen 1979, 318).

So many features in common cannot depend merely on chance. This led Stuart Piggott, who also brought in the evidence of pottery and causewayed camps, to put the question: 'Windmill Hill — East or West?'(1956). His conclusion that there was probably contact between the primary Neolithic cultures of Britain and the northern European Funnel Beaker Culture

seemed bold and at that time rested on slender evidence. Ten years later (1966) he again took up the question of a common northern European tradition for 'chamberless' long barrows from a British point of view. Since then the evidence has increased considerably – also on the question of causewayed camps – through well-documented studies from both the northern German and Danish areas (Schuldt 1972, 31, 102–5; Jazdzewski 1973, 65–72: Madsen 1979, 317–19 with references).

3,4 Kujavian barrow at Wietrzychowice, province of Wloclawek: above, *after excavation;* below, *after reconstruction. (Photos Muzeum Archeologiczne i Etnograficzne, Lodz, Poland.)*

The similarities between the northern German and Polish tombs and those described above are less tangible. Burnt mortuary houses appear but are exceptional. Tombs in northern German and Kujavian barrows are largely simple earth graves. In Kujavia these have also been found around the barrows.

Consequently one can no longer question the existence of a common tradition for northern European and British 'chamberless' long barrows, a tradition first argued by Piggott and recently convincingly proved in Denmark by Madsen (1979, 302, 318). In addition to the formal similarities there is also a chronological agreement between the Funnel Beaker Culture 'chamberless' long barrows and long barrows with stone chambers. There can appear in one and the same long barrow earth graves as well as megalithic tombs

80

and the tombs are not necessarily the last to have been constructed (Madsen 1979, 315). The construction of 'chamberless' long barrows continued during the Middle Neolithic as well, contemporary with passage graves and sometimes close by them (Schuldt 1972, 104).

The difference between the two types of long barrows would seem to be that single graves – one or more in succession – commonly appear in *'chamberless'* long barrows whereas in long barrows *with* stone chambers the skeletal remains of several individuals appear collectively.

The new investigation results are suggesting now that dolmens were being used primarily as graves for more than one individual even during the Early Neolithic (Raddatz 1979, 130–2, cf. however, Jörgensen 1977, 177). Surprisingly enough similar observations have been made in long barrows without stone chambers in Jutland (Madsen 1979, 311). This means – if the observations are valid – that in the 'chamberless' long barrows besides single graves there were also earth graves which were used for several successive interments. This suggests that the same burial ritual was practised in long barrows of both types, at least locally.

Which type of long barrow is the oldest within the Funnel Beaker Culture? Is the megalithic tomb a wooden construction transferred into stone, as a number of archaeologists claim (most recently e.g. Madsen 1979)? Or is it the other way round? The question is relevant for western Europe too, but cannot be answered in general terms.

In Denmark almost all known 'chamberless' long barrows are found in Jutland. The oldest rectangular dolmens – 'urdolmens' in long barrows – have their nucleus on Zealand where they begin to appear around the middle of the Early Neolithic (phase C). Although they are found during this period in Jutland too the great majority there were built at the beginning of the Middle Neolithic. Generally speaking, both types of long barrow are of equal antiquity within the Nordic Funnel Beaker Culture area. According to a more recent, and more fashionable, theory 'the megalithic graves involved no functional change, only an architectural one, which may or may not have its background in foreign influences' (Renfrew 1976, 200; Madsen 1979, 317). It can thus be established that the great similarities between the two types suggests a common tradition. Where this common tradition has its origin from a European perspective – North or East or West – is still an open question.

Polygonal dolmens Polygonal dolmens (ill. 6) present a different problem. Once the idea of a common origin

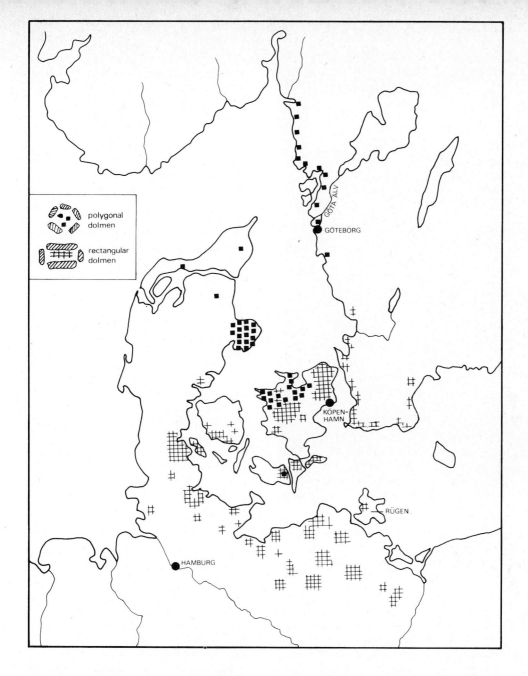

polygonal
dolmen

rectangular
dolmen

GÖTA ÄLV

GÖTEBORG

KÖPEN-
HAMN

RÜGEN

HAMBURG

for the two types of dolmen – that is, the rectangular and the polygonal – had been abandoned and each had been analysed individually, with account taken of the frequency of the different forms of the surrounding barrow, the solution to the problem of origin was in sight (Kaelas 1956, 10–14; Aner 1963).

Aner's analysis of the spread of rectangular and polygonal dolmens in Denmark and Schleswig-Holstein resulted in a survey map of the centres of the respective dolmen types (17, ill. 7). If Aner's map is supplemented with details from the south and west of

5 Areas where rectangular and polygonal dolmens predominate. (E. Aner 1963, with additions.)

Sweden (the counties of Scania, Halland, Bohuslän) and northern Germany (Mecklenburg) the picture is, if possible even more enlightening (ill. 2): Jutland (Djursland peninsula) and adjacent areas in north-western Zealand appear quite clearly as the central areas of the polygonal dolmens. With a few exceptions, on-ly polygonal dolmens are found on the west coast of

*6 Polygonal dolmen at Haga in Stala, isle of Orust,
Bohuslän. Note the 'heart'-shaped entrance. Similar
entrances are found in polygonal dolmens in Portugal.
(Photo Göteborgs arkeologiska museum (GAM).)*

Sweden (Bohuslän and modern Halland) opposite to
Jutland. It appears quite clearly from the map that
these polygonal dolmens of western European origin
reach the coastal area of the Kattegatt through Limfjorden (see also Aner 1963, 13, ill. 5.) (The earliest appearance of the polygonal dolmens is still considered to
date from phase C of the Early Neolithic). In other
parts of Zealand the rectangular dolmens predominate,
just as in Scania. Further eastwards, in Mecklenburg,
there are only rectangular dolmens. However, the map
showing the central areas of the respective dolmen
types should not be read as suggesting that within the
central areas in Denmark only one type in fact appears.
It shows only where the respective dolmen type is in
the majority. As a further comment on the map it can
be said that of the more than 300 identifiable polygonal

82

dolmens in Denmark and Schleswig-Holstein, 40 per
cent occur on Djursland and as many on north-western
Zealand (Aner 1963, 13).

Passage graves Many of the architectural and technical
details recently found through studies of the construction of passage graves in different geographical areas,
which were previously thought to be unique to or
prevailing in a particular area, have proved to be more
general in occurrence. One example of this state of af-
fairs is represented in the two types of passage graves,
the 'Lower Saxony' type (with the passage placed in
the middle of one of the long sides of the chamber) and
the 'Holstein' type (with asymmetrically placed
passage). The latter was considered typical of Holstein
and Mecklenburg. But more recent research has
shown that contrary to earlier belief both types are
equally common in Mecklenburg.

Another and yet more eloquent criterion is evident in
the division of the chamber into compartments (ill.
7), once believed to be unique to Västergötland. It is
now clear that such a division is not an isolated local
phenomenon but a general characteristic feature in the
layout of passage graves.

Chamber compartments are of course not uncom-
mon in western Europe. Prior to the extensive investigations in Mecklenburg I therefore regarded it as a
western European feature of the passage graves of the
Funnel Beaker Culture (Kaelas 1956, 22–3). It is now
difficult to maintain this view. The Mecklenburg investigations show in fact that chamber compartments
appear there in all types of megalithic tombs with the
exception of 'urdolmens'. The division of the
megalithic tombs of the Funnel Beaker Culture seems
to be related to their function, although with local
variations in design. However, it is surprising that
compartments of this type are not found in Denmark,
Schleswig-Holstein or Lower Saxony. Instead, in
these areas are found single, about human-length, par-
titions which divide the chamber transversely, usually
into two rooms. Is this a question of two different
traditions and functions?

According to observations in Mecklenburg,
chamber compartments can be dated to the early Middle Neolithic. They are primarily in the passage graves
and originated in connection with the process of
building (Schuldt 1972, 62). In my view this interpretation is substantiated both in Västergötland and in
Scania, one reason being that the stones in the walls of
the compartments are at the same depth as the chamber
walls. According to Strömberg (1971, 258), however,
the large number of compartments in passage graves –
in Scania up to thirteen, in Västergötland closer to
twenty, in Mecklenburg between seven and eight –

together with the fact that different compartments may have different floorings, speaks for the probability that they were not built in originally and not all at the same time. On the contrary, the compartments in dolmens are a later addition (Schuldt 1965, 49; 1969, 109; 1972, 62).

What was the function of the compartments? In the case of Mecklenburg, Schuldt (1966, 50–2; 1966, 76–9; 1972, 74) considers it proved that skeletal remains were interred in the burial chambers only after the bodies had lain for some time in another place. Ac-

7 Compartments in the excavated chamber of passage grave no.2 at Gnewitz, County Rostock, Mecklenburg, seen fromt the west. (Photo Klaus Nitsche, Schwerin, DDR.)

cordingly, the burial chambers had the function of ossuaries. He supports his view from observations which the majority of archaeologists have made, namely that skeletons from the primary burial period are never complete. They are always discovered in a preliminary evaluation suggests forty). Accordingly it is not known how many individuals the fragments in each compartment represent, or whether the remains of one and the same individual are to be found spread over several compartments. It is known, however, from earlier studies that in Västergötland the remains of several individuals have been found also in small compartments. The old ossuary theory, which is now over one hundred years old, has thus been given new relevance through this flood of new evidence. On the other hand, observations of bodies in a sitting position – mentioned in earlier excavation reports – must be questioned.

It should, however, be added that Strömberg, in an investigation of a passage grave in Scania, Carlshög at Hagestad, discovered skeletal fragments in such a position that she – although with certain reservations – considered this to indicate burial in a sitting position (1971, 289). If the observation is valid this suggests that megalithic tombs of the Funnel Beaker Culture in exceptional cases were used as burial places as such and not merely as ossuaries.

In what way was the body prepared before the bones were laid in the ossuary? The question has been discussed from different viewpoints but is still unanswered. It is possible that the unusual buildings of the Tustrup and Ferslöv type, of which there are at least six to seven in Jutland – all of the same type and age and all from the same period (that is, the Middle Neolithic period Ib, possibly at Herrup as early as period Ia and predating the first passage graves) – and of whose function nothing is known, may have had a role in this connection. However, according to Becker (1973, 79) they should rather be regarded as small sanctuaries or temples without direct connection with mortuary houses or funeral rites.

A large number of buildings which seem to have served as mortuary houses in the second half of the Middle Neolithic are found mainly in north-western and mid-Jutland. These are amongst the most remarkable discoveries which have been made in Funnel Beaker Culture burial ritual since the middle of the 1960s. The excavation of a passage grave at Vroue Hede between Viborg and Holstebro indicated that the sacrificial cult, traces of which are usually found outside the entrance of the passage in the so-called 'sacrificial cairn', had ceased at some time during the Middle Neolithic, period III. But at some distance from the passage entrance under level ground were found a large number of later graves, so called stone-packing graves dating from the Middle Neolithic, periods IV and V (Jörgensen 1977, 186). These human-length graves were in pairs and in rows next to their mortuary houses (ill. 9). This type of grave belongs to the

8 Funnel Beaker Culture bottom layer of agglomerated bones and bone fragments, bounded by partition walls into compartments. North-eastern part of the chamber in the passage grave at Rössberga, Valltorp, Västergötland, Sweden. (Photo Antikvariskt-Topografiskt Arkivet (ATA), Stockholm.)

more or less chaotic state, whether in compartments or in undivided burial chambers.

This view corresponds well with my own observations on visits during the excavation of the Rössberga passage grave in Västergötland (1962). The passage-grave chamber contained seventeen compartments. The lowest level of finds consisted almost wholly of a (30-cm thick) layer of bones bounded into compartments by the partition walls (ill. 8). Since the osteological analysis – twenty years after the dig – has not been published yet, it is still not known how many individuals are represented in the skeletal remains (a

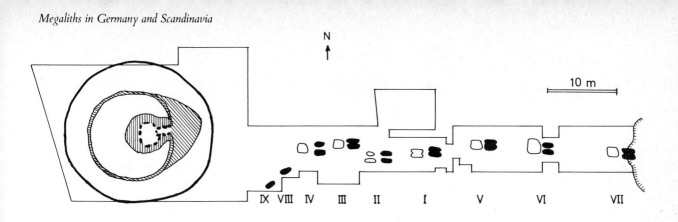

N

10 m

IX VIII IV III II I V VI VII

9 Passage grave and stone-packing graves (in black) with mortuary houses at Vroue Hede, Jutland. (Drawing by B. Jakobsson after Jörgensen 1977.)

second half of the Middle Neolithic, possibly originating as far back as the Middle Neolithic, period II (Becker 1967, 28–9). In addition, finds were made in the old sacrificial mound which, to judge from their position, were placed there by the stone-packing grave people. This indicates that the passage graves and their surroundings were still used as a cult and burial area also by a later Funnel Beaker Culture society (Jörgensen 1977, 110, 204–5, 207). These mortuary houses are important for future research because they suggest what traces such constructions leave behind. But in the meantime, the question of how these people treated the dead before the bones were laid in the passage-grave chamber or the dolmen must remain unanswered.

The 'Megalithic' Society

As the previous discussion has made clear, the questions still at the centre of research today, as they were fifteen years ago, are those of the architecture and dating of megalithic tombs, the function of such monuments and the cults connected with them and that of the origin of the tombs. But in addition greater interest is being taken in the question of the society that built them.

The tombs are a manifestation of the activity of a society – 'fossilized behaviour of extinct societies' as Childe expressed it. Under the influence of anthropological models postulated by American and British anthropologists, as well as the predominantly eastern European Marxist models, megalithic tombs are also being studied in their socio-economic aspects.

The construction of megalithic tombs must have been labour-intensive, especially if they are seen in relation to the estimates we have of the population of the societies. A precondition of such work would be a surplus of food supplies for the labour force involved, at least during the building period. How many individuals lived in a community which had the capacity to erect a passage grave? According to Paul Ashbee,

the construction of the Fussell's Lodge long barrow is calculated to have required nearly 5,000 days of labour for the mound alone (Clark 1977, 35). What was the basis of their economy?

Such considerations have made it essential to supplement excavations of tombs with a search for contemporary sites in the vicinity. As yet, few sites which can be assigned with certainty to the building period of a specific tomb are known.

Where are the Dwelling-Sites of the Tomb Builders?
Assuming that each megalithic tomb corresponds to one settlement unit, that is, one community, and that the monument marks the sphere of interest of the community – which is reasonable according to archaeological and ethnographic experience – traces of settlement should be found within the territory in question (cf. Renfrew 1976, 208). This view of the tombs is not new. However, systematic topographical studies and search for dwelling sites in the area around megalithic tombs have not generally been instigated. Where they have been for instance in connection with tomb investigations, good results have been obtained.

In Sweden, in the province of Scania, through systematic search Funnel Beaker Culture settlements have been found which have left culture deposit layers within an area of 1–1.5 km radius from the megalithic tomb, in some cases quite close and sometimes under the tomb as well. Similar results have also been obtained sporadically in other Nordic megalithic tomb areas. As mentioned above, the difficulty has been to connect the dwelling site chronologically to a specific tomb. This is not surprising. The tomb finds are different in composition and often contain a range of more 'valuable' objects than the dwelling-site finds. For a more definite connection it is necessary to have pottery

85

with complicated ornamentation from both the tomb and the dwelling-site in question. To get suitable samples from both sites for radiocarbon dating is also difficult. Up to now extremely few samples of this nature have been found.

In Jutland, however, they have succeeded in finding dwelling-sites beside a group of megalithic tombs at Karups Hede, south of Limfjorden. These sites were populated at the time of construction of the passage graves (Jörgensen 1977, 204). Dwelling-sites are also known near megalithic graves in Mecklenburg, but there too there are difficulties in establishing a chronological connection with the period of building. From Lower Saxony little knowledge exists. Practically no total investigations of dwelling-sites have been carried out there and dwelling-site excavations are also rare (Schirnig 1979, 19). On the other hand, cultural deposits contemporary with the tombs beside the 'chamberless' earthen long barrows are commonly found in Kujavia. Polish scholars generally consider these to stem from earlier dwelling sites above which long barrows have been built. Similar cultural deposits have also been found in connection with long barrows in Jutland, but have been differently interpreted there. It is thought 'that the cultural material was laid down in connection with the use of the structures' (Madsen 1979, 317), that is, as part of cult observances. This may be so, but until the Danish excavation reports are published it will not be possible to form an opinion.

Because of the difficulties commented on, megalithic tomb studies and dwelling-site studies have to some extent run parallel.

The Economy and Structure of Megalithic Tomb Societies
The two main questions are how foodstuffs were produced and how society was structured.

There has been renewed interest in the latter question since recent investigations have discovered earth graves in the areas of the passage graves, e.g. in Scania, Jutland and Lower Saxony. Sometimes the earth grave was very close to the passage grave (Strömberg 1971, 339–40; Tempel 1979, 111–13). Some of these graves are contemporary with the primary period of use of the passage graves (Tempel 1979, 114). Earlier known earth graves date almost exclusively from the non-megalithic groups of the Early Neolithic in southern Scandinavia. The premises for research have thus been changed.

Was it a sign of higher status that the bones were laid in a tomb rather than in an earth grave? Or can the presence of an earth grave beside a tomb possibly indicate an exogenous marriage to a person from a non-megalithic group of the Funnel Beaker Culture? The question must remain unanswered at present.

Archaeological surveys of the economy of megalithic communities and their structure are usually brief and generalized and, as is natural, based on the research of the natural sciences. These have shown considerable agreement between Scandinavia and northern Germany on such matters as cultivated plants and domestic animals. We know from these what the megalithic tomb-building Funnel Beaker Culture groups cultivated and what animals they kept.

Such determinations are, however, qualitative and understandably lack quantitative data. Accordingly they can say nothing about the importance of cultivation and cattle-breeding for the livelihood of these communities compared with what food-gathering, hunting and fishing could yield. Surveys give the general impression that the writer views 'the Neolithic revolution' as quantitatively important for food production.

Those who like myself have had the opportunity of sorting pottery sherds with alleged grain impressions (both in tomb-pottery and dwelling-site material) can hardly have avoided being surprised at the low frequency of sherds with such impressions. It may be claimed that the grains were not necessarily being handled in the same place as the pottery was made. But there also exist impressions which belong to wild edible plants. Fortunately, in certain areas one has the pollen diagram for comparison. But in the majority of cases the evidence of the tombs is the only starting point for judgment on the economy of the megalithic societies.

Since only a few dwelling-sites from the tomb-building period are known one must, in common with Grahame Clark, concentrate on the graves themselves and put the question if and to what extent their distribution pattern can be used for conclusions on the economy of the tomb builders (1977, 34–5). Clark's investigation is based on the hypothesis that 'under subsistence economy most food is obtained within an hour or so's radius of the focus of settlement'. This is an attempt at quantification. The same estimate of distance should also be valid for tomb building but should not be overstated. If anything, the transport of blue stones and sarsens to Stonehenge is proof that people are willing to undertake great exertions for ideological reasons, as Clark points out.

With due respect to the foregoing theory, traces of settlement in the neighbourhood of megalithic tombs suggest that the tombs *are* an indication of where people lived. And people settle down in areas which are favourable to their mode of subsistence.

As one example of this I would like to discuss the well-known inland concentration of passage graves in central northern Västergötland – Falbygden – in

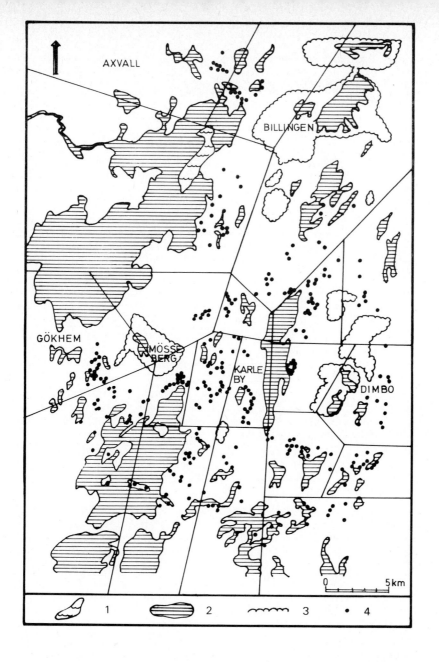

AXVALL

BILLINGEN

GÖKHEM

MÖSSE
BERG

KARLE
BY

DIMBO

0   5km

1   2   3   4

Sweden (ill. 10), also treated by Clark in his study of 1977.

The areas is a typical ecological niche. It comprises mainly a very small lime-rich Cambro-Silurian area – an island amid the vast primary rock terrain of which the rest of western Sweden consists. The Cambro-Silurian rock overlies the primary rock and forms an even surface, a plain, covered with moraine clays and surrounded by diabase-covered plateaux. Below the plateaux edges there are extensive marshes. The plain is subject to particular conditions of precipitation and drainage. Some small parts of the

10 Suggested classification of Falbygden's passage-grave area, based on the passage-grave groupings and natural boundaries. (Drawing by B. Jakobsson after Hyenstrand 1979.) 1 lake; 2 marshland; 3 plateaux; 4 passage grave.

area have even been defined ecologically as being of the same nature as the continental steppe. In these steppe-meadows we find a relict from a warmer period, the *Stipa pennata*, the only place it grows in Nordic countries. In this area the majority of Swedish passage graves are found, with 290 known examples, of which about 240 still remain. This means that four-fifths of all the passage graves in Sweden are concentrated in an area of 500 sq.km.

Falbygden today is a prosperous agricultural area. Was it also attractive as farming land for a megalithic tomb-society, when more favourable climatic circumstances existed than those of today? Clark, who mainly seems to rely on soil fertility, moraine clays above Cambro-Silurian lime bedrock, considers that the surplus of food symbolized by the tombs 'was derived substantially at least from farming'. To the extent that this interpretation relates to cereals cultivation it is supported neither by the comparatively few grain impressions on pottery sherds nor by palaeo-botanical studies. The pollen analysis of lake deposits in this area shows that, on the contrary, cereals cultivation during the Middle Neolithic was insignificant (Fries 1958, 31, 59). Magnus Fries, who started from the archaeological postulate according to which passage graves indicate cultivation, was surprised at the weak representation of cerealia in the pollen diagrams. According to his studies the area at this time was covered by deciduous forests, although with some open spaces, possibly man-made (ibid. 36).

When one discusses cereals cultivation during an age when agricultural implements were rudimentary one should remember that primitive cultivation demanded greater manpower than other means of sustenance in relation to yield. Prehistoric fields were small. Just how small they were during the Neolithic period we do not know. It is highly probable that cereals from the small clearings in Scandinavia during the Neolithic and also Bronze Ages were a luxury food. Basic nourishment must have come from other sources. For instance, Fries calls attention to the importance of acorns as human food.

The Silurian area's type of landscape provided better conditions for grazing than the surrounding western Swedish gneiss rock. But it would be too bold to conclude that the passage-grave people's sustenance was based on or dominated by cattle-raising.

On closer inspection of the position of the passage graves in the landscape described above, one finds that they appear in scattered groups, often beside the outskirts of the Silurian plain and adjacent to swamps. The diabase-clad plateaux and the vast marshlands form natural boundaries around the passage-grave area. Attempts have been made to divide the total of passage graves into some twenty groups comprising ten to fifteen graves, each in its own landscape setting (ill. 10), by assuming that an immediate area of 2–2½ km radius from each passage grave group was the supply area for food production (Hyenstrand 1979, 130).

In these settings there are plenty of small watercourses and they were once larger and more numerous. The watercourses, with their fish and waterbirds, together with the rich assets of forest wildlife in the vicinity, gave a good yield in relation to labour input. It is highly probable that such possibilities of sustenance were exploited. If this interpretation is correct, cattle-raising was only a complement to food-gathering, whereas sheep-wool and goat-hair were likely to have been more important. The importance of cereals cultivation was quite marginal. In such an ecological niche the conditions for the sustenance of a sedentary community would have existed all year round in each landscape setting.

Clark (1977, 40–2) points out the environmental circumstances of the west coast of Sweden, Bohuslän, as an example of how the nature of food production is crucial to the localization of megalithic tombs. All dolmens and 85 per cent of the passage graves are found within 3 km of the sea, some only a few metres from the waterline as it then was. Land that was arable by the techniques at that time consisted of washed-down moraine, a particularly meagre soil at the foot of the bare rocks. The pattern of distribution of the tombs cannot therefore depend on cultivation. The coastal meadows certainly were suitable for grazing, but the question is whether cattle-raising was an important means of sustenance in terms of quantity. The known major food supplies on the coast consisted of fish, shellfish, seals and sea birds, etc. The position of the megalithic-tomb communities can hardly have been decided by factors other than just these resources. As further proof of his theory Clark also analyses traces of coastal settlement before and after the Funnel Beaker Culture megalithic-tomb societies and their economy, which were similarly based on fishing and the sources of sustenance available on the coast.

Fishing and the abundance of shellfish in the Limfjord area in Jutland including the coast up to Djursland (where the majority of Jutland's 200 passage graves lie) would also have been decisive for the localization of the settlements and thus the tombs. The concentration of megalithic tombs to the north and south-east of Rügen is not explicable in any other light. In fact, this concentration was greater than what appears from the fifty-four surviving monuments. During the first half of the nineteenth century a good 250 stone-chamber tombs were registered on the island (with few exceptions all were so-called big dolmens with a rectangular chamber and passage on the gable end). This density of monuments clearly emphasizes the nature of food production on the protected bays on the east and south-east coast of the island.

On the other hand, if one studies the natural back-

ground to the megalithic tombs in the Mecklenburg hinterland one is struck by the abundance of watercourses. In this area there existed a rich ecological niche with freshwater fishing, game-hunting and edible herbs, with cattle-raising as a complement.

Mecklenburg has been divided into six different Neolithic settlement areas on the basis of the megalithic tombs, each with its characteristic tomb design (Schuldt 1972, 102 and distribution maps 3–9). Closer analysis of the landscape in these six dwelling areas together with grave finds may perhaps answer the question to what extent the different groups of tombs reflect groups with different economies.

Clark, by focussing on sources of sustenance as the basis for his study of the megalithic tombs distribution patterns, has opened up a fruitful avenue for continued productive research. The reason for the spread of the megalithic tombs along the Atlantic coast is according to his theory, 'the pursuit of fish'. It is an attractive hypothesis and as worth proving as any. The occurrence inland of megalithic tombs requires a different type of food production but not – as has been maintained – cereals cultivation.

The Community

What kind of community is symbolized by the megalithic tomb? One view is that the megalithic tomb is a grave and cult centre for an upper class among the Funnel Beaker Culture peasants (Strömberg 1968, 227). This notion is grounded mainly on the monumental nature of the tombs, since otherwise the finds show no difference in status between tombs and earth graves.

Another interpretation suggests that the megalithic tombs are indicative of a segmentary and thus egalitarian society (Renfrew 1976, 204–11).

Finds of copper objects in some twenty passage graves in Lower Saxony (mainly west of the Weser) show differences in economic resources, both during the Early Neolithic, phase C, and the beginning of the Middle Neolithic (Schlicht 1979, 169–78). Similar differences also occur in the area of the Funnel Beaker Culture earth graves (Tempel 1979, 114). In this respect, therefore, there is no difference between the tombs and the earth graves. At present the theory of segmentary societies seems superior as a working hypothesis.

According to Renfrew, the megalithic tombs of north-western Europe are to be interpreted as territorial markers. Examples cited by him (Renfrew 1976, ills 4, 6) show that each territory has one megalithic tomb as a marker of 'territorial behaviour'. Although the thesis seems reasonable it also awakens new questions. Can a group of ten to fifteen megalithic tombs in one and the same territory as those found in Västergötland bear the same significance? Do several contemporary monuments mean a stronger expression of territorial marking? And if so, is this true for all contemporary territorial groups?

A reasonable view is that each group of passage graves in Västergötland is a settlement unit with its own territory (Hyenstrand 1979, 74). In some groups the tombs are positioned in rows, such as in Karleby (10–12 passage graves) (ills 10–11), in others they lie more or less scattered in small clusters of just a few graves only 25–50m apart, thus symbolizing a village-like or more scattered unit of settlement. It is not likely that all passage graves of one and the same unit were built during the same building period. It is not possible to decide which and how many are contemporary without further investigations. Neither from the appearance of the tombs nor from topographical studies can one conclude as to the order of sequence of the, tombs. Finds from old studies are mostly of little use for determining the precise chronology of the building of the monuments. It is, however, probable that the passage graves in row formation were built successively – a few graves in each generation and depending on the size of the population. But this is only a hypothesis, which will need to be tested in future investigations.

Just as it is difficult to be precise about the chronological sequence of the tombs in each unit, it is also difficult to decide how many settlement units in this segmentary society were contemporary. Are all twenty settlement units of the same age? Which are the most ancient? In what direction did change take place? How long did the different units survive?

To answer these questions we should remember that the dating of finds shows that the building phase of the passage graves was brief and ended before the middle of the Middle Neolithic in southern Scandinavia and in Mecklenburg (in some parts even before period II, Kjaerum 1966/67, 332; Schuldt 1972, 62). The same is probably true of the Funnel Beaker Culture western group in Lower Saxony and Drenthe-Groningen in Holland. This view is partly supported by radiocarbon data. But to reach certainty on these questions comprehensive field studies will be required, especially of the social and economic aspects. This research is still in its initial stage. Research on the monuments stands in the forefront, as it did fifteen years ago.

In this survey I have stressed the importance of comprehensive studies of megalithic-tomb societies. Research into the tombs appears more and more as a means, albeit a necessary one, to the end of gaining new knowledge. This means that the search for settlement sites should be intensified; so should cooperation with the disciplines of the natural sciences. Different models from the field of anthropology should be tried out. The formulation of problems we have to work with will be increasingly dependent not only on archaeological concepts but also on the general aims and methods of the social sciences.

Translated by Bryan Errington

Bibliography

ANER, E. 1963 'Die Stellung der Dolmen Schleswig-Holsteins in der nordischen Megalithkultur', *Offa* XX, 9–38.

BECKER, C.J. 1947 'Mosefundne Lerkar fra yngre Stenalder', *Aarbøger for nordisk Oldkyndighed og Historie*.

1967 'Gadefulde jyske stenaldergrave', *Nationalmuseets Arbejdsmark*, 19–30.

1973 'Problems of the Megalithic "Mortuary Houses" in Denmark, in Daniel, G. and Kjaerum, P. (eds), *Megalithic Graves and Ritual*, Copenhagen, 75–9.

CLARK, J.G.D. 1977 'The Economic Context of Dolmens and Passage Graves in Sweden', in Markotic, V. (ed.), *Ancient Europe and the Mediterranean*, Warminster, 35–49.

FRIES, M. 1958 'Vegetationsutveckling och odlingshistoria i Varnhemstrakten, Acta Phytogeographica' *Suecica* XXIX, Uppsala.

HYENSTRAND, Å. 1979 *Ancient Monuments and Prehistoric Society*, Stockholm.

JAZDZEWSKI, K. 1973 'The Relations between Kujavian Barrows in Poland and Megalithic Tombs in northern Germany, Denmark and western European Countries', in Daniel, G. and Kjaerum, P. (eds), *Megalithic Graves and Ritual*, Copenhagen, 63–74.

KAELAS, L. 1956 'Dolmen und Ganggräber in Schweden', *Offa* XV, 5–24.

1966/67 'The Megalithic Tombs in South Scandinavia —Migration or Cultural Influence?' *Palaeohistoria* XII, 287–321.

KJAERUM, P. 1966/67 'The Chronology of the Passage-Graves in Jutland', *Palaeohistoria* XII, 323–33.

MADSEN, T. 1979 'Earthen Long Barrows and Timber Structures: Aspects of the Early Neolithic Mortuary Practice in Denmark', *Proc. Preh. Soc.* XLV, 301–20.

PIGGOTT, S. 1956 'Windmill Hill – East or West', *Proc. Preh. Soc.* XXI, 96–101.

1966/67 'Unchambered Long Barrows in neolithic Britain', *Palaeohistoria* XII, 381–93.

RADDATZ, K. 1979 'Zur Funktion der Grosssteingräber', in Schirnig H. (ed.), *Grosssteingräber in*

Niedersachsen, Hildesheim, 127–41.

RENFREW C. 1976 'Megaliths, Territories and Populations', in De Laet, S.J. (ed.), *Acculturation and Continuity in Atlantic Europe*, Brugge, 198–220.

SCHIRNIG, H. 1979 'Einführung', in Schirnig, H. (ed.), *Grosssteingräber in Niedersachsen*, Hildesheim, 1–26.

SCHLICHT, E. 1979 'Handels- und Kulturbeziehungen auf Grund von Importfunden aus niedersächsischen Grosssteingräbern', in Schirnig, H. (ed.), *Grosssteingräber in Niedersachsen*, Hildesheim, 169–78.

SCHULDT, E. 1972 *Die Mecklenburgischen Megalithgräber*, Berlin.

STRÖBERG, M. 1968 'Der Dolmen Trollasten', *Acta Archaeologica Lundensia*, VIII, no. 7, Lund.

1970 'Die Megalithgräber von Hagestad', *Acta Archaeologica Lundensia*, VIII, no. 9, Lund.

TEMPEL, W.-D. 1979 'Flachgräber der Trichterbecherkultur', in Schirnig, H. (ed.), *Grosssteingräber in Niedersachsen*, Hildesheim, 111–16.

7 Megalithic Graves in Belgium — A *Status Quaestionis*

Sigfried J. De Laet

ONLY A FEW megalithic tombs exist in Belgium, as distinct from its neighbouring countries, France, the Netherlands and Germany. Just five are known, three of which still exist, the remaining two having been destroyed at the end of the nineteenth century. Though so few in number, they are of interest because of their geographical location which may make it possible to determine the links existing between different cultures in the third millennium BC.

These five tombs are concentrated in a small triangular area, with sides of about 50, 45 and 30 km, lying in the provinces of Namur and Luxemburg and covering part of the Condroz and the Famenne (ill. 2). Very probably they all belong to the Seine-Oise-Marne (SOM) culture; I shall return to this later. First we should study the graves and their contents.

The two best-preserved tombs (still visible) are situated at Wéris, in the north of the province of Luxemburg (Corbiau 1978, 286 ff.). The smaller of these

1 Plan of the two megalithic graves at Wéris (after de Loë 1928). 1 the sunken allée couverte; *2 the gallery-grave built above ground.*

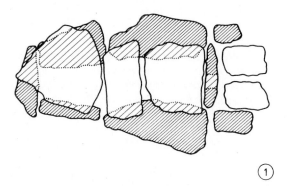

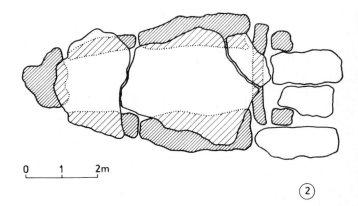

0   1   2m

①   ②

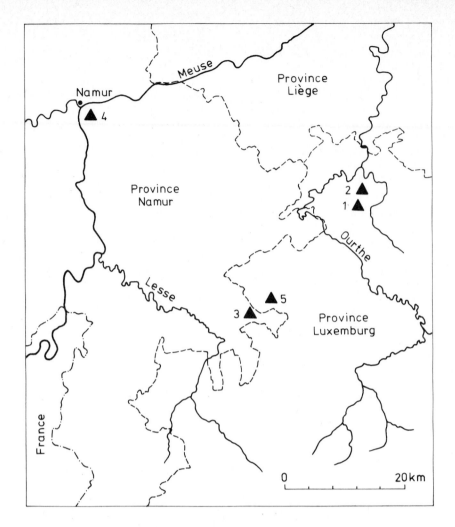

2 Location of the Belgian megalithic graves: 1 sunken gallery-grave (allée couverte) at Wéris; 2 gallery-grave, built above ground, at Wéris; 3 gallery-grave (?) at Jemelle, partly destroyed; 4 destroyed megalithic grave at Velaine (Jambes), type unknown; 5 destroyed megalithic grave (long cist ?) at Jemeppe-Hargimont.

is a gallery-grave, an *allée couverte* of the Paris Basin type, sunk below ground level up to the capstones (ill. 1). The walls of the funerary chamber (length 4.6 m, width 1.2 m: internal dimensions) are made of two pairs of opposing orthostats, and of one slab closing off the chamber at the rear end; the roof is composed of three massive horizontal slabs. Leading to this chamber is an antechamber, only two orthostats of which are left. As a result of the rather questionable restoration of 1906 (Rahir 1928, 71 ff.), this antechamber is now paved with two slabs which are probably fragments of a

broken capstone. Chamber and antechamber are separated by a transverse slab, pierced by a round hole. The interstices between the orthostats were filled in with dry-stone masonry. This tomb was discovered in 1888 and 'excavated' the same year by A. Charneux using the rather clumsy methods customary at that time. If the very cursory report published on this occasion (Charneux 1888a) can be trusted, the grave-chamber yielded traces of a 'hearth' (ritual fire?), human bones, animal bones, artifacts made of flint (scrapers, arrowheads, polished axes) and of sandstone (hammer-stones), sherds of very coarse, thick-walled and plain pottery (probably SOM pottery) and a few sherds of (bell-beaker?) pottery decorated with a herring-bone pattern.

All these finds seem since to have disappeared. When in 1906 the monument was bought by the State and restored, new excavations were carried out but these yielded no results (Rahir 1928, 71–2). The larger megalithic tomb at Wéris is much the same in plan; but it is a gallery-grave built above ground and was originally covered with an earth mound. Here too the chamber (length 5.50 m, width 1.75 m: internal dimensions) is made of two pairs of opposing orthostats, and of one slab closing off the chamber at the rear end. The roof is composed of two capstones, one now broken. Again, funerary chamber and antechamber are separated by a transverse slab pierced by a door-shaped hole. Of the antechamber, only two rather narrow orthostats are left. When the restoration took place in 1906, three slabs lying on the ground in and next to the antechamber were interpreted as paving-stones, but are probably the remains of a broken capstone originally covering this antechamber. *Allées couvertes* of the Paris Basin type almost certainly belong to the SOM, but gallery-graves built above ground and covered by a barrow are less frequent in this culture (Bailloud 1964, 156). Both megalithic tombs at Wéris are made of pudding-stone, coming from a site approximately 3 km distant. The second megalith, which has long been known and publicized, had of course been robbed some time ago. According to local tradition, it had contained several skeletons. When, in 1888, the *allée couverte* was discovered and excavated, Charneux took the opportunity to dig the gallery-grave as well, but he found only traces of a 'hearth' (ritual fire?), some bones and a few flint and sandstone artifacts, and sherds of coarse pottery, all scattered in and around the tomb (Charneux 1888b). When the monument was acquired by the State in 1906 and restored, new excavations were carried out by the Musées royaux d'Art et d'Histoire (Brussels), but they yielded only a single sherd of coarse pottery from the chamber and very few remains scattered around the grave (Rahir 1928, 71).

The two megalithic tombs at Wéris seem to have formed part of a big religious complex, a sacred area (ill. 3). Indeed, on a straight strip about 5 km long and orientated NNE-SSW are to be found successively the site of the menhir of Tour (municipality of Heyd), which was destroyed at the end of the nineteenth century (Danthine 1947a); the gallery-grave at Wéris; a second menhir, 3.6 m high, which had been toppled and buried in a field, but rediscovered in 1947 and reinstated (Danthine 1947b); the *allée couverte* of Wéris; and finally, the three menhirs of Bouhaimont at Oppagne (municipality of Wéris). The last named, the largest of which is 3.6 m high, had also been toppled and subsequently buried, but they were reinstated in 1906 (Rahir 1928, 73–4). All five menhirs were made of the same material as the megalithic graves, namely pudding-stone from the site previously referred to. Another element has possibly to be added to

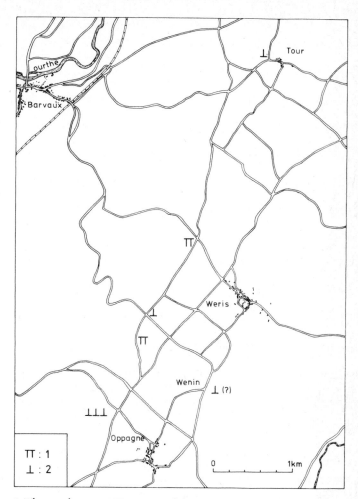

3 The sacred area at Wéris: 1 megalithic grave; 2 menhir.

this group: the so-called 'Pas Bayard' at Wenin (municipality of Wéris), a large pudding-stone about which several local legends have grown up, but it is not possible to tell whether it is a fragment of a broken menhir or the remains of a megalithic grave.

The third megalithic tomb was discovered as recently as September 1976 near the farm of Lamsoul at Jemelle (province of Namur) (Chardome 1979). It was excavated in 1976 and 1977 by a group of amateurs. This tomb, which had been robbed and largely destroyed, appears to have been built above ground and was originally covered by a barrow, some traces of which were discovered. Of the tomb itself only part of the funerary chamber remains: seven orthostats, two of which had fallen down, and one roof-slab. No traces of a possible antechamber were found and therefore it is rather difficult to determine the exact type of this monument, although it is likely to have been some kind of gallery-grave. The excavators found some human bones, sherds of coarse, probably SOM pottery, but also a few Gallo-Roman sherds.

As far as the two graves destroyed at the end of the nineteenth century are concerned, practically nothing is known of the one at Velaine (municipality of Jambes, province of Namur), apart from the fact that it was called 'Pierre du Diable'; there are no clues as to its type (Knapen-Lescrenier 1970, 146 ff.). A little more is known about the megalithic tomb at the 'Bois des Lusce' at Jemeppe-Hargimont (province of Luxemburg) (Corbiau 1978, 119–20; see also Mariën 1952a, 152–4). This tomb – which, according to some traditions, contained several skeletons – was 15 m long and 1.25 m wide (internal dimensions). Very probably it was a dug-out tomb, although this is not mentioned explicitly in the publications. The chamber was bounded by a vertical slab at each end, while its side walls consisted of dry-stone masonry. No roof-slabs are mentioned and it is possible that the tomb originally had a wooden ceiling. There is no mention either of an antechamber or of a pierced slab between chamber and antechamber. From this description, one gets the impression that this tomb is much closer to the West German *einteilige Galeriegräber* than to the *allées couvertes* of the Paris Basin. We will come back to this point later.

For the sake of completeness, I should mention the discovery in 1970 at Gomery (municipality of Bleid, province of Luxemburg) of a jumble of buried blocks of stone, which some amateurs interpreted – wrongly in my opinion – as remains of a megalithic grave (Corbiau 1978, 60–1). In fact, on investigation this structureless heap of stones yielded neither bone remains nor any grave contents whatsoever and I think that they were dumped there fairly recently. An earth-sample taken from *under* the stones was subjected to a palynological analysis by J. Heim of the University of Louvain and showed a typical sub-Atlantic composition with 40 per cent *Carpinus*. Furthermore, charcoal from a hearth discovered at a depth of 70 cm in the immediate neighbourhood of the stone heap gave a radiocarbon date of AD 1390 ± 110 (Lv–496) (Gilot 1971, 50).

In the general context of the European megalithic graves, the Belgian group is rather isolated, geographically speaking. It is situated at least 100 km from the nearest megalithic tombs, namely those of the Ardennes department in France (as can be seen in Kaelas 1967, map on page 307). Notwithstanding the loss of the grave goods almost in their entirety, however, it is generally admitted that the Belgian megalithic graves belong to the SOM culture (Mariën 1952a; De Laet

1958; De Laet-Glasbergen 1959; Bonenfant 1969; De Laet 1974; 1976; 1979): there is the *allée couverte*, of a type characteristic of this culture, and there are the gallery-graves of Wéris and Jemelle, which are paralleled in the SOM, besides the references to 'coarse pottery', which practically always indicate SOM ceramics in the reports concerning Neolithic sites in the regions we are considering. Furthermore, there is the presence in the neighbourhood of very numerous caves, which in the basin of the Meuse and its tributaries have been used as collective graves by the SOM people (after having been, long before, the dwelling-places of Middle and Later Palaeolithic hunters). In Belgium, there are at least eighty caves and rock-shelters which have been used as ossuaries (ill. 4). Most of these belong to the SOM culture, as shown for example by the grave goods. Collective inhumation in caves, however, was continued in this particular region during the whole of the Bronze Age and even during the Hallstatt period. I have discussed this subject more thoroughly elsewhere (for the most recent data, see De Laet 1979, 270 ff.), so there is no need to say more about it here, except to stress the fact that the Belgian megalithic tombs, although isolated as such, are clearly situated in the northernmost part of the SOM area. Naturally, the latter point is a further argument to link these tombs to the SOM culture.

A few decades ago, it was still generally conceded that the SOM was only poorly represented in Belgium (see for instance Mariën 1950, 1952b). Now we know, however, that not only the whole northern half of France, but also Belgium and even part of the southern provinces of the Netherlands lay within the area of SOM culture and that in Belgium the SOM was even the main Neolithic culture of the third millennium BC, surviving there, at least in some regions, during an important part of the Bronze Age (*status quaestionis*: De Laet 1979, 265 ff.). We need only glance at the distribution map for Belgium, however (ill. 4), to see that the SOM occupation there was much denser in the Meuse basin, from the French border to Dutch Limburg, than it was in the Scheldt basin. It has been stressed for some time that there exist striking similarities between the Westphalian and Hessian *Galeriegrab-Kultur* and the SOM, mainly as far as the structure of some megalithic tombs is concerned (recent bibliography in De Laet 1976, to which should be added Louwe Kooijmans 1976; Schrickel 1976; Fischer 1979 and Schwellnus 1979). Dutch Limburg can probably be identified as the main contact zone between the two cultures. It was in this region that P.J.R. Modderman (1964) discovered and excavated the important tomb at Stein, a non-megalithic version of the *allées couvertes*: its structure can best be compared

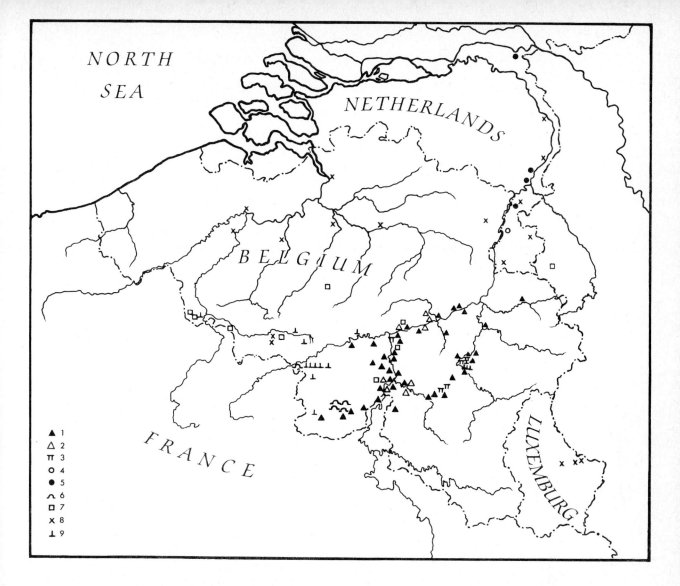

to that of a number of non-megalithic SOM tombs in France; part of the grave goods point to relations with the *Galeriegrab-Kultur*, while other elements present features analogous to those of the SOM (Modderman 1964; De Laet 1979, 284 ff). Since this discovery, other finds have come to light in Dutch Limburg which present the same mixed character: this 'Limburgs midden-neolithicum' (Middle Neolithic of Limburg) has been studied mainly by Modderman (1964) and L.P. Louwe Kooijmans (1976). All these elements suggest the existence of contacts between the SOM and the *Galeriegrab-Kultur*; one can probably add to that the already mentioned megalithic cist of Jemeppe-Hargimont, which up till now has never been discussed in this particular context. As far as its type can be identified from the older publications which do not include plans or photographs, it seems to be very much

4 Distribution map of the SOM culture in Belgium and in the southern part of the Netherlands
1 sepulchral cave; 2 group of sepulchral caves; 3 megalithic grave; 4 the non-megalithic grave at Stein; 5 site of the 'Middle Neolithic of Limburg'; 6 Bronze Age barrow with SOM pottery; 7 SOM settlement; 8 SOM stray find; 9 menhir.

akin to some dug-out megalithic non-segmented West German tombs (the *einteilige Galeriegräber*). In his recent book on the Hessian Wartberg group W. Schwellnus (1979) too has touched upon the problem of the contacts between the German gallery-graves and the French *allées couvertes*; he seems to be unaware of the importance of the SOM culture in the Meuse basin in Belgium and in the southern part of the Netherlands, believing the contacts between the two cultures to have been established by way of the Moselle valley. The remains he uses as a basis for this theory are not well known and much poorer than those from the Meuse valley. Of course, it may be that the Moselle was also used as a contact route between the two cultures, but as far as our actual knowledge goes, it was a much less important one than the Meuse route.

From the information available at present, I can only conclude that the small group of Belgian megalithic graves constitute a far from negligible factor when considering contacts and mutual influences between the SOM and the *Galeriegrab-Kultur*. Some years ago the study of this particular problem led me to propose (De Laet 1976) a new solution for another problem, that of the origins of the *allées couvertes* of the Paris Basin type, a question which Glyn Daniel has broached on several former occasions (Daniel 1941; 1955; 1960; 1967; 1973). Till then it was generally accepted that

the Hessian and Westphalian tombs, presenting the same structure as the French *allées couvertes*, derived from the latter, but I tried to demonstrate that the oldest tombs of this type were not those of the SOM but on the contrary those of West Germany, and that the origins of the SOM *allées couvertes* were to be looked for in Germany, the Meuse valley being the main contact route between the two areas. In Germany the *allées couvertes* with chamber and antechamber separated by a pierced vertical slab can easily be derived from the non-segmented dug-out gallery-graves, the *einteilige Galeriegräber*, of which the grave of Jemeppe-Hargimont probably constitutes one of the westernmost specimens. It was quite a joy for me to see my thesis accepted by my friend Glyn Daniel (Daniel 1978), who completed it by suggesting that the ancestry of both the *Galeriegräber* and the *allées couvertes* is to be found in the long-houses of the Linear Pottery people. It is now my turn to stress my full agreement with his view on the subject.

Bibliography

BAILLOUD, G. 1964/1974 *Le néolithique dans le Bassin Parisien,* 2nd edn, Paris, with 'mise à jour' 1972, 387–429.

BONENFANT, P.-P. 1969 *Civilisations préhistoriques en Wallonie. Des premiers cultivateurs aux premières villes,* Brussels.

CHARDOME, J.-M. 1979 'Le monument mégalithique de Lamsoul à Jemelle', *Conspectus MCMLXXVIII = Archaeologia Belgica* CCXIII, 44–8.

CHARNEUX, A. 1888a 'Un second dolmen à Wéris', *Annales Institut archéologique Luxembourg* XX, 203–5.

1888b 'Les fouilles à l'ancien dolmen de Wéris' *Annales Institut archéologique Luxembourg* XX, 207ff.

CORBIAU, M.-H. 1978 *Répertoire bibliographique des trouvailles archéologiques de la province de Luxembourg,* Brussels.

DANIEL, G.E. 1941 'The dual nature of the megalithic colonisation of prehistoric Europe', *Proc. Preh. Soc.* VII, 1–49.

1955 'The *allées couvertes* of France', *The Archaeological Journal* CXII, 1 – 19.

1960 *The Prehistoric Chamber Tombs of France,* London.

1966 'The Megalith-Builders of the SOM', *Neolithic Studies in Atlantic Europe = Palaeohistoria* XII, 199–208.

1973 'Spain and the Problem of European Megalithic Origins', *Estudios dedicados al Professor Dr. Luis Pericot* Barcelona, 209–14.

1978 Review of S.J. DE LAET (ed.), *Acculturation and Continuity in Atlantic Europe, mainly during the Neolithic period and the Bronze Age* (Bruges 1976), in *Helinium* XVIII, 268–9.

DANTHINE, H. 1947a 'Le champ mégalithique de Wéris (Luxembourg)', *Archéologie* 1947, 2 (= *L'Antiquité Classique* XVI, 2), 358.

1947b 'Wéris (Luxembourg). Découverte d'un menhir', *Archéologie* 1947, 2 (= *L'Antiquité Classique* XVI, 2), 358.

DE LAET, S.J. 1958 *The Low Countries,* London and New York.

1974 *Prehistorische Kulturen in het Zuiden der Lage Landen,* Wetteren.

1976 'L'explication des changements culturels: modèles théoriques et applications concrètes. Le cas du S.O.M.' in DE LAET, S.J. (ed.) *Acculturation and continuity in Atlantic Europe, mainly during the Neolithic period and the Bronze Age. Papers presented at the IV.Atlantic Colloquium, Ghent 1975 (= Dissertationes archaeologicae Gandenses* XVI), Bruges, 67–76.

1979 *Prehistorische Kulturen in het Zuiden der Lage Landen.* 2nd edn, Wetteren.

DE LAET, S.J. AND GLASBERGEN, W. 1959 *De Voorgeschiedenis der Lage Landen,* Groningen.

DE LOË, A. 1928 *Belgique ancienne. Catalogue descriptif et raisonné.I.Les âges de la pierre,* Brussels.

FISCHER, U. 1979 'Europäische Verbindungen der niedersächsischen Groszsteingräber', in *Groszsteingräber in Niedersachsen,* Hildesheim, 27–42.

96

GILOT, E. 1971 Louvain 'Natural Radiocarbon Mea-
surments X', *Radiocarbon* XIII, no.1, 45–51.

KAELAS, L. 1967 'The Megalithic Tombs in South
Scandinavia. Migration or cultural influence?' *Neolithic Studies in Atlantic Europe = Palaeohistoria* XII,
287–321.

KNAPEN-LESCRENIER, A.-M. 1970 *Répertoire bibliographique des trouvailles archéologiques de la province de Namur*,
Brussels.

LOUWE KOOIJMANS, L.P. 1976 'Local developments in
a borderland. A survey of the neolithic at the Lower
Rhine', *Oudheidkundige Mededelingen van het Rijks-
museum van Oudheden te Leiden*, 57, 227–97.

MARIËN, M.E. 1950 'Poteries de la civilisation de
Seine-Oise-Marne en Belgique', *Bulletin des Musées
royaux d'Art et d'Histoire* XXII, 79–85.

1952a *Oud-België, van de eerste landbouwers tot de komst
van Caesar*, Antwerp.

1952b 'La civilisation de Seine-Oise-Marne en Belgique', *L'Anthropologie* VI, 87–92.

MODDERMAN, P.J.R. 1964 'The neolithic burial vault
at Stein', *Analecta praehistorica Leidensia* I, 3–16.

RAHIR, E. 1928 *Vingt-cinq années de recherches, de res-
taurations et de reconstitutions*, Brussels.

SCHRICKEL, W. 1976 'Die Galeriegrab-Kultur West-
deutschlands. Entstehung, Gliederung und Bezie-
hung zu benachbarten Kulturen' in Schwabedissen,
H. (hrsg.von-) *Die Anfänge des Neolikums von Orient
bis Nordeuropa, Teil V b, Westliches Mittel-Europa*,
188–233.

SCHWELLNUS, W. 1979 *Wartberg-Gruppe und hessische
Megalithik*, Wiesbaden.

8   Chambered Tombs and Non-Megalithic Barrows in Britain

Lionel Masters

To the graves, then, of our earliest ancestors, must
we mainly turn for a knowledge of their history and
of their modes of life; and a careful examination and
comparison of their contents will enable us to arrive
at certain data on which, not only to found theories,
but to build up undying and faultless historical
structures.

Llewellynn Jewitt,
Grave Mounds and their Contents (1870)

THREE DECADES have passed since the publication of
Glyn Daniel's seminal work on *The Prehistoric Chamber Tombs of England and Wales* (1950). Many changes
have occurred since the publication of that work. It
would indeed be surprising if they had not, for an ac-
tive discipline should thrive on changes in perspective
and approach. Two of the more important changes
have been the application of radiocarbon dating, and
the acceptance by many scholars of a more insular
interpretation for the development of prehistoric
cultures in Britain. The former has given us a greatly
extended time-scale for the Neolithic period in Britain
as elsewhere, and the latter has challenged us into considering new approaches in explanation of the origins

and functions of chambered tombs and NM (non-
megalithic) barrows.

Major works of synthesis have appeared since the
publication of *The Prehistoric Chamber Tombs of
England and Wales*. Of outstanding importance is
Henshall's *The Chambered Tombs of Scotland* (1963,
1972), a work to which I have already paid tribute
(Masters 1974). The wealth of detail provided in these
two volumes has greatly facilitated not only the study
of the Scottish monuments, but also from Henshall's
assessment and speculation, the consideration of chambered tombs in general. Sadly, there is still no *corpus* of
chambered tombs for England and Wales, a fact which
must be a disappointment to Glyn Daniel, for he has
championed and encouraged the publication of *corpora*
for other areas (Daniel 1976, 187–9). *Megalithic Enquiries in the West of Britain* (Powell *et al.* 1969) does,
however, provide useful lists of the tombs in North
Wales, the Severn-Cotswold area and the Clyde area,
in addition to the respective authors' detailed considerations of the monuments. The NM series of long
barrows was considered by Ashbee in *The Earthen
Long Barrow in Britain* (1970), and the recent publication of a *corpus* of Neolithic round barrows and ring-
ditches has drawn attention to this less well

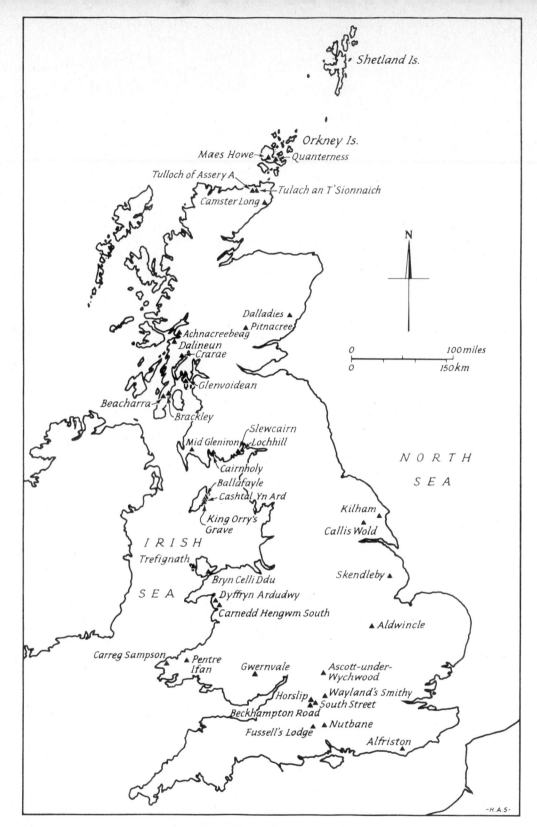

Shetland Is.

Orkney Is.
Maes Howe — Quanterness
Tulloch of Assery A
— Tulach an T'Sionnaich
Camster Long

N

Dalladies
Pitnacree
Achnacreebeag
Dalineun
Crarae

0   100 miles
0   150 km

Glenvoidean

Beacharra
Brackley

NORTH
SEA

Slewcairn
Mid Gleniron — Lochhill

Cairnholy
Ballafayle
— Cashtal Yn Ard
King Orry's
Grave

Kilham
Callis Wold

IRISH

Trefignath

Skendleby

SEA

Bryn Celli Ddu
Dyffryn Ardudwy
Carnedd Hengwm South

Aldwincle

Carreg Sampson
Pentre
Ifan   Gwernvale   Ascott-under-
Wychwood

Horslip   Wayland's Smithy
South Street
Beckhampton Road
Nutbane
Fussell's Lodge   Alfriston

-H.A.S-

1 Map of principal sites mentioned.

documented series of funerary monuments (Kinnes 1979). These works, together with the many excavation reports of chambered tombs and NM barrows, provide the information on which to base an assessment of the origin, function and role of the monuments themselves.

As comprehensive summaries have recently been published of the state of knowledge concerning the Neolithic period in Britain (Smith 1974, 100–36; Ashbee 1978), it is not necessary here to go into detail on the general background. Suffice it to say that the chambered tombs and NM barrows occupy a place in time contemporary with the causewayed enclosures of southern England, and that some monuments must be contemporary with the developing series of stone circles and henge monuments in the latter half of the third millennium BC. In other aspects of material culture, pottery, flint and stone objects of Neolithic date are encountered in both chambered tombs and NM barrows. The significance of such deposits for the understanding of the function of the monuments is discussed later.

One point does, however, demand more detailed consideration. It is generally accepted that the earliest Neolithic in Britain was initiated by people from the continent of Europe. What particular area or areas provided the immediate impetus for settlement in Britain is still a matter for debate. For the initial pioneering phase, Case (1969, 3–27) has cogently argued that the settlers may have brought little of their material culture with them to Britain and Ireland because of the sea journeys involved. He also suggests that the building of large monuments, demanding in terms of communal effort, would not have formed part of the initial colonizing process. This would not rule out the possibility that simple structures were built, some of which may later have been incorporated into monumental mounds. Nor does it rule out the possibility of contact at later stages between established communities in Britain and those of western and northern Europe.

If the arguments put forward by Case are accepted, it makes it all the more difficult to seek a European source for the earliest Neolithic settlers in Britain. In a recent study, Whittle has looked to 'the Linear Pottery culture tradition of the Rhineland and its environs and of northern France . . . as the most likely source of population to have filled Britain from the earlier fourth millennium bc onwards' (1977, 238). General similarities in pottery, flint and stone tools can be demonstrated, as can possible antecedents to the causewayed enclosures. Whilst the characteristic long houses of the Linear Pottery culture have been notoriously absent from Britain, they have frequently been

considered as providing the inspiration behind the form of the NM long barrow. Yet the people of the Linear Pottery culture did not themselves engage in the building of monumental mounds. The question of origins for both chambered tombs and NM barrows in Britain may, therefore, not lie with the initial movements of colonization. Kinnes (1975, 18) has, however, drawn attention to some examples of 'enclosed-space interment', in pits lined and roofed with wood, amongst the flat grave cemetery at the Linear Pottery culture site at Elsloo. It is possible that such unspectacular monuments could provide the basis for the development of the NM series in Britain, and even have formed part of the initial colonization process.

Questions concerning the origin and development of chambered tombs are frequently bound up with the model of the past in current vogue. A general consideration of this is given elsewhere in this volume, but it is necessary here to mention some of the approaches which have a direct effect on the British monuments, for the acceptance or rejection of some of them is of crucial importance to the understanding of origins, developments and function.

Approaches to Interpretation

Piggott (1973, 9–15) has drawn attention to the problems associated with the interpretation of chambered tombs. These may be outlined as questions concerning the nature of the distribution pattern and whether it is the result of independent invention, diffusion or migration, or a combination of two or more of these major determinants of culture change. Tomb typology still looms large in current thinking, though a straightforward linear typology from simple to complex or vice versa may no longer fit the available information. Furthermore, there is the realization that under a term such as 'collective burial' there is a wide variety of modes of deposition, and the questionable assumption that 'grave-goods' represent the personal property of the deceased. At a completely mundane level, the flint knife and the broken pot in a Scottish chambered tomb might represent no more than the detritus of a meal taken in the chamber by a passing traveller sheltering from the cold! I do not make this point too seriously, but it might serve to remind us that, if chambered tombs were left open in the Neolithic period, disturbance of the burial deposit could have taken place for reasons other than the insertion of further burials. The question of dating, and particularly the provenance of samples for radiocarbon dating of chambered tombs, is of crucial importance, and Piggott's strictures on these should be in the minds of every chambered tomb

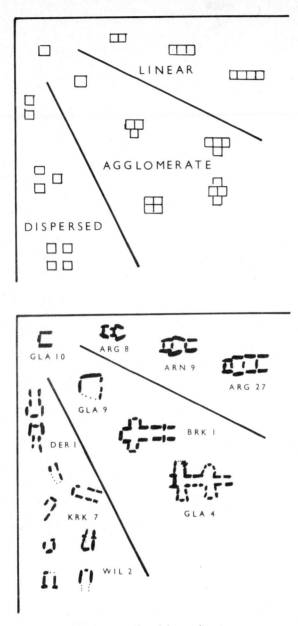

2 (Upper) *Systems of modular combination.*
(Lower) *Modular systems in practice. (After Kinnes.)*

excavator. Finally, there are the questions of function and ritual 'which perhaps by their nature will always remain insoluble' (Piggott 1973, 13). With these important points in mind, we can now turn to consider some of the new approaches to the interpretation of British chambered tombs and NM barrows.

Fleming (1972, 1973) has looked at the question of the design of chambered tombs, and has seen design as the major control for monument typology. He isolates as the main features the requirements of the ritual, the appearance of the monument at varying stages, the number of chambers, and the nature of any pre-existing structures. Adopting a modular approach the wide variety of plans in British chambered tombs can be seen as the combining and recombining of the existing elements in the architect's repertoire. For the Severn-Cotswold tombs, Fleming suggests that the builders 'may already have been engaged in "systems building"' in thinking of forecourts and trapezoidal cairns as modules to be arranged in the most convenient way. On the function of the tombs themselves, Fleming has considered them as 'attention-focussing devices, part of a signalling system designed to reinforce the existing patterns of leadership' (1973, 190).

The concept of modules has been taken up by Kinnes when he puts forward the view that 'A simple scheme of modular manipulation according to need and intent forms a plausible alternative to linear taxonomy *qua* typology' (1975, 19–20). What is envisaged here (ill. 2) is that a simple box-type chamber can be arranged in three grouping patterns – linear, agglomerate and dispersed. By combining the basic box-type chamber in the groupings suggested, it is possible to reproduce many of the varieties of plans of the chambers of chambered tombs without recourse to external influences. Thus a linear grouping would account for the segmented chambers of the Clyde and court cairns, the agglomerate grouping for the transepted Severn-Cotswold tombs and the transepted court cairns, and the dispersed grouping for the laterally chambered tombs in the Severn-Cotswold, Bargrennan and Clyde cairns.

Acceptance of these ideas 'does much to undermine the diffusionist approach to the study of the origins of British types of megalithic tomb' (Fleming 1972, 66), a point echoed by Kinnes (1975, 20). But it might be considered that whilst these ideas have considerable validity, they are as yet still as incapable of proof as the linear typologies which they seek to replace.

A possible relationship between long barrow length in Britain and the length of long houses in the Linear Pottery and Rössen cultures of Europe has been discussed by Reed (1974, 33–57). It is suggested that a doubling of the length and width of long house dimensions is involved in the consideration of long barrow measurements. There is some evidence that a strict adherence to 'length requirements was the rule among long barrow builders' (Reed 1974, 56), and this is used to promulgate the view that particular lengths might be related to discrete groups. On this basis, movement of the group and settlement strategy may be inferred. This is an interesting series of ideas which could, perhaps, be considered in more detail if and when a full series of radiocarbon dates has been obtained from NM long barrows.

Attempts to define territory using the distribution patterns of chambered tombs and long barrows have been made by Ashbee and Renfrew. For southern England, Ashbee (1970, 104–5) has pointed out that in some areas groups of long barrows are associated with one or more causewayed enclosures. In a more recent account he has developed this concept further (Ashbee 1978) and has pointed to the close association between henge monuments and chambered tombs.

The defining of territories on a more limited basis has been attempted by Renfrew for the islands of Arran and Rousay (1973, 132–42; 1979, 13–20, 216–17). The results for Rousay have suggested that each of the thirteen tombs on the island might represent a population of about twenty people, assuming they were all built and used at the same time. Although the radiocarbon dates for the Knowes of Yarso, Rowiegar and Ramsay support the view that they were all in use during the latter half of the third millennium bc, there are no radiocarbon dates for the putative early tombs like Bigland Round, Knowe of Craie or Cobbie Row's Burden. It may also be inappropriate to make estimates of group size for Rousay on the basis of skeletal remains preserved in the Mainland tomb of Quanterness. At this site parts of 157 individuals were recovered from the partially excavated main chamber and one of the six side chambers. The majority of the Rousay cairns have been excavated, admittedly excavated and published (or not published) to widely different standards, but the skeletal evidence ranges from a skull at the Knowe of Craie, two adults at Blackhammer, to the twenty-five individuals at Midhowe and twenty-nine at the Knowe of Yarso. It might, therefore, be necessary to consider that some of the Rousay monuments are not 'equal access' tombs after the manner of Quanterness, with consequent results for any estimate of population.

Although Renfrew has concluded that 'Quanterness housed the dead of a living group, whose numbers at any time may have been some twenty in number' (1979, 172), and also that because there was no differentiation in the age or sex of the people buried in the tomb, that burial was accorded to every member of the group, this does not appear to be the case for other areas of Britain. A study of the burials from NM long barrows led Atkinson to conclude, on the basis of thirty-five excavated sites, that the population represented would range from 1,500 to 3,000 individuals for the whole of the Neolithic period (1968, 86). Kinnes (1975, 25–6) has also considered this question in relation to NM barrows, arriving at a figure of eighty

people at any one time throughout the whole of the long barrow territory. Even allowing for a population explosion, the figure is unlikely to exceed 250. It is concluded that the burial privilege was reserved for a more socially dominant group. Any apparent conflict between the concept of a more hierarchical society in the south of Britain and Renfrew's 'small-scale, autonomous, segmentary societies' lacking 'indications of high rank or prominent status' (1979, 217) for those buried at Quanterness, can be resolved by the simple expedient that different social orders would prevail at different times and in widely separate areas. It could also be resolved by accepting the last of the new approaches mentioned here.

That some groups of chambered tombs and NM barrows should be considered not as burial places for human remains, but as shrines, has been suggested by Case (1973, 193–5). Following the excavation of the pits at Goodland, Co. Antrim, which are considered to have been filled with settlement debris, Case has pointed to the occurrence of similar deposits in some of the Irish court cairns and NM barrows of England. Assuming that settlement debris was associated in the mind of Neolithic man with soil fertility, it is argued that the 'closed foundation deposits' in the court cairn chambers may have been an attempt by magic rites to provide for the needs of the living against the effects of predatory Neolithic farming and consequent soil-deterioration. This hypothesis has been adopted by Ashbee, who would appear to see the majority of chambered tombs and NM barrows, not as mausolea, but as *fana* where dedicatory deposits were made 'as a response to developing soil deterioration' (Ashbee 1978, 85). This is a stimulating hypothesis, and one which deserves careful consideration in the light of the increasing knowledge of the contemporary environment. But I doubt if it provides a *raison d'être* for all chambered tombs, and I hope it will not be misunderstood if I continue to refer to tombs, chambers and burials, rather than to *fana*, repositories and dedicatory deposits.

This account of new approaches to the problems posed by chambered tombs in Britain has involved considerations of tomb typology and challenges to the assumption of linear typological development and to whether chambered tombs are really tombs at all. Such a maelstrom of conflicting hypotheses makes it difficult to see any clear pattern developing amongst the disparate groups of chambered tombs and NM barrows. Nevertheless, in a period of at least one and a half millennia during which these monuments were built and used, it is hardly surprising that ideas concerning their function may well have changed through time, and in response to local needs and circumstances.

It now remains to outline the current state of research and to examine some of the more important results from the large number of excavations which have taken place on both chambered tombs and NM barrows. Obviously such a survey must be selective, but I have tried to indicate those lines of research which seem most profitable for future speculation.

NM Barrows and Cairns

Included in this section are those monuments variously described as 'earthen' or 'unchambered' barrows and cairns which have either proved after excavation to have features similar to those encountered under NM barrows, or can be suspected from fieldwork to belong to this series. Their distribution in Britain is well known, from southern and eastern England to eastern Scotland. From the all too few radiocarbon dates available, they were being built and used throughout the latter half of the fourth millennium and almost all of the third millennium bc (Whittle 1977, 248–9).

A general semblance of unity among the series is provided by the regular occurrence of a long mound, generally trapezoidal in plan, although rectangular and oval plans are also found, the latter recently demonstrated at Alfriston, East Sussex (Drewett 1975). Lengths range from about 18 m to over 120 m, but generally are less than 70 m. The possibility has been put forward 'that differential lengths of Long Barrow were quite deliberate and established according to precise principles' (Reed 1974, 34). Following excavation, the mounds have been shown to cover a wide variety of timber and stone structures. It can also be pointed out that round barrows or cairns can cover structures similar to those found under long mounds (Kinnes 1979).

Following Piggott (1967, 381–93) and Manby (1970, 1–27), three main types of structural feature have been discovered under the mounds. First, there are mortuary structures, generally containing cremated or inhumed bone, pottery, flint, charcoal and, on occasions, dark soil. Second, there are timber enclosures which might be small, as at Nutbane (Morgan 1959, 32–3) or large, as at Fussell's Lodge (Ashbee 1966, 6–7) and Kilham (Manby 1976, 119–23). Finally, there are forebuildings or porches set in line with the mortuary structure, and represented by post holes at Fussell's Lodge (Ashbee 1966, 7), Wayland's Smithy (BRK 1) (Atkinson 1965, 130) and in stone at Lochhill (KRK 14) (Masters 1973, 99).

Not all of these features need occur under any one mound. Indeed some barrows have proved to have none of them, as at Horslip, where only a series of intersecting pits was recorded (Ashbee *et al.* 1979,

207–28). At the nearby barrows of Beckhampton Road and South Street, there were no indications of mortuary structures or burials, but there was evidence from both for the division of the barrows into a number of bays defined by timber fences (Ashbee *et al.* 1979, 228–75). A similar feature has also been found under the Severn-Cotswold long barrow at Ascott-under-Wychwood (OXF 6) (Selkirk 1971, 7–10).

This is not the place to pursue a detailed comparison of all the features found under long barrows, but a few general comments can be made.

The position of mortuary structures is generally at right angles to the proximal end of the barrow, but exceptions to this can be seen at Dalladies (KNC 8) (Piggott 1974) and Skendleby (Phillips 1936), where the mortuary structures are located transversely to the long sides of the barrows. The basic form of the mortuary structure comprises a linear area, generally defined by low banks or stone walls. Pits, which may or may not have held posts, sometimes serve to subdivide the mortuary structure. The presence of posts at some sites has led Ashbee to claim that the basic form of these structures is that of a pitched-roof mortuary house. Objections to such an all-embracing reconstruction have been made (Simpson 1968, 142–4; Ashbee and Simpson 1969, 43–5), and with the objectors the present writer would agree. Piggott's careful analysis of the successive mortuary structures at Dalladies offered no conclusive evidence for a pitched roof. Mortuary structures are generally quite narrow, sometimes less than 2 m in internal width, a factor which could be used to argue against a pitched roof. There is also some evidence to suggest that the posts may pre-date the mortuary structure. At Pitnacree, the first phase was marked by two large posts, but the stone wall of the second phase mortuary structure clearly overlies the cavity of the western phase one post (Coles and Simpson 1965, 39–41). It is considered that the posts of the first phase mortuary structure at Dalladies had rotted away before the second phase structure, with its boulder walls, was built. Kinnes has proposed that a simpler solution to the pitched roof could be provided by a flat roof resting on the flanking banks or walls of the mortuary structure (1975, 19). Nevertheless, Ashbee continues to maintain his position regarding pitched-roof chambers (1978, 70), and this certainly seems to be a convincing reconstruction for Wayland's Smithy I (Atkinson 1965).

The contents of mortuary structures have been shown to be very variable. At Dalladies only a fragment of a child's skull, a cup-marked stone and a plano-convex flint knife were found. It is doubtful in this instance if the structure was used for mortuary purposes, unless the removal of skeletal remains prior to the building of the barrow is invoked. At the other end of the scale is the burial of the disarticulated remains of between fifty-three and fifty-seven individuals in the area covered by the flint cairn at Fussell's Lodge. In Yorkshire, *in situ* cremation deposits have been found at a number of sites including Garton Slack C34, Helperthorpe, Market Weighton, Rudston, Westow and Willerby Wold (Manby 1970, 10). Inhumation burials do occur, as at Kilham (Manby 1976, 113–14) and, on a stone pavement flanked at either end by massive post pits, at the Callis Wold 275 round barrow (Coombs 1976, 130–1).

The timber enclosures found under some mounds as, for example, at Fussell's Lodge and Kilham, have sometimes been assumed to be free-standing enclosures pre-dating the construction of the mound. The proximal end is sometimes marked by more massive timbers, suggesting the presence of a timber façade, analogous with the stone façades of some chambered tomb groups. At Lochhill, a free-standing timber façade has been shown to pre-date the construction of a trapezoidal long cairn and stone façade (Masters 1973, 96–9). In some cases it can be suggested that the free-standing timber enclosure was later used to revet the barrow.

Arrangements of post holes, variously interpreted as porches or forebuildings, have been found at Wayland's Smithy I and Fussell's Lodge. A similar arrangement has also been found in the forecourt of the Severn-Cotswold tomb at Gwernvale (BRE 7) (Britnell 1979, 132–4). These may be compared with the stone-built porch at Lochhill, and it is interesting to speculate that the covered passage at Pitnacree, incompletely excavated because of tree cover, may have been a similar feature. These porches are normally located in line with the mortuary structure and in front of the façade, but the occurrence of 'avenues' of post holes at Kilham and Kemp Howe (Manby 1976, 148; Brewster 1969, 13) may, as Manby suggests, 'be the ultimate development of an entrance approach'.

The final act at these NM barrows can be seen as the construction of a covering mound, the material being derived from flanking quarry ditches in many cases, but also by turf or stones. How long after the construction and use of mortuary structures is not known with any precision, but it has generally been assumed that the enmounding took place after an appreciable lapse of time. Ashbee has even suggested that the long barrows did not assume their final form 'until more than a millennium after the laying down of the foundation deposit' (1978, 97). That the interval was not so long may be suspected from some sites, but the lack of radiocarbon dates from each of the sequences of construction makes it very difficult to offer any convinc-

ing estimate of time-lapse between one stage and the next. A number of stages are clearly involved before the construction of the mound, as can be clearly seen at Nutbane (Morgan 1959), Aldwincle (Jackson 1976) and Kilham (Manby 1976), but less complex monuments also exist, such as the oval barrow at Alfriston covering only two pits, one of which contained a crouched inhumation burial (Drewett 1975, 119–52).

The presence of round barrows in the Neolithic has been known for some time (Piggott 1954, 111–12), but the extent of their presence has recently been demonstrated by Kinnes (1979). From the eighty-eight acceptable Neolithic sites, Kinnes has been able to show that the earlier sites cover features such as crematoria and linear mortuary structures, similar to those found under NM long mounds. Among the later developments, however, is a tendency towards a single-grave tradition with distinctive grave-goods, as at Liff's Low. The important point is made that this development took place well before any beaker presence.

Before concluding this section on the NM monuments, an account can be given of two cairns which clearly belong with the NM series. These sites are situated some 6 km apart in the Stewartry District of Dumfries and Galloway Region.

Excavation at Lochhill (ill. 3) produced evidence for a first phase mortuary structure, consisting of a rectangular trench edged by a low boulder wall, and containing three pits, the end ones of which had held large split tree-trunks, whilst the central pit had held two posts. The mortuary structure contained a burnt plank floor, some small deposits of cremated bone, charcoal, small boulders and dark soil. Associated with the mortuary structure was a timber façade, with four granite orthostats in front forming a porch. The second phase comprised a trapezoidal long cairn, which covered the mortuary structure and timber façade. The cairn was provided with a stone façade, which closely copies the plan of the preceding timber one and was linked to the earlier porch by an additional slab and a panel of dry-walling. Unfortunately, it is not known what interval of time elapsed between the first phase mortuary structure and the building of the cairn. As there were no voids in the cairn above the post pits, the presumption must be that the split timbers had rotted away before the cairn was built. Final activity at the site was marked by the blocking of the forecourt and long cairn walls (Masters 1973, 96–100).

Excavations at Slewcairn (KRK 12) are still in progress, so the account given here must be tentative pending completion of the work (Masters 1973 to 1979). Broadly the same sequence as revealed at Lochhill has been repeated at Slewcairn (ills 3,4). A first phase rectangular mortuary structure contained

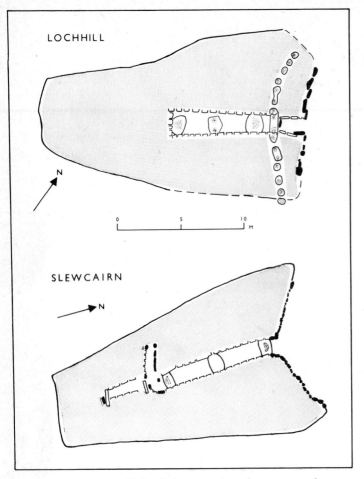

LOCHHILL

SLEWCAIRN

3 Lochhill and Slewcairn: plans of main structural features.

three pits, the outermost of which had held split tree-trunks. The filling of the centre pit proved to be ambiguous, but it may have held two posts in the first phase of its use. The mortuary structure had a filling similar to that at Lochhill, but cremated bone, mostly in the form of minute fragments, was found throughout the length of the structure. Cremated bone was also found in the pits, and it is suggested that the posts had rotted away before the mortuary structure was infilled. No indications of a timber façade have as yet been found, but at the southern end of the mortuary structure there is a setting of vertical stones which might be considered as the equivalent of the porch at Lochhill. When the long cairn was built, these stones were incorporated into a small 'chamber' approached by a passage from the west side of the long cairn. There is, however, one other feature which must be considered to belong to the primary phase. In line with the

mortuary structure, but separated from it by the 'porch' was a paved area bounded by a kerb on its east and west sides, a recumbent block to the north, and a recumbent block and vertical stone over 1 m in height to the south. Scattered over the paving were some sixty sherds of undecorated Neolithic pottery. The major building stage comprised the construction of a trapezoidal long cairn with a concave façade at its north end. Activity within the forecourt area is attested by the finds of over three hundred small sherds of undecorated Neolithic pottery, together with flint scrapers, leaf-shaped arrowheads and knives. Finally, as at Lochhill, the forecourt was blocked and the cairn wall concealed by deliberately placed extra-revetment material.

Taken with the evidence from Dooey's Cairn, Co. Antrim (Evans 1938; Collins 1976) and Ballafayle (Henshall 1978, 172), Lochhill and Slewcairn can be seen as the western outliers of the NM barrow series of eastern and southern Britain.

The Chambered Tombs

It is a daunting task to contemplate the considerable amount of work and speculation which has been undertaken on British chambered tombs within the last decade or so. The perennial problems of chronology, typology and relationships still figure largely in many of the considerations, and changing views are detectable as a reflection of the changing model of the past from one which relied on continental parallels for the monuments to one which sees insular development playing the prominent role. Powell summed up the situation envisaged some three to four decades ago when he wrote 'At that time it was a much discussed working hypothesis that the more elaborate tombs of the British Isles stood at the head of an introduced building tradition for which there existed very general comparisons in "Atlantic Europe"' (1973, 33). Today the general mood is to reverse such a proposition, and to see within the various tomb groups a sequence which begins with simple structures and develops towards more elaborate monuments. Such a process can be illustrated by the sequence proposed for the Maes Howe group. In Piggott's (1954, 245) scheme, followed by Henshall (1963, 131; 1972, 238; 1974, 155), Maes Howe itself is seen as the prototype. Two lines of development are envisaged leading to a slackening of the general plan of the prototype on the one hand, and to a multiplicity of side chambers on the other. Henshall sees a possible origin for the group in the Irish cruciform passage graves (1972, 283; 1974, 155). Renfrew envisages a different situation in which relatively simple tombs are the earliest monuments,

4 Slewcairn: façade and mortuary structure from north. (Photo C. Provan.)

followed by a local evolutionary pattern towards stalled cairns in one direction, and his Quanterness-Quoyness group in the other. Maes Howe is seen as the end of the sequence within the Quanterness-Quoyness group. Despite the radiocarbon dates used to support this sequence, the beginning of it rests on the fact that Renfrew 'implicitly accepts that the Orkney tombs of the Orkney-Cromarty class (such as Bigland Round, Sandyhills Smithy and the Knowe of Craie) are part of a tomb building tradition brought to Orkney by the first Neolithic colonists' (1979, 210), a belief for which there is as yet no absolute proof, but seems reasonable in the light of present-day thought. Thus the sequence has been reversed and, at first sight, the 'foreign' connections dismissed. But Renfrew does leave open the possibility of contact between Orkney and Ireland when he writes 'Some scholars have wished to see a connection between the two groups, and this seems perfectly possible' (1979, 210).

This example could be repeated for virtually all the major tomb groups in Britain, and illustrates very well the dilemmas still surrounding questions of origin and development. Chronological problems of a detailed nature cannot as yet be solved by the available radiocarbon dates. Too many of them are, for quite valid

reasons, related either to pre-monument activity, or to the use of the chambers, rather than to the construction of the monument. All that can safely be said is that chambered tombs in Britain were being built and used from towards the end of the fourth millennium to the end of the third millennium BC.

The problems of local development and imported influences can be illustrated by reference to the Clyde group. In his detailed study of these monuments in south-west Scotland, Scott (1969, 175–222) postulated that the earliest were simple closed-box chambers (protomegaliths) set in minimal cairns. This was followed by elaboration at one end to produce an entrance with a pair of portal stones, and later still a second pair of stones could be added to form a two-compartment chamber divided by a septal slab. The next major stage sees the introduction, possibly from the Severn-Cotswold region, of trapezoidal cairns with flat façades. Later developments include more concave façades, an increase in the length of the chamber and its division by septal stones, and finally, influences

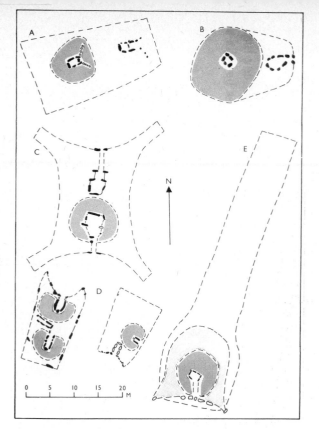

5 *Excavated multi-period chambered tombs in Britain*
(after Corcoran):
A *Dyffryn Ardudwy*
B *Achnacreebeag*
C *Tulloch of Assery A*
D *Mid Gleniron I and II*
E *Tulach an-t' Sionnaich*

from Irish court cairns, detectable in the 'dual court' cairn at Barmore Wood (ARG 9) and in the jambs and septal slabs at such sites as Achnagoul II (ARG 8). The sequence is supported to some extent by the pottery evidence and by Scott's own excavations at Brackley (ARG 28), Crarae (ARG 11) and Beacharra (ARG 27) (1958, 22–54; 1963, 1–27; 1964, 134–58). The excavation of the Mid Gleniron cairns (WIG 1, 2) could also be used to support the sequence, for it is claimed that the long cairns at these sites were added to pre-existing chambers set in minimal cairns (Corcoran 1969a, 29–90).

Leaving aside for the moment the subject of multi-period tombs, Scott has used the evidence of the Clyde sequence to reinterpret the rather unusual plan of Cairnholy I (KRK 2) (1969, 193–5; excavation: Piggott and Powell 1951, 103–23). According to Scott, the first phase could comprise the closed inner compart-

ment with its tall end-stones, to be followed by the addition of the first one, and then another pair of tall stones to form an outer compartment. The final phase would see the building of the long cairn and slightly concave façade. But it would also be possible to see Cairnholy I as a megalithic version of the mortuary structure and porch at Lochhill, with the tall stones of the closed chamber recalling the wooden posts at either end of the Lochhill mortuary structure, and the outer compartment of the Cairnholy I chamber fulfilling a role similar to the porch at Lochhill. As it is considered that the trapezoidal cairn at Lochhill formed part of the original design plan, the same might apply to Cairnholy I. I do not wish to press this point too strongly, for further excavation would be necessary to solve these differences in conjecture. I do, however, use it as an illustration of the differences in view between those who see multi-period sites developing in distinct stages, not necessarily related directly to each other, and those who see multi-period as merely the planned stages in a unitary design, analogous with the situation envisaged for NM sites like Nutbane and Aldwincle (Kinnes 1975, 19).

Some of the more recent hypotheses on the origin and development of tomb groups have, however, been based on the premise that multi-period tombs reached their final form as the result of one or more distinct, and not necessarily related, additional building phases to an original monument. The evidence was conveniently summarized by Corcoran (1972, 31–63) and by Henshall (1974, 137–64), so only a brief statement is necessary here with the addition of a few more recent examples.

Excavations by Corcoran (ill. 5) at Tulach an-t' Sionnaich (CAT 58) and Tulloch of Assery A (CAT 69), together with the evidence from the two cairns at Mid Gleniron (WIG 1, 2), led him to suggest that the monuments had reached their final form as the result of a number of distinct building phases (1967, 1–34; 1969a, 29–90). It should be noted that the evidence for Tulloch of Assery A being a multi-period site is not considered in the original excavation report, but in Corcoran's later consideration of multi-period tombs in general (1972, 34). Taken with the evidence from Dyffryn Ardudwy (MER 3) (Powell 1973, 1–49), what seems to be involved is the encapsulation by means of a long cairn of earlier simple chambers set in minimal cairns. Evidence for addition to an original cairn is provided by the site of Achnacreebeag (ARG 37), where a round cairn with a closed chamber was subsequently enlarged to accommodate a small passage grave (Ritchie 1973, 31–55). At Dalineun (ARG 3), however, Ritchie was able to show that a large cist, visible in the cairn to the south-west of a small Clyde type chamber, was a secondary insertion into the cairn (1974, 48–62).

To this collection of sites, together with the clear evidence for two periods at Wayland's Smithy (Atkinson 1965, 126–33), we can now add information from Camster Long (CAT 12) (ill. 6). At the time of his death, Corcoran had excavated most of the northeastern half of the cairn, in which are situated the two known passages and chambers. The present writer has now assumed responsibility for the rest of the excavation (Masters 1978, 453–4, 459). Corcoran's work has shown that the simple polygonal passage grave was originally enclosed within a circular cairn, bounded by a well-built dry-stone wall a little over 1 m in height (ill. 7). The round cairn wall meets the passage at a point where the latter takes a slight bend to the right. This change in passage alignment is further emphasized by a pair of orthostats set into the dry-walling of the passage indicating, perhaps, the original entrance to the tomb. As access was still required to the chamber, the building of the long cairn involved a lengthening of the passage by some 6 m. The second chamber at Camster Long belongs to the classic Camster type as defined by Henshall (1963, 69–70). There are hints from Anderson's excavation that this chamber was also enclosed within a round cairn (Anderson 1870, 484), but further investigation will have to take place before this point can be resolved.

Brief notes of work at Trefignath (ANG 1) have indicated that this is a most interesting multi-period site

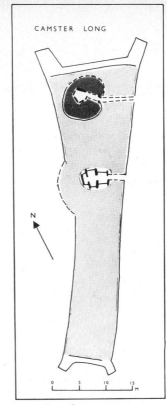

6 Plan of Camster Long.

7 Camster: round cairn enclosing simple passage-grave, from west; wall of long cairn in foreground. (Photo Crown Copyright Reserved.)

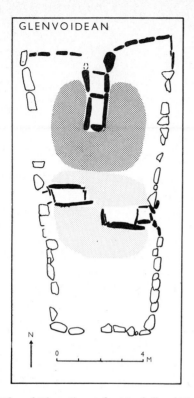

8 Plan of Glenvoidean (after Marshall and Taylor).

chamber. Still within the primary phase, a pair of tall portal stones may have been added to the north end of the chamber to form a porch. A second phase is represented by the two lateral chambers, enclosed within a separate oval cairn which abuts the earlier one. It is suggested that the lateral chambers may have started as simple closed structures, to which were added pairs of stones to form porches, and then with the addition of end-stones, outer compartments. The third phase comprised the incorporation of these earlier structures by a trapezoidal long cairn, and within this phase a second pair of stones, one represented now only by a hole, may have been added to the axial chamber to form an outer compartment opening from the centre of the façade. Such a sequence, if accepted, would support Scott's sequence of development for the Clyde cairns (Scott 1969, 175–222). But the excavators emphasize that 'it is very difficult to determine the chronological sequence for the various stages', and they themselves stress that no great period of time need have elapsed between the first and second stages (Marshall and Taylor 1979, 14).

In the absence of a radiocarbon sequence for any of the composite tombs mentioned, considerations of whether the various features form part of a single design plan, or whether they are separate and distinct entities conceptually unrelated to the additions which follow, is something which has to be decided on the basis of the excavation evidence. At the moment, there seems to be no easy way of solving this dilemma, and personally held views will sway the evidence one way or another. In my own view, the evidence from Camster Long is strongly indicative of a situation in which the simple passage grave was built without there being any intention of enclosing it within a long mound. I suspect that the same situation may have prevailed at Mid Gleniron I, but I am not so sure about Glenvoidean. The excavators rightly stress the tentative nature of their interpretation and, apart from the pitching of the cairn stones, I can see little evidence for three distinct phases at this site. The Scottish legal verdict of 'not proven' may be appropriate in this case.

I have considered in some detail the subject of multiperiod sites, for they have become a dominant theme for some writers on chambered tombs. Henshall has, perhaps, made most of the opportunities provided by considering that the final appearance of the monuments was the result of different building phases (Henshall 1972, 198–264). On the basis of fieldwork, sometimes supported by evidence from earlier excavations, it can be suggested that sites such as Oban nam Fiadh (UST 25), Rudh' an Dunain (SKY 7), Ormiegill (CAT 42) and Vementry (ZET 45) may be multiphase in development. In a recent study of the Isle of

(Smith 1978, 445; 1979, 340). Formerly classified by Lynch as a long grave (1969, 296), it can now be seen that the western group of stones are the remains of a simple passage grave contained within a circular cairn. The next stage was marked by the construction of a portal dolmen to the east, and set in a wedge-shaped cairn, which also incorporated the cairn of the passage-grave. Provision was made, however, for continued access to the passage-grave chamber. Blocking of the forecourt area of the portal dolmen was subsequently removed and a second portal dolmen was constructed in the forecourt of the first. The second portal dolmen was contained within an extension of the wedge-shaped cairn. Lynch's percipient comment that 'the possibility that Trefignath is a composite monument, with chambers juxtaposed over a period of time' (1969, 114) has proved to be correct.

Finally, the evidence for multi-period construction at Glenvoidean (ill. 8) (BUT 1) may be considered (Marshall and Taylor 1979, 1–39). The excavators suggest that the primary monument here was the northern closed chamber, set in its own round cairn. A radiocarbon date of 2910 ± 115 bc (I–5974) was obtained from burnt material under the west slab of this

Man tombs, Henshall has put forward evidence for different building phases at King Orry's Grave and Cashtal yn Ard (1978, 171–6), and Lynch has considered that the cairn at Pentre Ifan might be of two-period construction, the enlargement of the cairn occurring when the façade was added to the portal dolmen (1972, 70–7). A similar situation may have prevailed at Carnedd Hengwm South (MER 6) (Lynch 1976, 69).

Henshall has recently stated that she regards 'all tombs as multi-period constructions, believing that most eccentric plans are due to difficulties of adapting or incorporating earlier structures in later additions', and also that 'there is plenty of evidence, once it is looked for, that this is a valid line of enquiry' (1974, 143). Not everyone would agree that all tombs are even potentially multi-period, but the line of enquiry is certainly valid, bearing in mind the difficulties of interpretation at unexcavated and often ruined sites.

If any general conclusions are to be reached concerning the earliest chambered tombs in Britain, it appears that present opinion would suggest that the earliest examples are simple structures. Into this category can be placed the simple box-like chambers set in minimal cairns. Portal dolmens might also be considered to be early in date on the basis of the pottery found in the forecourt pit of the western chamber at Dyffryn Ardudwy. Although the origins of the portal dolmen are by no means clear, it can be postulated that it could be derived from the simple box-like chambers, with which they share a similar concept of enclosed space burial. Irish evidence might appear to be in conflict with an early date for portal dolmens, if the accepted derivation of this type of monument from the lateral chambers of court cairns is accepted (de Valera and Ó Nulláin 1972, 162–8). This view has now been challenged by Flanagan, who would prefer to see court cairns and portal dolmens 'treated as a continuum instead of two distinct types' (1977, 26).

By using the evidence from Scottish multi-period sites, and the early Neolithic pottery from Carreg Sampson, Lynch (1975, 25–35) has suggested that passage graves with small polygonal chambers and short passages might be considered as early in date. The group, if indeed it can be called a group, has a widespread distribution from southern Brittany to the north of Scotland, and would include such sites as Broadsands, Devon Ty Newydd (ANG 3) and Camster Long (CAT 12).

Subsequent developments in many of the tomb groups seems to proceed towards elaboration of the chambers, and takes such diverse forms as segmented chambers in the Clyde group, tripartite and stalled chambers in the Orkney-Cromarty group, and transepted chambers in the Severn-Cotswold group. The problem of the origin of the long cairn, common to all three groups, is still not resolved, but it is still possible to look to the trapezoidal long barrows of the NM series as a possible progenitor.

The more elaborate passage graves, such as Barclodiad y Gawres (ANG 4) (Powell and Daniel, 1956) and Bryn Celli Ddu (ANG 7) (Hemp 1930, 179–214) can then be seen as later Neolithic monuments related to the Irish cruciform tombs of the Boyne Valley. At the latter site, a late date is indicated for it has been demonstrated that the tomb post-dates a henge monument (O'Kelly 1969, 17–48). The radiocarbon dates from the ditch at Maes Howe would also indicate a late date for this monument.

That we are still unable to offer a more precise picture of the development of the tomb groups is a measure of our ignorance of the chronology and human motivation behind the development of the tomb series. Nevertheless, further fieldwork analysis and excavation, together with sequences of radiocarbon dates, may resolve some of these problems and enable us to see more clearly the history of the various chambered tomb groups.

Origins

Any attempt to seek origins for the NM and chambered tombs of Britain is bound to be bedevilled with difficulties and we can only point to various possibilities.

In the present climate of thought, waves of colonists from Europe introducing various types of chamber plan are less acceptable now than they were three or four decades ago. Acceptance for Britain of a model which emphasizes insular and localized developments during the Neolithic period, following an initial colonization from Europe, still leaves the problem of accounting for the observed similarities in monument plan and function over wide areas of western and northern Europe. Recourse to the transmission of ideas, unaccompanied by archaeologically significant movements of people, or the acceptance of a view that people faced with similar problems will react in broadly similar ways are two constructive lines of approach. Alternatively, consideration can be given to MacKie's version of modified diffusionism, and accept that the passage graves of western Europe, the rite of collective burial, and knowledge of practical astronomy and geometry were disseminated by a professional priesthood. Basing his hypothesis on Darlington's *The Evolution of Man and Society* (1968), MacKie envisages that his professional priesthood may have been formed in Iberia 'due to the genetic and cultural mixing of two or more different ethnic groups of talented people', or even

109

that the priesthood was brought to Iberia 'perhaps from the proto-urban societies of the Near East' (1977, 191). Whatever one's views of MacKie's hypothesis, there is the awesome spectre of Childe's megalithic missionaries returning once more, in different guise, to western Europe.

Whichever hypothesis, or series of hypotheses, is taken to account for the distribution of the chambered tombs and NM barrows, we are still likely to conclude, as Daniel did, by saying that 'in the absence of written evidence we may go on arguing for ever about the historical role of the megalith builders' (1958, 125). It seems reasonable, however, still to think of two broad traditions – that of the NM barrows of northern Europe, and of the chambered tombs of western Europe, which was the position envisaged by Daniel (1967, 313–17).

For the British NM series, many scholars have looked to the North European Plain as a source of origin (Piggott 1955, 96–101; 1961, 557–74; 1967, 381–93; Ashbee 1970, 87–99; Jazdzewski 1973, 63–74), but chronological difficulties, as well as significant differences in material culture, precluded a derivation of the British series from one specific European source. Recent excavations in Denmark have added greatly to our information, and these have been summarized by Madsen (1979, 301–20). Three basic groups are distinguished. The first comprises the gabled and ridge-roof mortuary houses of Konens Høj type, for which there are now between fourteen and sixteen examples. The Troelstrup type consists of rectangular mortuary structures built entirely of wood, or a combination of wood and stone. The third group is characterized by earth graves. Long covering mounds have also been recognized, generally rectangular in plan, but with some trapezoidal examples. The similarities of the Danish examples with the British series can be summarized as a common interest in an east-west orientation of the mound, timber façades and palisade enclosures, transverse rows of poles sectioning the barrows, and mortuary structures. Differences there certainly are, such as the position and number of the mortuary structures and in the burial rite, but the plans of some of the sites, Bygholm Nørromark for example, might not look out of place in the southern British Neolithic. Radiocarbon dates at present available would place some of the monuments in the first half of the third millennium bc, contemporary with the British series. Madsen concludes that the similarities seen in the long barrows of northern Europe are 'the result of structurally similar solutions to religious, ritual and sociopolitical problems' (1979, 319).

The passage graves of western Europe present similar problems of interpretation to those posed by the NM series. Iberia and Brittany can be considered as potential areas of origin on the basis of TL dates for Portuguese examples (Whittle and Arnaud 1975, 5–24) and early fourth millennium bc radiocarbon dates for some Breton passage graves. The two areas need not be connected, however, and both could have had separate origins and developments. It may be possible, as Whittle has suggested (1977, 221), to introduce into Britain those simple passage graves with short passages, although the dating evidence for this is slight, as Lynch has demonstrated (1975, 25–35).

Within Britain it is still possible to offer, with varying degrees of conviction, a whole set of different ideas to account for the various tomb groups. To take but one example, it could still be maintained that the transepted terminal chamber plan in the Severn-Cotswold group was derived from progenitors in the southern Morbihan and the mouth of the River Loire (Daniel 1939, 143–65; 1950, 158). The difficulties over a 'foreign' origin for the trapezoidal cairn could be resolved by accepting influences from the British NM series (Piggott 1962, 59–64). These hypotheses were accepted by Corcoran, who developed the foreign influences theme even further by suggesting that the Severn-Cotswold lateral chambers could be derived from the passage graves of the Hérault, and that more locally, blind entrances were derived from the frontal appearance of portal dolmens. Thus for Corcoran, the Severn-Cotswold group was the result of 'an amalgam of external influences' (1969b, 102). But the present climate of thought would see the Severn-Cotswold group and the NM series as 'expressions of the same set of ideas' with parallel developments and 'adaptation of one kind of idea to suit local needs' (Whittle 1977, 218).

Similar situations could be postulated for almost all the major tomb groups in Britain. Chronological difficulties, differing views on the nature of Neolithic society, and judgments as to whether independent invention, diffusion or migration, should be held to account for the appearance of the monuments in space and time, will inevitably lead to the many views seeking to account for their origin, role and function.

In writing this essay I recall with pleasure the hours spent as an undergraduate discussing with Glyn Daniel the chambered tombs of western Europe. That we have not yet constructed Llewellynn Jewitt's 'undying and faultless historical structures' will come as no surprise to him!

Bibliography

ANDERSON, J. 1870 'On the Horned Cairns of Caithness: their Structural Arrangements, Contents of Chambers &c', *Proc.Soc.Antiq.Scot.* VII, 480–512.

ASHBEE, P. 1966 'The Fussell's Lodge Long Barrow Excavations 1957', *Archaeologia* C, 1–80.

1970 *The Earthern Long Barrow in Britain*, London.

1978 *The Ancient British*, Norwich.

ASHBEE, P. AND SIMPSON, D. D. A. 1969 'Timber Mortuary Houses and Earthen Long Barrows Again', *Antiquity* XLIII, 43–5.

ASHBEE, P., SMITH, I. F. AND EVANS, J. G. 1979 'Excavation of Three Long Barrows near Avebury, Wiltshire', *Proc. Preh. Soc.* XLV, 207–300.

ATKINSON, R. J. C. 1965 'Wayland's Smithy', *Antiquity* XXXIX, 126–33.

1968 'Old Mortality: Some Aspects of Burial and Population in Neolithic England', in Coles, J. M. and Simpson, D. D. A. (eds) *Studies in Ancient Europe*, Leicester, 83–93.

BREWSTER, T. C. M. 1969 'Kemp Howe', in *Archaeological Excavations*, 1968, 13.

BRITNELL, W. 1979 'The Gwernvale Long Cairn, Powys', *Antiquity* LIII, 132–4.

CASE, H. 1969 'Settlement-patterns in the North Irish Neolithic', *Ulster J. Archaeol.,* 32, 3–27.

1973 'A Ritual Site in North-East Ireland', in Daniel, G. and Kjaerum, P. (eds) *Megalithic Graves and Ritual*, Copenhagen, 173–96.

COLES, J. M. AND SIMPSON, D. D. A. 1965 'The Excavation of a Neolithic Round Barrow at Pitnacree, Perthshire, Scotland', *Proc. Preh. Soc.* XXXI, 34–57.

COLLINS, A. E. P. 1976 'Dooey's Cairn, Ballymacaldcrack, County Antrim', *Ulster J. Archaeol.* 39, 1–7.

COOMBS, D. 1976 'Callis Wold Round Barrow, Humberside', *Antiquity* L, 130–1.

CORCORAN, J. X. W. P. 1967 'Excavation of Three Chambered Cairns at Loch Calder, Caithness', *Proc. Soc. Antiq. Scot.* XCVIII, 1–75.

1969a 'Excavation of Two Chambered Cairns at Mid Gleniron Farm, Glenluce, Wigtownshire', *Trans. Dumfriesshire Galloway Natur. Hist. Antiq. Soc.* XLVI, 29–90.

1969b 'The Cotswold-Severn Group', in Powell, T. G. E. (ed.) *Megalithic Enquiries in the West of Britain*, Liverpool, 13–104.

1972 'Multi-Period Construction and the Origins of the Chambered Long Cairn in Western Britain and Ireland', in Lynch, F. and Burgess, C. (eds) *Prehistoric Man in Wales and the West*, Bath, 31–63.

DANIEL, G. E. 1939 'The Transepted Gallery Graves of Western France', *Proc. Preh. Soc.* V, 143–65.

1950 *The Prehistoric Chamber Tombs of England and Wales*, Cambridge.

1958 *The Megalithic Builders of Western Europe*, London.

1967 'Northmen and Southmen', *Antiquity* XLI, 313–17.

1976 'Megaliths Galore', *Antiquity* L, 187–9.

DE VALERA, R. AND Ó NUALLÁIN, S. 1972 *Survey of the Megalithic Tombs of Ireland*, III, Dublin.

DREWETT, P. 1975 'The Excavation of an Oval Burial Mound of the Third Millennium bc at Alfriston, East Sussex, 1974', *Proc. Preh Soc.* XLI, 119–52.

EVANS, E. E. 1938 'Doey's Cairn, Dunloy, County Antrim', *Ulster J. Archaeol.* I, 59–78.

FLANAGAN, L. N. W. 1977 'Court Graves and Portal Graves', *Ir. Archaeol. Res. Forum* IV (Part 1), 23–9.

FLEMING, A. 1972 'Vision and Design: Approaches to Ceremonial Monument Typology', *Man* VII, 57–73.

1973 'Tombs for the Living', *Man* VIII, 177–93.

HEMP, W. J. 1930 'The Chambered Cairn of Bryn Celli Ddu', *Archaeologia* LXXX,179–214.

HENSHALL, A. S. 1963 *The Chambered Tombs of Scotland*, vol. 1, Edinburgh.

1972 *The Chambered Tombs of Scotland*, vol. 2, Edinburgh.

1974 'Scottish Chambered Tombs and Long Mounds', in Renfrew, C. (ed.) *British Prehistory: A New Outline*, London, 137–64.

1978 'Manx Megaliths Again; An Attempt at Structural Analysis', in Davey, P. (ed.) *Man and Environment in the Isle of Man,* Brit. Archaeol. Rep. 54 (i), Oxford, 171–6.

JACKSON, D. A. 1976 'The Excavation of Neolithic and Bronze Age Sites at Aldwincle, Northants, 1967–71', *Northamptonshire Archaeol.* XI, 12–70.

JAZDZEWSKI, K. 1973 'The Relationship between Kujavian Barrows in Poland and Megalithic Tombs in Northern Germany, Denmark and Western European Countries', in Daniel G. and Kjaerum, P. (eds) *Megalithic Graves and Ritual*, Copenhagen, 63–74.

KINNES, I. 1975 'Monumental Function in British Neolithic Burial Practices', *World Archaeol.* VII, 16–29.

1979 'Round Barrows and Ring-ditches in the British Neolithic', *Brit. Mus. Occasional Paper,* 7.

LYNCH, F. 1969 'The Megalithic Tombs of North Wales', in Powell, T. G. E. (ed.) *Megalithic Enquiries in the West of Britain*, Liverpool, 107–48.

1972 'Portal Dolmens in the Nevern Valley, Pembrokeshire', in Lynch, F. and Burgess, C. (eds) *Prehistoric Man in Wales and the West*, Bath, 67–84.

1975 'Excavations at Carreg Sampson Megalithic Tomb, Mathry, Pembrokeshire', *Archaeol. Cambrensis* CXXIV, 15–35.

1976 'Towards a Chronology of Megalithic Tombs in Wales', in Boon, G. C. and Lewis, J. M. (eds) *Welsh Antiquity, Essays Presented to H. N. Savory*, Cardiff, 63–79.

MacKie, E. 1977 *The Megalith Builders*, London.

Madsen, T. 1979 'Earthen Long Barrows and Timber Structures: Aspects of the Early Neolithic Mortuary Practice in Denmark', *Proc. Preh. Soc.* XLV, 301–20.

Manby, T. G. 1970 'Long Barrows of Northern England; Structural and Dating Evidence', *Scot. Archaeol. Forum* II, 1–27.

1976 'Excavation of the Kilham Long Barrow, East Riding of Yorkshire', *Proc. Preh. Soc.* XLII, 111–59.

Marshall, D. N. and Taylor, I. D. 1979 'The Excavation of the Chambered Cairn at Glenvoidean, Isle of Bute', *Proc. Soc. Antiq. Scot.* CVIII, 1–39.

Masters, L. J. 1973 'The Lochhill Long Cairn', *Antiquity* XLVII, 96–100.

1973–9 'Slewcairn' in *Discovery and Excavation in Scotland*.

1974 'The Chambered Tombs of Scotland', *Antiquity* XLVIII, 34–9.

1978 'Camster Long Chambered Cairn', in Department of the Environment Summary Reports, *Proc. Preh. Soc.* XLIV, 453–4, 459.

Morgan, F. de M. The Excavation of a Long Barrow at Nutbane, Hants.', *Proc. Preh. Soc.* XXV, 15–51.

O'Kelly, C. 1969 'Bryn Celli Ddu, Anglesey: A Reinterpretation', *Archaeol. Cambrensis* CXVIII, 17–48.

Phillips, C. W. 1936 'The Excavation of the Giant's Hills Long Barrow, Skendleby, Lincs.', *Archaeologia* LXXXV, 37–106.

Piggott, S. 1954 *The Neolithic Cultures of the British Isles*, Cambridge.

1955 'Windmill Hill – East or West?' *Proc. Preh. Soc.* XXI, 96–101.

1961 'The British Neolithic Cultures in their Continental Setting', in *L'Europe à la fin de l'âge de la pierre*, Prague, 557–74.

1962 *The West Kennet Long Barrow: Excavations 1955–56*, London.

1967 '"Unchambered" Long Barrows in Neolithic Britain', *Palaeohistoria* XII, 381–93.

1973 'Problems in the Interpretation of Chambered Tombs', in Daniel, G. and Kjaerum, P. (eds) *Megalithic Graves and Ritual*, Copenhagen, 9–15.

1974 'Excavation of the Dalladies Long Barrow, Fettercairn, Kincardineshire', *Proc. Soc. Antiq. Scot.* CIV, 23–47.

Piggott, S. and Powell, T. G. E. 1951 'The Excavation of Three Neolithic Chambered Tombs in Galloway, 1949', *Proc. Soc. Antiq. Scot.* LXXXIII, 103–61.

Powell, T. G. E. 1969 (ed.) *Megalithic Enquiries in the West of Britain*, Liverpool.

1973 'Excavation of the Megalithic Chambered Cairn at Dyffryn Ardudwy, Merioneth, Wales', *Archaeologia* CIV, 1–49.

Powell, T. G. E. and Daniel, G. E. 1956 *Barclodiad y Gawres*, Liverpool.

Reed, R. C. 1974 'Earthen Long Barrows; A New Perspective', *Archaeol. J.* CXXXI, 33–57.

Renfrew, A. C. 1973 *Before Civilization*, London.

1979 *Investigations in Orkney*, Reports of the Research Committee of the Society of Antiquaries of London, no. 38, London.

Ritchie, J. N. G. 1973 'Excavation of the Chambered Cairn at Achnacreebeag', *Proc. Soc. Antiq. Scot.* CII, 31–55.

1974 'Excavation of a Chambered Cairn at Dalineun, Lorn, Argyll', *Proc. Soc. Antiq. Scot.* CIV, 48–62.

Scott, J. G. 1958 'The Chambered Cairn at Brackley, Kintyre', *Proc. Soc. Antiq. Scot.* LXXXIX, 22–54.

1963 'The Excavation of a Chambered Cairn at Crarae, Loch Fyneside, Mid Argyll', *Proc. Soc. Antiq. Scot.* XCIV, 1–27.

1964 'The Chambered Cairn at Beacharra, Kintyre, Argyll, Scotland', *Proc. Preh. Soc.* XXX, 134–58.

1969 'The *Clyde* Cairns of Scotland', in Powell, T. G. E. (ed.) *Megalithic Enquiries in the West of Britain*, Liverpool, 175–222.

Selkirk, A. 1971 'Ascott-under-Wychwood', *Curr. Archaeol.* XXIV, 7–10.

Simpson, D. D. A. 1968 'Timber Mortuary Houses and Earthen Long Barrows', *Antiquity* XLII, 142–4.

Smith, C. 1978 'Trefignath Burial Chambers, Holyhead, Anglesey', in Department of the Environment Summary Reports, *Proc. Preh. Soc.* XLIV, 445.

1979 'Trefignath Burial Chambers, Holyhead, Anglesey', in Department of the Environment Summary Reports, *Proc. Preh. Soc.* XLV, 340.

Smith, I. F. 1974 'The Neolithic' in Renfrew, C. (ed.) *British Prehistory: A New Outline*, London, 100–36.

Whittle, A. W. R. 1977 *The Earlier Neolithic of Southern England and its Continental Background*, Brit. Archaeol. Rep. Suppl. Ser. 35, Oxford.

Whittle, E. H. and Arnaud, J. M. 1975 'Thermoluminescent Dating of Neolithic and Chalcolithic Pottery from Sites in Central Portugal', *Archaeometry* XVII, 5–24.

9　The Megalithic Tombs of Ireland

Michael J. O'Kelly

I DOUBT if Glyn Daniel remembers our first meeting. It was when he and Terence Powell were on a visit to Seán P. Ó Ríordáin in Cork. I had just begun to study archaeology but knew absolutely nothing of the subject at the time and I was very impressed by the fact that two Cambridge students should deign to visit Cork! I have no very clear memory now either of that visit except that they would not look at anything that was not a megalithic tomb. Time mellowed them both and when they were back in Ireland after the war, they were very ready to look at many things that were not megalithic! I was involved with them again at the excavation of Barclodiad y Gawres and they both many times visited my Newgrange excavations which began in 1962; various pieces about it have appeared in *Antiquity* over the years since. I have benefited so much from my continuous contact and association with Professor Daniel that it gives me the greatest pleasure to contribute this piece on the megalithic tombs of Ireland to a *Festschrift* that he so well deserves.

Since the 1930s, Irish megalithic tombs have attracted much attention and several archaeologists have devoted themselves to their particular study. Early in the field were Professor Daniel himself as well as his fellow student the late Professor Terence Powell. In the north of Ireland Professor Estyn Evans, Oliver Davies and the late Dr John Corcoran contributed mightily to the study as also did the late Professor Seán P. Ó Ríordáin in the south. In more recent times a new generation has taken over the field and contributions have been made by Pat Collins, the late Dudley Waterman and Lawrence Flanagan in Belfast. In Dublin, the leading scholar of the new generation has been the late Professor Ruaidhrí de Valera who devoted his whole archaeological working life from his student days to his untimely death in 1978 to an intensive study of the tombs, and while he was Archaeology Officer at the Ordnance Survey, initiated the official survey of the megalithic tombs of Ireland. Because of all this, de Valera's influence on the course the research has taken has been very great and his lines of thought have been accepted by his co-workers and students. They in turn have made their own considerable contributions and amongst them are the works of Dr Seán Ó Nualláin, who in 1957 succeeded to the post in the Ordnance Survey when de Valera became professor in University

College, Dublin. Dr Michael Herity of the same College, also much influenced by de Valera, has dealt with aspects of the portal– and wedge-tombs and has published a major study of the passage-tombs. The art of the passage-tombs has been studied comprehensively by Dr Elizabeth Twohig of University College, Cork, and the Boyne Valley art in particular by Claire O'Kelly. Professor George Eogan, UCD, has also contributed to this aspect in connection with his excavations at Knowth, Co. Meath.

In what I have written here, I have made constant reference to and use of the published work of all these writers and I thank them, one and all not only for their writings, but for information freely given over a long number of years. It is inevitable that different interpretations can be put upon the same archaeological evidence and as will be seen below, my views differ from those of my friends and colleagues in various ways. I trust that they will find my views as interesting as I have found theirs, even when I have drawn as long a bow of speculation as they have done.

The survey of the megalithic tombs of Ireland has been in progress for twenty years and the fieldwork is now well nigh completed. The work has been done by the late Professor Ruaidhrí de Valera of University College, Dublin and by Dr Seán Ó Nualláin, Archaeology Officer to the Ordnance Survey. So far, three volumes have been published and others are in preparation. Since the recent and lamented death of Professor de Valera, the work is being continued by his collaborator, Dr Ó Nualláin, who hopes to bring it all to a successful published conclusion during the next seven or eight years. Volume I (1961) dealt with the tombs of Co. Clare, Volume II (1964) with those of Co. Mayo and Volume III (1972) with those of the counties of Galway, Roscommon, Leitrim, Longford, Westmeath, Cavan, Laoighis, Offaly and Kildare. No proven tombs have been discovered in the three latter counties. The volumes are published by the Stationery Office, Dublin. They have been produced to a very high standard and it is to be hoped that despite present-day costs, it will be possible to maintain this standard throughout.

The survey has given many interesting results. It has shown that there are at least 1,200 megalithic tombs in the whole of Ireland and that this cannot have been the original total. A study of the literature published in the past and of other sources of information has shown that much destruction of sites has taken place and that this destruction has gone on even in recent times. Some sites seen by the surveyors and given a preliminary recording had disappeared when they went back to do a full survey. In the absence of a blanket preservation by the state and because of the land improvement schemes that are in progress throughout the country, sites which have now been fully recorded, will alas also disappear.

The majority of the 1,200 known sites have been classified into four main types but there is a residue which, for a variety of reasons, remains unclassified. Unfortunately, too, there are megalithic structures, which, though they have been examined, have been excluded from publication because in the opinion of the surveyors they were not recognizable by them as tombs. Such sites could have been included in appendices under some heading such as 'doubtful sites' so that other workers holding differing views would be made aware of their existence and so could make their own judgments.

In Volume III, the first which covers an area that includes passage-tombs, a curious policy has been followed. Because this type occurs in cemetery groups, they are to be treated

> separately from other types which do not have a nucleated distribution pattern. The cemeteries will be dealt with as units but examples of Passage-tombs occurring outside the main cemeteries are surveyed during the county surveys. It is proposed to publish plans and descriptions of these scattered sites from time to time in *ad hoc* papers and eventually to include all Irish Passage-tomb cemeteries and isolated sites in one or more volumes of the survey entirely devoted to this class. In the meantime, lists of Passage-tombs, where they occur, will be published in the relevant county volumes (de Valera and Ó Nualláin, 1972, xiii).

Because Dr Michael Herity of the Department of Archaeology, University College, Dublin, is interested in the finds from each class of tomb, the finds will not be published in the survey volumes – they will be published separately by Dr Herity. This means that the survey volumes will not present the complete information which one would expect them to contain. These, however, are minor criticisms and are greatly outweighed by the very valuable body of information now on record.

The four types of megalithic tombs in Ireland are now called court-tombs (329 examples), portal-tombs (160), wedge-tombs (400) and passage-tombs (150), a

change in nomenclature made since Volumes I and II were published (de Valera and Ó Nualláin 1972, xiii). In them the names were court-cairns, portal-dolmens, wedge-shaped gallery-graves, and passage-graves, names for the types which had long been current in the literature. The fourfold classification has received widespread acceptance, though there is an appreciable residue of structures which remains outside it. For instance, there is in the south-west of Ireland (Cork/Kerry) a group of fifty-two structures known in the past as 'boulder dolmens' but now called 'boulder burials' by Ó Nualláin (1978). These might have been called 'boulder-tombs' since they are overground structures, the reason given for the change from passage-grave to passage-tomb etc. (de Valera 1979, 102). Only one of them has been excavated – that at Bohonagh, Co. Cork (Fahy 1961). This did contain a cremated burial (no grave goods or dating evidence), but is one out of fifty-two sufficient to enable them all to be called burial structures without even the addition of a question mark? They consist of a large boulder capstone resting on three or more small boulders and some of them stand adjacent to or within stone circles.

The distribution patterns revealed by the megalithic survey are of much interest. The court-tombs (ill. 1) have a very marked northern distribution, all except five of the 329 lying north of a line drawn across the country from Dundalk on the east to Galway on the west. Of the five south of this line, two are in Co. Clare, and one each in the counties of Waterford, Kilkenny and Tipperary (ills. 5 and 6). There is a strong concentration of the tombs in the west particularly in the coastal regions of Mayo, Sligo and Donegal and a lesser one on the east coast in Louth and Down around Carlingford Lough. Apart from these two areas of density there is a general scatter of the tombs throughout the northern third of Ireland. The portal-tomb distribution is also very northern lying within the court-tomb area, though there is a small group in Co. Clare in the west and a spread of them from Dublin to Waterford in the south-east where some very impressive examples are to be seen. There are at least two in Co. Cork (ill. 2).

The wedge-tombs are the largest and most widespread group though they are most strongly represented in the western half of the country from south-west Cork to Donegal. The densest concentrations are in south-west Cork/Kerry, Tipperary and Clare, the latter county having over a hundred tombs (ill. 3).

The passage-tombs also have a northern distribution (ill. 4), but the most impressive of them lie in a cross-country band from the Dublin/Drogheda east coast to Sligo in the north-west and this band includes the four great cemeteries of the Boyne and Loughcrew in Co.

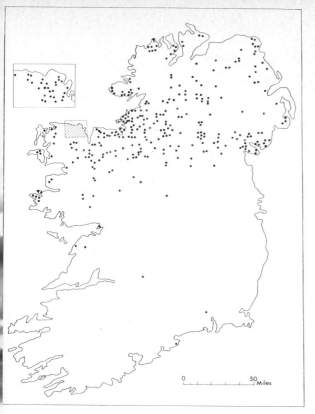

1 Distribution of court-tombs.

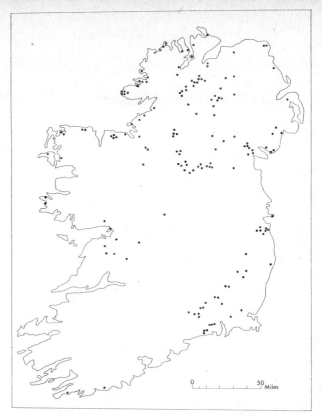

2 Distribution of portal-tombs.

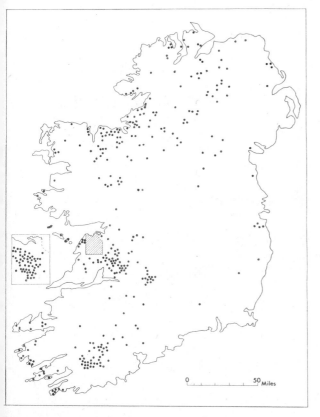

3 Distribution of wedge-tombs.

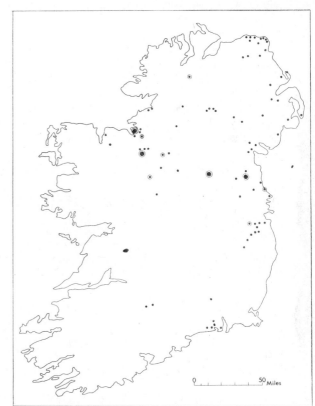

4 Distribution of passage-tombs.

1–4 Courtesy Irish Megalithic Survey.

5 Conjectural reconstruction drawing of court-tomb at Shanballyedmond, Co. Tipperary. (From JCHAS LXIII (1958).)

6 Plan of court-tomb at Shanballyedmond, Co. Tipperary. (From JCHAS LXIII (1958).)

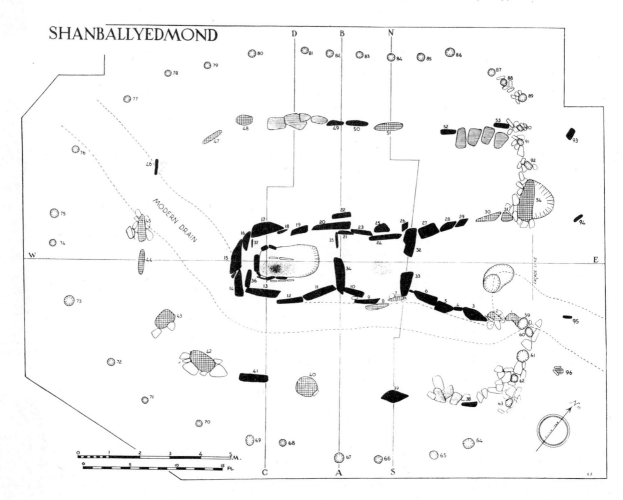

Meath and Carrowkeel and Carrowmore in Co. Sligo. There are small, more scattered groups in the Dublin/Wicklow mountains, in Donegal, in north Antrim and in Co. Waterford. A single slab bearing typical passage-tomb ornament, now in the Cork Public Museum (O'Kelly 1949; Powell 1966, 115), is the only surviving evidence of a site on Clear Island off the coast of south-west Cork. The site was destroyed over one hundred years ago. There is a single passage-tomb in east Co. Limerick.

The passage-tombs differ from the rest of the Irish megaliths in their cemetery groupings and in their hill-top sitings as well as in grave furniture. They have been found to contain personal ornaments such as beads, pendants, bone and antler pins, the enigmatic 'marbles' and round-bottomed pottery called Carrowkeel ware after the Sligo cemetery of that name, but no objects of everyday use in flint or stone. Arrowheads, javelin heads, axes and pottery of types known from domestic sites have been found in the court- and portal-tombs and some of the same objects in the wedges.

The numbers of tombs of all types that have been partially or fully excavated is very small – 37 court-tombs, 19 wedges, about 40 passage-tombs and 20 portal-tombs – a rather small statistical sample of the 1,200 total. The sample is poor in the case of the court-tombs and particularly so in the case of the wedges. The passage-tomb sample may seem large, but one must remember that it is not a random one – over half of it is made up of the two very close-knit groups at Newgrange and Knowth in the Boyne Valley, four sites recently excavated in the Carrowmore cemetery and fourteen of the rest are the old excavations at Carrowkeel of Macalister (*et al.*) in 1912. It does not include the very old 'excavations' of the middle of the last century at Dowth, Loughcrew and Carrowmore.

In the most recently published general statements on the megalithic tombs of Ireland, little that is new has been said (de Valera 1979; Ó Nualláin 1979; Herity and Eogan 1977; Herity 1974). It is assumed that the Neolithic way of life was introduced into Ireland by an incursion/invasion of new people who 'would have found virtually if not totally virgin country' (de Valera 1979, 1). In other words, a denial of a Mesolithic presence in Ireland. It is assumed that the court-tombs, the passage-tombs and the wedge-tombs represent 'three major colonizations by different groups of tomb builders' (de Valera 1979, 102) – people who came from the west of France and Brittany and who landed on the Irish coast at different points from which they extended their colonies into the country. The portal-tombs alone of the four types evolved in Ireland (central Ulster) from the court-tombs. Thus the court-

tomb builders landed in the west around Killala Bay in Co. Mayo and spread eastward across Ulster and eventually into Scotland and the Isle of Man. The passage-tomb builders arrived on the east coast and set up the Boyne Valley cemetery from where the general movement was westward resulting in the founding of the cemeteries at Loughcrew, Carrowkeel and Carrowmore in that order (Herity and Eogan 1977, 57). The wedge-tomb builders came from Brittany, landed in Kerry in the south-west and spread northward to Donegal and in time occupied the greater part of the western half of Ireland.

In the matter of date there is in the accounts cited an ambivalence towards radiocarbon and while dates obtained by this means seem to be accepted where they fit, there is a constant emphasis on the unreliability of the method. The court-tombs are said to be the earliest of the four types, the passage-tombs beginning a little later, but continuing to be built for the same period of time as the court-tombs. The floruit of the portal-tombs is contemporary with the later part of the court-tomb building activity, while the wedge-tombs are the latest and belong to the end of the Neolithic and to the Beaker/Early Bronze Age period. So much for what has recently been said.

There is now emerging quite acceptable evidence that there was a strong early Mesolithic in Ireland. Two recently excavated sites, Mount Sandel, Co. Derry (Woodman 1978, 220) and Lough Boora, Co. Offaly (Ryan 1978) have been shown to be seasonal settlement sites with radiocarbon dates ranging from 6500 to 7000 bc. At Mount Sandel a number of circular huts with hearths, rubbish pits and flint-knapping floors have been uncovered. Animal, bird and fish bones as well as hazelnut shells give some indication of diet, and very numerous microliths of several kinds display a high-level flint technology. Polished stone axes were also in use. All the same things except the hut sites have been found at Lough Boora. The polished axes have occasioned some surprise as it has been so firmly held in the past that such tools were not in Ireland before the Neolithic period proper had begun. It seems likely that these first colonizing immigrants to Ireland came from northern Britain (Woodman 1978), and while they may have come dryshod across landbridges, these connections were cut by the rising sea by 6500 bc and thereafter the people must have had boats. Even though our knowledge of them is still very meagre, they were obviously an able people for whom the developing Irish Sea became a highway, not a barrier, and by 4000 bc they were travelling the length and breadth of it and had maintained their contacts in Britain and probably established others farther afield in north and north-west France. I imagine some of them trading animal skins and furs, smoked salmon and other fish and dried venison as well as raw flint out of Ireland and coming back with calves and lambs, kids and young pigs and probably a new wife or two as well as friends *invited* into Ireland. In due time after other visits abroad, they came back with round-bottomed shouldered bowl pots and sacks full of seed wheat and barley. Thus the Neolithic way of life was introduced by a slow and complicated process resulting from overseas contacts – there was no invasion and no arrival of a great colony of foreigners. But see Case's discussion of the matter (1969).

By 3000 bc, pastoralism and agriculture were well established and an increasing population had developed a settled way of life and a firm social structure. The food supply was assured and abundant, and thought could be given to matters other than just the daily round. Foreign contacts had continued of course, and thus by the later part of the fourth millennium, megalithic tomb-building and its associated cult of the dead was coming into fashion in Ireland, the passage-tomb builders beginning their experiments with the cult in the Carrowmore cemetery in Co. Sligo as the radiocarbon dates that we now have suggest. Site no. 7 there has a date of 3290 ± 80 bc (LU–1441). This has been shown to be a very simple tomb structure with just a hint of a passage, the whole set within a circular kerb of boulders within which there never had been a covering cairn (Burenhult 1980). Site 27 in the cemetery had a simple cruciform structure without a passage proper and just the basal layer of a cairn within the circular boulder kerb. Its radiocarbon date is 3090 ± 80 bc (LU–1698).

As was to be expected these two sites show a local elaboration within a cemetery now reduced to thirty-one monuments from an original one hundred or more. Did the Carrowmore cemetery begin to come into existence out of the same stream of influences that affected Denmark and south Sweden and which way was the stream flowing – Scandinavia to Ireland or the reverse? Clear evidence has come from the excavations at Newgrange (O'Kelly et al. 1978) and Knowth (Eogan 1969, 13) that simple passage-tomb types can be and are earlier than the great tombs on the Boyne, and so if there is an evolutionary sequence at all, it must be from the simple to the complex. Thus the three great mounds in the Boyne cemetery mark the zenith of the passage-tomb sect of the cult in Ireland, not the beginning as has so often been said (de Valera 1965, 24; Herity and Eogan 1977, 57). The radiocarbon dates for the building of Newgrange centre on 2500 bc, five hundred radiocarbon years later than at least two of the Carrowmore sites. Meanwhile, be-

tween Carrowmore in the west and the Boyne Valley in the east other passage-tomb builders were carrying out their own experiments at Carrowkeel, Loughcrew and elsewhere. New excavatains and more radiocarbon dates will in time place them in the sequence of events.

But what of the other megalithic tomb types in Ireland? We have now been stuck for a long time with the arguments about whether the court-tomb builders entered Ireland in the east at Carlingford Lough or in the west at Killala Bay, this because of the concentrations of the tombs in these two areas. In the last written statement he made before he died, de Valera firmly favoured the western entry and a devolution eastward, but he was constrained to say that

> Excavation has produced evidence of a Neolithic date for the court-tombs . . . The dating evidence . . . does not as yet warrant a judgment between the theory of east-west evolution or that of west-east devolution. The finds from court-tombs present coherent evidence for a Neolithic dating and this is confirmed by radiocarbon determinations. It is clear that examples of both the simpler and more complex types were built in Neolithic times (de Valera 1979, 108).

De Valera has argued that the seven transepted court-tombs which he and Ó Nualláin have found in the north-west of Ireland are very early in the series and that they indicate an origin for the court-tombs in the west of France (1965, 29), but seven sites, some of them very doubtful, can hardly be taken as good evidence of an invasion mounted from the Loire estuary – and where did they pick up the courts? They are not known in the putative homeland of the invaders. The cruciform plans of these sites are more likely due to an idea borrowed from the Sligo passage-tomb builders. But what if no flotillas of boats came up the Irish Sea to Carlingford or sailed up the west coast of Ireland to Mayo from the mouth of the Loire? Is it not more likely that we are dealing here with long settled groups of Irish farmers who had now got themselves caught up in another sect of the megalithic cult of the dead and who were doing their own thing in different parts of Ireland at the same time? Taken as a whole the court-tombs must be an Irish invention sparked off perhaps by influences coming from Scotland and northern Britain amongst other places (Waddell 1978, 122).

It has also been firmly said that the court-tombs are the earliest of the four types and that they were built by the first Neolithic invaders (de Valera 1960, 85), but the radiocarbon dates do not support this view. The earliest dates now available are from the court-tomb at

Ballymacdermot, Co. Armagh, but there are great discrepancies between the four dates obtained from charcoal from chamber 3 of the gallery. These range from 770 ± 75 and 1010 ± 75 *both ad* to 2345 ± 90 and 2880 ± 95 *both bc* (UB-705, 697, 695 and 694) and, therefore, one can have little confidence in them. The dates from the Ballyglass court-tomb site (Ó Nualláin 1972) are for the pre-existing house. They average at 2600 ± 45 bc (S1–1450–54) and so all one can say of this site is that the tomb is later. It may be indeed that earlier dates will be obtained for the court-tombs, but as yet there is no evidence that they belong to the very beginning of the Neolithic period.

Likewise we have been stuck for a long time with theories about the wedge-tombs which are unsupported by the evidence, but which have been repeated so often that their protagonists and others have come to believe them as true and they are no longer prepared to question them or look at any other options. Here the statistics must be emphasized: 400 tombs, 19 excavations, 7 no pottery finds, beaker pottery from 6, tanged-and-barbed arrowheads from 3, fragments of stone moulds for bronze objects very doubtfully associated with 2 (Ó Nualláin 1979, 15), yet on this basis we are told that

> Though several [wedge-tombs] especially in Cork and Kerry, were very poor in finds and produced no primary pottery, *the frequent occurrence of Beaker pottery* [italics mine] and the barbed-and-tanged arrowheads which are typical of the beaker-using people securely assigns the type to the Early Bronze Age. A coarse bucket-shaped pottery is likewise very frequent. A few metal finds are also present (de Valera 1979, 128).

The coarse bucket-shaped pottery is the Neolithic ware that is well known from the court-tombs and from Neolithic domestic sites such as those at Lough-Gur in Co. Limerick (Ó Ríordáin 1954). The six most recently excavated wedge-tombs in the south of Ireland, four in Kerry in the very area where the builders from Brittany are said to have come ashore (Herity 1970, 10; Herity and Eogan 1977, 122) one in Co. Cork (O'Kelly 1958) and one in Tipperary (O'Kelly 1960), contained no beaker pottery, no tanged-and-barbed arrowheads and no evidence that the builders had a knowledge of metal. Herity (1970, 11) said 'No grave furniture has been found . . . though four tombs have been excavated. It may be that no pottery was ever deposited in the tombs, or that it has disintegrated in conditions unfavourable for its preservation . . . a cremated burial from one tomb is the only definite trace of ancient interment . . . ' The four tombs he is talking about are those excavated by

himself in the Ballinskelligs/Waterville area of Co. Kerry and in spite of the lack of evidence from them, he repeats the arguments so often put by de Valera and Ó Nualláin for 'a close association of the Beaker-makers and the wedge-builders' (Herity 1970, 10).

The group of potsherds from burial 1 in the wedge-tomb at Baurnadomeeny, Co. Tipperary, seems to have most affinity with the Neolithic shouldered bowl ceramics while the coarse ware sherds from under the cairn are also of late Neolithic type (O'Kelly 1960, 112). Beaker sherds have been found in the wedge-tomb at Lough Gur (Ó Ríordáin and Ó hIceadha 1955) as one element in a late Neolithic complex of sherds, but beaker material has been found in almost every type of early monument in that area so it is not surprising that it should have been intruded into the tomb. The other wedge-tombs that have contained the ware are in the northern half of Ireland in areas where, like Lough Gur, beaker ware is generally found on domestic sites, and it is probably intrusive in the wedges where it was found. No evidence has come up since 1960 when in writing about Baurnadomeeny (ills. 7 and 8) I said: 'We feel therefore that for the present, caution is necessary and suggest that the beaker-wedge equation should not be allowed to harden in our minds until more evidence in support of it is forthcoming from the monuments of Munster' (O'Kelly 1960, 113). If, as now seems likely, there were no Beaker people as such – that beaker pottery was part of the paraphernalia of a cult practice the ideas for which began to be disseminated in late Neolithic times (Burgess and Shennan 1976, Burgess 1978, 213) – wedge-tombs must represent another sect of the megalithic cult of the dead which Irish farmers evolved in the northern part of Ireland, the cult and tomb type later spreading into the deep south of the country. There is no good reason to derive the tombs from the *allées couvertes* of Brittany (Waddell 1974, 36). The detailed forms which the tombs took are no evidence of an invasion of Beaker or other people into this country.

As a support for the Beaker/Bronze Age dating for the wedge-tombs, the distribution pattern of the latter is linked with the distribution of copper ores and a close relationship between the two is seen particularly in the south-west in the Cork/Kerry area, and in the counties of Tipperary, Wicklow and Mayo (Herity 1970, 13: de Valera 1979, 123; Ó Nualláin 1979, 15) and this despite the absence of any hard evidence that Beaker people had anything to do with the wedge-tombs in these areas (Harbison 1973, 125, 129) or that the wedge-tomb builders, whoever they were, had anything to do with copper-mining (Harbison 1978, 103–4). The densest concentration of wedge-tombs,

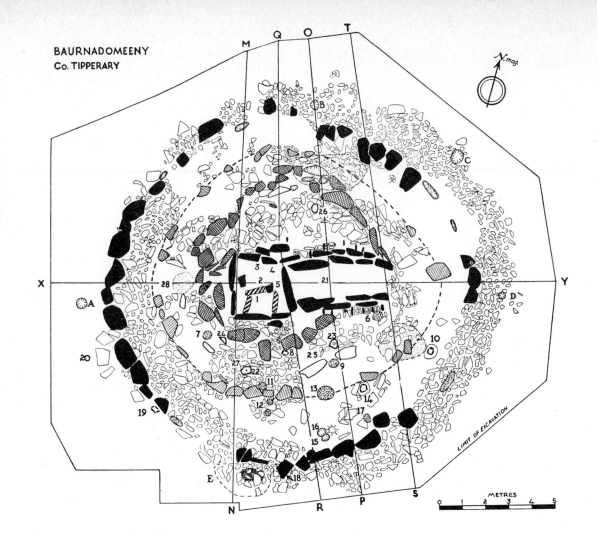

BAURNADOMEENY
Co. TIPPERARY

*7 Plan of wedge-tomb at Baurnadomeeny, Co. Tipperary.
(From* JCHAS *LXV (1960).)*

about seventy, is on the upper limestone plateau of
north-west Co. Clare, a region that has no known
metalliferous deposits. The reason given for this particular concentration is that the plateau provided grazing for cattle throughout the winter (de Valera 1979,
123; Ó Nualláin 1979, 15). Because most wedge-
tombs are situated on hill-slopes and uplands, this is
taken by the same writers to mean that the builders
were mainly pastoralists, not cultivators, and, living
near their tombs, they were on soils which would not
have been forested so there would have been round-
the-year grazing for their stocks. While all of this is
possible and may even be true, there is no hard
evidence for any of it. Settlements in upland areas that
might even be thought of as belonging to the wedge-

tomb builders are not known (Herity 1970, 13). In
some areas in Kerry not far from a few wedge-tombs,
field systems enclosed by stone-built fences have
become apparent as the blanket peat has been cut away
for use locally as domestic fuel, but as yet there is no
evidence to connect these fields with the tomb
builders, though in time it may be shown that this is
the case. Similar field systems recently found under the
peat in Co. Mayo by Herity and Caulfield (1977, 50)
are said to have belonged to the court-tomb builders of
that area.

   The most recently offered evidence in support of the
wedge-tomb/Early Bronze Age equation is a comparison of the distributions of the wedges and Early
Bronze Age cist graves and it is said that because the
two distributions are complementary and mutually exclusive, the two types of burial must be contemporary,
the wedge-tomb builders invading from the west, the
cist-grave people invading from the east (de Valera

1979, 126, Harbison 1977, 20). Ó Nualláin (1979, 15) repeats this assertion and says 'The picture is one of two communities living side by side but each preserving its own distinct traditions'. As there is no real evidence to show that the four hundred wedge-tombs were built in the Early Bronze Age, this distribution map comparison is a dubious exercise to say the best of it. Nor indeed is it certain that all the cists on the map made by Waddell (1970, 103) are of the Bronze Age, since several have had no grave-goods associated with the burials and have not been dated by any other means. It may be that some of them are late Neolithic, because the fashion for single-grave burial was already in vogue well before the end of the floruit of the megalithic tomb-building era.

In some respects it is strange that the current theory in regard to the portal-tombs should regard them so positively as an Irish invention with a firm birth-place in central Ulster. The theory of an origin there is based on similarities in structural detail between the portal-tombs and the court-tombs and undoubtedly some similarities do exist, though they are not more compelling than the structural similarities which one can find in all four main classes of tomb if one looks for *similarities* rather than *differences*. From central Ulster

there was an outward spread to east and west and thence down the coasts to Waterford on the one hand and to Clare and Cork on the other, with an extension to Wales and Cornwall from the Waterford limb (de Valera 1979, 112; Ó Nualláin 1979, 9). If one were imbued with an invasionist belief it would be easy to argue on the same evidence for a movement of people from Cornwall via Wales to Waterford and ultimately to central Ulster. The Dyffryn Ardudwy portal-tomb in Wales is an important staging point on the route whichever way the people were marching, for it produced characteristic shouldered bowl pottery of a kind as early as any in these islands (Powell 1963). I do not believe in a mass movement of people in either direction. The portal-tomb is another expression of the house-for-the-dead cult and as portal-tomb builders were living side-by-side with the people of the three other megalithic sects, there was much communication between them all and hence the similarities in their cult buildings.

8 Wedge-tomb at Baurnadomeeny, Co. Tipperary after excavation and conservation. (From JCHAS LXV (1960); photo M.J. O'Kelly.)

9 Portal-tomb at Kilmogue, Co. Kilkenny. (Photo M.J. O'Kelly.) (Visible height of right-hand upright: 3m.)

Thirteen of the twenty excavated portal-tombs have produced grave-goods that are comparable with those from the court-tombs: Neolithic period shouldered-bowl and flat-based coarse ware, leaf- and lozenge-shaped arrow- and javelin-heads and hollow scrapers, and all one can argue from this is the contemporaneity of the two classes of monument throughout the floruit periods of both. There is no real evidence for the derivation of one from the other.

Mound or cairn shape for the portal-tombs has occasioned much discussion and no conclusion has been reached. There is good evidence for a primary round mound – Dyffryn Ardudwy is an instance of an excavated site. There it could be shown that the long mound was an addition. This is no surprise because excavation has shown that some of the other tomb types were multi-period structures as for instance Site K, a satellite passage-tomb at Newgrange (O'Kelly et al. 1978) and the court-tomb at Annaghmare, Co. Armagh (Waterman 1965, 21, 37). No portal-tomb is known where an appreciable amount of mound survives and in my view this is because there never was a high mound. It is inconceivable that having erected the usually enormous capstone poised high over the entrance portals and sloping downward to the rear, its builders would have done anything to detract from their great feat (ill. 9). The piling up of a high mound would have done this. Just enough stone packing was put around the orthostats to keep them firm. Where some evidence of a long mound is present, this is no more than a token fulfilment of the local cult rule.

Orientation was important to the builders of many Neolithic monuments – easterly for court-tombs and some portal-tombs, south-west/north-east for most wedge-tombs, while in passage-tombs no very strong rule can as yet be determined. The dramatic effect of the orientation of Newgrange to the rising sun at the winter solstice has to be seen to be believed.

The carvings on the structural slabs of the passage-tombs have for long excited interest and comment and have been seen as decoration and art, as anthropomorphs and representations of the Earth Mother or Mother Goddess, as symbols of religion or magic, as indications of male and female sex, and more recently as a written language which, if we could only read it, would give us all the answers. Maybe indeed it contains elements of all these things and surely it had a significance for those who created the patterns and did the carvings as well as for those who just saw them in passing. But to what extent are all the interpretations and explanations of it merely the figments of the imaginations of modern-day scholars conditioned consciously or subliminally by the psychological climate in which they have lived? In my years of work at Newgrange I have heard from the general visitor as well as from experts in many fields, explanations and interpretations conceivable and inconceivable, sane and lunatic, all expressed with such conviction that it was often difficult to avoid being influenced and thereby being led into making a false record of what was actually carved on the stone. But the record is now made for Newgrange and will soon be published and all are welcome to make what they like of it. The work has been done by Claire O'Kelly who has also made a detailed study of the Boyne Valley carvings in general (1973; 1978) and I agree with her when she comments as follows:

Within the relatively restricted framework of geometrical motifs it is clear that there was ample scope for Irish passage-grave builders to express individuality by characteristic groupings of motifs to which names such as Newgrange style, Loughcrew style etc., can be applied. Generally speaking, there is a definite similarity between all the decorated stones of a particular tomb. How much of the various styles are idiosyncratic, how much the product of particular or even personal, beliefs or cults . . . is one of the intriguing problems yet to be solved. Wide as the divergence between the different styles appears to be, it is minimal, however, compared with that between Irish passage-grave art and the Iberian and Breton examples with which it has been so often linked. Heretofore, the tendency has largely been to concentrate attention on alleged anthropomorphic and representational elements in the Irish material . . . This has led to a linking of Irish carvings with a variety of media far removed spatially as well as chronologically. Irish passage-grave art has been said to be derived from the stone idols, amulets, stone plaques and small anthropomorphic figures found in Iberian tombs, for example, as well as from the designs engraved and painted on the walls of the tombs themselves.

Gavrinis in Brittany, has repeatedly been brought forward as an example, if not an exemplar, of Irish art, often without due regard to the fact that this tomb is an exotic in the context of both Breton and Irish art. Petit Mont (Arzon) has also been cited as an Irish parallel mainly on the strength of its zigzag and radial lines, but non-Irish motifs such as feet, axes and shields (*écussons*) are also present. Other putative sources are designs on pottery from Iberia and Scandinavia, but unless all or any of these proposed models can at the very least be shown to antedate the Irish examples, there is little point in the comparisons . . . Now that Newgrange has been shown to belong to the mid-third millennium BC, many of the above comparisons can be ruled out. Moreover, the overtly representational nature of much of the Breton and Iberian carvings indicates a fundamental difference which is not negatived by the fact that a small range of motifs such as arcs, U's, circles, radials, zigzags, etc., is held in common (O'Kelly, C. 1973, 28–9).

As Fleming (1969, 259) would have it: 'The mothergoddess [from Iberia & Brittany] has detained us for too long; let us disengage ourselves from her embrace.'

10 *Kerbstone 52 at Newgrange — detail. (Reproduced by permission of the Commissioners of Public Works in Ireland.)*

11 *Back of kerbstone 13 at Newgrange. (Reproduced by permission of the Commissioners of Public Works in Ireland.)*

12 Newgrange now. (Reproduced by permission of the Commissioners of Public Works in Ireland.)

Conclusions

The introduction of the Neolithic way of life into Ireland was a complicated process which was initiated by late Mesolithic Irishmen who were constantly travelling abroad and returning. Pastoralism probably came first and cereal cultivation a little later. Food production was well established here by 4000 bc.

Continuing to travel abroad, the Irish farmers became caught up in the megalithic cult of the dead and by 3000 bc were introducing at home the ideas of the various sects, and so, while international threads can be seen in the tomb types, the tombs are native versions built on these ideas.

124

All four types of Irish tombs were being built during more or less the same period of time. There was much communication between the sects and many borrowings took place. Each tomb built was an individual effort so that even within the sects there were many experiments and elaborations. Many tombs are multi-period structures, additions having been made as circumstances demanded.

By 2000 bc, so much man-time/effort had been spent on tomb building that there was an economic collapse (Whittle 1978, Burgess 1978, 207). One has only to think of the strain put upon the economy of the Boyne Valley by the profligacy shown in the building of the three great passage-tombs – Newgrange, Dowth and Knowth.

There is little evidence to support the oft repeated Beaker/Early Bronze Age/wedge-tomb equation. Researches still in progress on the late Neolithic/Beaker period pottery complex around the edge of the

Newgrange passage-tomb are showing that *all* the pottery types including the best beaker ware were locally made. The high-tin bronze axe from this horizon shows that metallurgy was well established in Ireland long before 2000 bc and long before Beaker pottery came upon the scene (O'Kelly and Shell 1978).

Irish archaeologists have so concerned themselves with searches abroad for the origins of Irish megalithic tombs that they have not had time to 'glory in the great achievement of Irish megalithic architecture in the 4th and 3rd millennia bc irrespective of where the first seeds came from. Newgrange is one of the great wonders of the prehistoric world of ancient Europe and far surpasses any comparable achievement in Spain or Brittany' (Daniel, *in lit.*, 21 December 1979). I wholeheartedly agree (ill. 12).

Bibliography

BAR *British Archaeological Reports*
JCHAS *Jour. Cork Hist. and Arch. Soc.*
JRSAI *Jour. Roy. Soc. Antiquaries Ireland*
PPS *Proceedings Prehist. Soc.*
PRIA *Proceedings Roy. Irish Academy*
UJA *Ulster Jour. Archaeology*

BURENHULT, G. 1980 'The Archaeological Excavation at Carrowmore, Co. Sligo. Ireland', in Malmer, M. P. (ed.), *Theses and Papers in North-European Archaeology 9*, Inst. of Archaeology, Univ. of Stockholm.

BURGESS, C. 1978 'The Background of Early Metalworking in Ireland and Britain', in Ryan, M. (ed.), *The Origins of Metallurgy in Atlantic Europe*, Proceedings of the Fifth Atlantic Colloquium, Dublin, 30 March to 4 April 1978, 207–14.

BURGESS, C. AND SHENNAN, S. 1976 'The Beaker Phenomenon: Some Suggestions' in Burgess, C. and Miket, (eds), *Settlement and Economy in the Third and Second Millennia BC*, *BAR* British Series 33, Oxford, 309–31.

CASE, H. J. 1969 'Settlement Patterns in the North Irish Neolithic', *UJA* XXXII, 3–27.

DE VALERA, R. 1960 'The Court Cairns of Ireland', *PRIA* 60, C, 9–140.

1965 'Transeptal Court Cairns', *JRSAI* XCV, 5–37.

1979, in S. P. Ó Ríordáin, *Antiquities of the Irish Countryside* 5th edn, London, 1–28.

DE VALERA, R. AND O NUALLAIN, S. 1972 *Megalithic Survey of Ireland* III, Dublin.

EOGAN, G. 1968 'Excavations at Knowth', *PRIA* 66, C, 299–400.

1969 'Excavations at Knowth, Co. Meath, 1968', *Antiquity* XLIII, 8–14.

1974 'Report on the Excavations at Knowth', *PRIA* 74, C, 11–112.

FAHY, E. M. 1961 'A Stone Circle, Hut and Dolmen at Bohonagh, Co. Cork', *JCHAS* LXVI, 93–104.

FLEMING, A. 1969 'The myth of the mother-goddess' *World Archaeology* I, 247–61.

HARBISON, P. 1973 'The Earlier Bronze Age in Ireland – Late 3rd Millennium – *c.* 1200 BC', *JRSAI* CIII, 93–152.

1977 'The Bronze Age' in Cone, P. (ed.), *The Treasures of Early Irish Art 1500 BC to 1500 AD*, New York, 18–24.

1978 'Who were Ireland's First Metallurgists?' in Ryan, M. (ed.), *The Origins of Metallurgy in Atlantic Europe*, Proceedings of the Fifth Atlantic Colloquium, Dublin, 30 March to 4 April 1978, 97–105.

HERITY, M. 1970 'The Prehistoric Peoples of Kerry: A Programme of Investigation', *Jour. Kerry Archaeological & Hist. Soc.* no. 3, 4–14.

1974 *Irish Passage Graves*, Dublin.

HERITY, M. AND EOGAN, G. 1977 *Ireland in Prehistory*, London.

MACALISTER, R.A.S., Armstrong, E.C.R. and Praeger, R. L1. 1912 'Bronze Age Cairns on Carrowkeel Mountain, Co. Sligo', *PRIA* 29, C, 311–47.

O'KELLY, C. 1973 'Passage-grave art in the Boyne Valley', *PPS* XXXIX, 354–82.

1978 *Illustrated Guide to Newgrange and the other Boyne Monuments*, Cork.

O'KELLY, M. J. 1949 'An Example of Passage-Grave Art from Co. Cork' *JCHAS* LIV, 8–10.

1958 'A Wedge-shaped Gallery-grave at Island, Co. Cork', *JRSAI* LXXXVII, 1–23.

1960 'A Wedge-shaped Gallery-grave at Baurnadomeeny, Co. Tipperary', *JCHAS* LXV, 85–115.

O'KELLY, M. J., LYNCH, F. M. AND O'KELLY, C. 1978 'Three Passage-graves at Newgrange', *PRIA* 78, C, 249–352.

O'KELLY, M. J. AND SHELL, C. A. 1978 'Stone objects and a Bronze Axe from Newgrange, Co. Meath', in Ryan, M. (ed.), *The Origins of Metallurgy in Atlantic Europe*, Proceedings of the Fifth Atlantic Colloquium, Dublin, 30 March to 4 April 1978, 127–44

Ó NUALLÁIN, S. 1972 'A Neolithic House at Ballyglass near Ballycastle, Co. Mayo', *JRSAI* CII, 49–57.

1978 'Boulder Burials', *PRIA* 78, C, 75–114.

1979 'The Megalithic Tombs of Ireland, *Expedition XXI, 6–15.*

Ó RÍORDÁIN, S.P. 1954 'Lough Gur Excavations: Neolithic and Bronze Age Houses on Knockadoon' *PRIA* 56, C, 297–459.

Ó RÍORDÁIN, S. P. AND Ó HICEADHA, G. 1955 'Lough Gur Excavations: The Megalithic Tomb', *JRSAI* LXXXV, 34–50.

POWELL, T. G. E. 1963 'The Chambered Cairn at Dyffryn Ardudwy', *Antiquity* XXXVII, 19–24.

1966 *Prehistoric Art*, London.

RYAN, M. 1978 'Lough Boora Excavations', *An Taisce* (Ireland's Conservation Journal), II, no. 1 Jan/Feb., 13–14.

WADDELL, J. 1970 'Irish Bronze Age Cists', *JRSAI* C, 91–139.

1974 'On Some Aspects of the Late Neolithic and Early Bronze Age in Ireland', in Scott, B. G. and Walsh, D. E. (eds.), *Irish Archaeological Research Forum*, Belfast, 32–8.

1978 'The Invasion Hypothesis in Irish Archaeology' *Antiquity* LII, 121–8.

WATERMAN, R. D. 1965 'The Court Cairn at Annaghmare, Co. Armagh', *UJA* XXVIII, 3–46.

WHITTLE, A. W. R. 1978 'Resources and population in the British Neolithic', *Antiquity* LII, 34–42.

WOODMAN, P. C. 1978 *The Mesolithic in Ireland: Hunter Gatherers in an Insular Environment*, BAR British Series 58, Oxford, 1–360.

Index

Page numbers in *italics* refer to illustrations

agriculture 88, 118, 124
Alfriston 102–3
allées couvertes 16, 17, 24, 27, *91*, 92–6, 119; typology 92
Anta dos Gorginos 32
Anta dos Tassos 32
Antiquity 18, 113
Araslov 78
architects 68–70
Arran 12–13
art, in Ireland 122–3, Malta 67, 70

Ballymacdermot 119
Bari-Taranto tombs 46–8
Barnenez 26
Baurnadomeeny 119, *120, 121*
Beaker culture 32, 35, 119, 124–5
Beira Alta 31–2
Belgium 91–6; location of megaliths *92, 95*
Bisceglie 47
Bougon 24, 26–7
boulder-materials 114
Boyne valley 14–15, 109, 117–18, 122, 124
Britain 97–110; colonization in Neolithic 99; maps of sites *98*; origins of monuments 109–110
Brittany *16*, 20, *22*, 27
burial patterns 10–15
burial practices 23–5, 43–4, 47–8, 51, 65, 80: *see also* mortuary practices

Cairnholy 106
cairns 26–7, 102–4; typology 26, 102–4
Camster Long 107–9, *107*
Carapito 31–2
Carenque 33
Carrowmore cemetery 118
Castelluccio dei Sauri 53, *54*
cemeteries 11, 14–15, 34, 36, 38, 45, 115, 118
centre, emergence of 15
chambered tombs 16, 24, 26, 46–8, 80, 97–110; typology 46–7, 106–9
chamberless long barrows *see* unchambered long barrows
Childe, Gordon 30

cists, stone 46, 48–9, 51–3, 55–6, 58, 77, 121; typology 48–51, *50*
coffres *see* cists, stone
collective burial 11, 21, 23, 32–4, 43–4, 80, 94, 99, 109
corbelled tombs 30
Corsica 46, 48–9, 53, 55–6, *56*, 58–9; list of sites 63
court cairns 13, *15*, 101, 106, 109, 114
court-tombs 114, *115, 116*, 117–22
cremation 23

Dalladies 102
Daniel, Glyn *Antiquity* 18, 113; the person 8, 17, 64; publications on megaliths 8–9, 18, 22, 29, 30, 33, 39, 58, 77, 96, 97, 110, 125; undergraduate 113
Daniel, Ruth 8, *9, 16*
dating techniques 21; *see also* radiocarbon dating and thermoluminescence dating
Denmark 77–82, 110
destruction of sites, in France 19–20; Iberia 35; Ireland 114
diffusion: Britain 99–100, 110; Central Mediterranean 58–9; France 21; Iberia 30, 34; Ireland 117; Malta 74–5; northern Europe 79–80, 95–6
dolmens 46–9, 51–5, 58, 74, 77–8, 83, 88; polygonal 80–2; portal 108–110, 114; rectangular 82; typology 48–9
dwelling sites 85–6
Dyffryn Ardudwy 106, 109, 121–2

economy of megalith communities 14, 86–9
El Barranquete 32, 35, 36, 39
Evans, J. D. 47, 64–5, 69, 73–5

Falbygden 86–8
Filetto 55
Fonelas 37, *38*, 39
France 18–27, *16, 19*; destruction of sites 19–20; recent excavation 20; surveys of monuments 18, 20

Funnel Beaker culture 77–80, 82, *84*, 85–6, 88–90
Fussell's Lodge 102–3

Galeriegrab-Kultur 94–6
gallery graves *23*, 27, 46, 48, *91*, 92–4, 96, 114; typology 46; *see also tombe di giganti*
Genna Arrele 55
Germany 77–90
Ggantija 65–7, 76
Giorina 46
Giovinazzo 46–7
Glenvoidean 108
Gnewitz 83
grave-goods 23, 25, 44, 51, 92, 94, 99, 117, 122

Haga 82
Hagar Qim 66–8, *68*, 71, *71*, 76
Hal Saflieni 69, 76
Herdade da Farisoa 32
hierarchy 12, 14–15, 89, 101; sociospatial in Neolithic Wessex *12*
hypogea 21, *24*, 25, *67*, 69–71; typology 69–70

Iberia 29–39; dating of sites 31–3; destruction of sites 35; distribution of sites 34–7; maps of sites *31, 36*–7; origins of megaliths 29–30, 33; recent excavations 35
ideas, transmission of 22, 48, 59, 109
independent invention of megaliths 9, 22, 58–9, 64, 74, 99, 104–5, 109, 118
Ireland 113–25; distribution maps 115; surveys of megaliths 113–14
Iron Age 44–4, 48–9, 52, 54–5
Italy 42, 44–8, 53–4; list of sites 61

Jemelle 93–4
Jemeppe-Hargimont 94–6

Karleby *89*, 90
Karups Hede 86
Kilham 102–3
Knowth 117–18
Kordin 65–6, 73, *73*, 76
Kujavian Barrow 80

La Chaussée-Tirancourt *23*, 24
La Houge 24, 26
La Hoguette 23–4, 26
Le Montiou 24, 26
Les Mournouards 25
Les Peirières 25
Linear Pottery culture 99–100
Lochhill 102–4, 106
long barrows 27, 78–9, 86, 101; typology 79–80
Los Millares 11, 32, 36, *37*, *38*, 39
Los Rurialillos *38*
Lough Boora 117
Lough Gur 119

Maes Howe 14–15, 104–5, 109
Malta 48, 53, 64–75, *72*; development of temples 66–7; list of sites 61; list of temples and rock-cut tombs 76
Mecklenburg 77–8, 82–3, 86, 89–90
Mediterranean, central 42–59, *43*, *45*, *52–3*, *57*; see also Corsica, Italy, Sardinia and Sicily
megaliths, in Belgium 91–6; Britain 97–110; France 18–27; Germany and Scandinavia 77–90; Iberia 29–39; Ireland 113–25; Malta 64–75; central Mediterranean 42–59; associated settlement remains 10, 85–6; chronology 21, 31, 44, 47–8, 51–2, 55, 57, 90; distribution in Europe *9*, *13*, *16*, *19*, *31*, *36–7*, *43*, *45*, *52–3*, *57*, *72*, *79*, *81*, *87*, *92*, *95*, *98*, *115*; function 8–9, 65, 101; origins of 29–30, 34, 64, 105–6, 109–10, 117–18, 121; rebuilding 26, 51; skeletal remains 14, 23–5, 39, 44, 47, 51, 84, 103; spatial patterning 9–10, 12–13, 35–7; technology of construction 26, 67–8, 77
menhir 27, 45, 47–9, 52–8, 75, 93; statue- 47, 49, 53, *54*, 55, *56*, 57–9
Merina 10–11
Mesolithic 117
Mgarr 66
Mid Gleniron 106, 108
Mnajdra 67, *69*, 76
modules, concept of 100
mortuary houses 80, 84–5, 102–4, 110
mortuary practices 23–6, 30, 33–4; see also burial practices
mother goddess 59, 71, 122–3
Mount Sandel 117

Neuvy-en-Dunois 23

Newgrange 117–18, 122, *123–4*, 125
Nuragic culture 51–2, 57
Nutbane 102–3

Orca de Seixas 31
Orca dos Castenairos 31
Oridda 51, 62
Orkney 13–14, 105
ossuaries 21, 25, 83–4, 94
Otranto tombs 46–8, 53–5, 74–5
Ozieri culture 44

Pagliau 48, 55, 57, 63
passage graves 14–15, *15–16*, 17, 21, 24, 26, 29, 31–3, 49, 78, 82, *83–4*, 85–90, 109–10, 114; typology 32, 49, 82
passage-tombs 114, *115*, 117–18, 122, 124
patterned behaviour 9–11, 16
Piggott, Stuart 99–100
Pitnacree 102–3
places of worship 66, 70
Poco da Gateira 32
political grouping 71–2
Pontevecchio 55
population estimates, NM long barrows 101; Rousay 101
portal-tombs 114, *115*, 117, 121–2
Portugal see Iberia
pottery, Beaker culture 119
Powell, T. G. E. 113
priesthood 71, 109–10
Proto-Apennine 47

Quanterness 14, 101, 105

radiocarbon dating 33, 97, 99; of megaliths 8–9, 14, 21, 23–4; 31–3, 44, 51, 57–8, 64, 86, 101, 108, 118; of Mesolithic 117
religious complex 93
Renfrew, A. C. 31, 33–4, 36–7, 44, 69, 71–2, 80, 85, 89–90, 101, 104–5
Ring of Brogar 14–15
Roaix *24*, 25
rock-cut tombs 21, 25, 30, 32, 42–6, 51–2, 54–5, 58, 65, 70; distribution in Mediterranean 42, *43*; plans of *44*; typology 42–4
Rössberga 84, *84*
round barrows 103
Rousay 16, 101

sacrifice 84; animal 71
Saint-Just 27

Sardinia 42–6, 48–9; *50*, 55, 58–9; list of sites 62
Scandinavia 77–90
segmentary societies 12–14, 17, 89–90, 101
Seine-Oise-Marne culture 91–6
settlement pattern 10–11, 12, 15
Shanballyedmond *116*
Shardana 57–8
shrines 101
Sicily 42, 44–5, 64
skeletal remains 14, 23–5, 39, 44, 47, 51, 84, 103
Skorba *64–5*, 66–7, 71, 74–5
Slewcairn 103–4, *105*
social change, processes of 34–5
social structure 71, 86
Spain see Iberia
spatial patterning 9–13, 35–7
statue-menhirs see menhirs
Stonehenge 12, 15
stone-packing graves 84–5
Stones of Stenness 14
surveys of megaliths, in France 18, 20; Ireland 113–14

Ta Hammut 75
Tarxien 61, 66, *67–8*, 67–9, 70, 71, 74, 76
Ta Trapna 65
temple 65–74, 84; distribution *72*; evolution *65*
territorial definition 16, 36, 72, 90, 101
thermoluminescence dating 31–3, 110
tholoi 32–3
tombe a poliandro 49, 51
tombe di giganti 49–52, 55, 58; typology *50–1*
trade 59, 118
Trefignath 107–8
typology, comparative 47

unchambered long barrows 14, 78, 79, 80, 102–4
urdolmens 77–8, 80, 82

Velaine 94
Vierville 24
Vrone Hede 84, *85*

Wayland's Smithy 102–3
wedge-tombs 114, *115*, 117, 119–22, 124
Weris 91, *91–2*, 93–4